CHICAGO PUBLIC LIBRARY

R0008290170

CHILTON'S REPAIR & TUNE-UP GUIDE
CHEVETTE 1976 to 1980

Covers all Chevette models

Managing Editor KERRY A. FREEMAN, S.A.E.
Senior Editor RICHARD J. RIVELE, S.A.E.
Editor David Stanley

President WILLIAM A. BARBOUR
Executive Vice President JAMES A. MIADES
Vice President and General Manager JOHN P. KUSHNERICK

CHILTON BOOK COMPANY
Radnor, Pennsylvania
19089

TL
215
.C48
C47
1979

SAFETY NOTICE

Proper service and repair procedures are vital to the safe, reliable operation of all motor vehicles, as well as the personal safety of those performing repairs. This book outlines procedures for servicing and repairing vehicles using safe, effective methods. The procedures contain many NOTES, CAUTIONS and WARNINGS which should be followed along with standard safety procedures to eliminate the possibility of personal injury or improper service which could damage the vehicle or compromise its safety.

It is important to note that repair procedures and techniques, tools and parts for servicing motor vehicles, as well as the skill and experience of the individual performing the work vary widely. It is not possible to anticipate all of the conceivable ways or conditions under which vehicles may be serviced, or to provide cautions as to all of the possible hazards that may result. Standard and accepted safety precautions and equipment should be used when handling toxic or flammable fluids, and safety goggles or other protection should be used during cutting, grinding, chiseling, prying, or any other process that can cause material removal or projectiles.

Some procedures require the use of tools specially designed for a specific purpose. Before substituting another tool or procedure, you must be completely satisfied that neither your personal safety, nor the performance of the vehicle will be endangered.

Although information in this guide is based on industry sources and is as complete as possible at the time of publication, the possibility exists that the manufacturer made later changes which could not be included here. While striving for total accuracy, Chilton Book Company cannot assume responsibility for any errors, changes, or omissions that may occur in the compilation of this data.

PART NUMBERS

Part numbers listed in this reference are not recommendations by Chilton for any product by brand name. They are references that can be used with interchange manuals and aftermarket supplier catalogs to locate each brand supplier's discrete part number.

ACKNOWLEDGMENTS

Chilton Book Company thanks the Chevrolet Motor Division of the General Motors Corporation for assistance in the preparation of this book.

Information has been selected from the Chevette Service Manual.

Chevrolet special tools mentioned in some procedures can be ordered through your Chevrolet dealer or directly through Kent-Moor Tool Division, 28635 Mound Road, Warren, MI., 48092

Copyright © 1979 by Chilton Book Company
All Rights Reserved
Published in Radnor, Pa., by Chilton Book Company
and simultaneously in Ontario, Canada
by Nelson Canada, Limited

Manufactured in the United States of America
34567890   876543210

Chilton's Repair & Tune-Up Guide: Chevette 1976–80
ISBN 0-8019-6836-4 pbk.
Library of Congress Catalog Card No. 78-20248

CONTENTS

1 General Information and Maintenance
- **1** How to Use this Book
- **2** Tools and Equipment
- **3** Routine Maintenance and Lubrication

2 Tune-Up
- **18** Tune-Up Procedures
- **19** Tune-Up Specifications

3 Engine and Engine Rebuilding
- **26** Engine Electrical
- **32** Engine Service and Specifications
- **51** Engine Rebuilding

4 Emission Controls and Fuel System
- **70** Emission Controls
- **75** Fuel System

5 Chassis Electrical
- **81** Accessory Service
- **83** Instrument Panel Service
- **84** Lights, Fuses and Flashers

6 Clutch and Transmission
- **87** Clutch
- **91** Manual Transmission
- **93** Automatic Transmission

7 Drive Train
- **97** Driveshaft and U-Joints
- **98** Rear Axle

8 Suspension and Steering
- **101** Front Suspension
- **106** Rear Suspension
- **109** Steering

9 Brakes
- **118** Front Brakes
- **122** Rear Brakes
- **125** Brake Specifications

10 Body
- **131** Repairing Scratches and Small Dents
- **135** Repairing Rust
- **141** Body Care

11 Troubleshooting
- **144** Problem Diagnosis

178 Appendix
182 Index

74 Chilton's Fuel Economy and Tune-Up Tips

Quick Reference Specifications For Your Vehicle

Fill in this chart with the most commonly used specifications for your vehicle. Specifications can be found in Chapters 1 through 3 or on the tune-up decal under the hood of the vehicle.

Tune-Up

Firing Order _____

Spark Plugs:

    Type _____

    Gap (in.) _____

Point Gap (in.) _____

Dwell Angle (°) _____

Ignition Timing (°) _____

    Vacuum (Connected/Disconnected) _____

Valve Clearance (in.)

    Intake _____   **Exhaust** _____

Capacities

Engine Oil (qts)

    With Filter Change _____

    Without Filter Change _____

Cooling System (qts) _____

Manual Transmission (pts) _____

    Type _____

Automatic Transmission (pts) _____

    Type _____

Front Differential (pts) _____

    Type _____

Rear Differential (pts) _____

    Type _____

Transfer Case (pts) _____

    Type _____

FREQUENTLY REPLACED PARTS

Use these spaces to record the part numbers of frequently replaced parts.

PCV VALVE	**OIL FILTER**	**AIR FILTER**
Manufacturer_____	Manufacturer_____	Manufacturer_____
Part No._____	Part No._____	Part No._____

General Information and Maintenance

HOW TO USE THIS BOOK

Chilton's Repair and Tune-Up Guide for the Chevette is intended to give you a basic idea of how your car works and how to save money by servicing it yourself. The first two chapters will be the most frequently used, since they contain maintenance and tune-up information and procedures. The following chapters concern themselves with the more complex systems of the Chevette. Operating systems from engine through brakes are covered to the extent that we feel the average do-it-yourselfer should get involved. Chilton's *Chevette* won't explain rebuilding the transmission for the simple reason that the expertise required and the investment in special tools make this task uneconomical. We will tell you how to change your own brake pads and shoes, replace your spark plugs, and do many more jobs that will save you money, give you personal satisfaction, and help you avoid problems.

Before loosening any bolts, please read through the entire section and the specific procedure. This will give you the overall view of what will be required as far as tools, supplies, and you. There is nothing more frustrating than having to walk to the bus stop on Monday morning because you were short one metric bolt during your Sunday afternoon repair. So read ahead and plan ahead.

The sections begin with a brief discussion of the system and what it involves. Adjustments and/or maintenance are then discussed, followed by removal and installation procedures and then repair or overhaul procedures where they are feasible. When repair is considered to be out of your league, we tell you how to remove the part and then how to install the new or rebuilt replacement. In this way you at least save the labor costs. Backyard repair of such components as the alternator are just not practical.

Two basic mechanic's rules should be mentioned here. One, whenever the left side of the car is referred to, it is meant to specify the driver's side of the car. Conversely, the right side of the car means the passenger's side of the car. Second, most screws and bolts are removed by turning counterclockwise and tightened by turning clockwise. Safety is always the most important rule. Constantly be aware of the dangers involved in working on an automobile and take the proper precautions. Use jackstands when working under a raised vehicle. Don't smoke or allow an exposed flame to come near the battery or any part of the fuel system. Always use the proper tool and use it correctly; bruised knuckles and skinned fingers aren't a

2 GENERAL INFORMATION AND MAINTENANCE

mechanic's standard equipment. Always take your time and have patience; once you have some experience and gain confidence, working on your car will become an enjoyable hobby.

TOOLS AND EQUIPMENT

Since the Chevette is built using mainly metric bolts and screws, you're going to need metric tools. Standard wrenches are either too tight or too loose to be used on metric fasteners. With the tools described below you'll be able to perform most of the procedures outlined in this guide.

1. Metric socket wrenches with various length drives.
2. Metric open end wrenches.
3. A ⅝ in. spark plug socket.
4. Round wire spark plug gauge.
5. Slot and phillips head screwdrivers.
6. Timing light.
7. Tachometer.
8. Torque wrench. This assures proper tightening pressures and helps avoid stripped threads.
9. Oli filter wrench.
10. Vice-grips.
11. Heavy duty jackstands. Safety is a primary concern when working underneath any car.

HISTORY

The Chevette was introduced in 1976 as Chevrolet's answer to imported cars. When it was first introduced it featured the lightest curb weight, smallest body style and smallest turning circle of any Chevrolet to date.

The first Chevettes came with 1.4 litre, single overhead camshaft engines with 4-speed manual transmissions. 3-speed automatic transmissions were available as an option. The 1.6 litre engine was listed as an option in 1976 but in 1978 it was made standard and the 1.4 was discontinued.

The H.O. (High Output) engine was introduced in 1978. It is the same size as the base 1.6 litre engine but offered more power.

The four door body style was also introduced in 1978. Not only does it increase the leg room and cargo space, but also the wheelbase and overall length of the car.

With 1979 came the introduction of a 2 bbl Holley carburetor to once again boost power and a revised suspension system with softer rate front springs for a more comfortable ride.

Minor changes were made to improve the braking system for 1980.

SERIAL NUMBER IDENTIFICATION

Vehicle

The serial number is located on the top left-hand side of the instrument panel, visible through the windshield. A typical vehicle serial number tag yields manufacturer's identity, vehicle type, model year, assembly plant and production unit number when broken down as shown in the following chart.

Engine

The engine identification number is located on a pad on the right side of the cylinder block below the No. 1 spark plug.

Transmission

The transmission identification number on the four speed manual is centered on a pad

Serial Number Breakdown

Mfr Identity [1]	Series Code Letter [2]	Body Style [3]	Engine Model [4]	Model Year [5]	Assy Plant [6]	Unit No. [7]
1	B	08	A	6	Y	100025

1. Manufacturer's identity number assigned to all Chevrolet vehicles.
2. Series.
3. Body Style.
4. Engine code.
5. Last number of model year (1976).
6. Assembly plant (Y—Wilmington).
7. Unit numbering will start at 100001.

GENERAL INFORMATION AND MAINTENANCE

on the lower right side of the case. On models with automatic transmissions, the number will be found on a tag on the right side of the transmission.

ROUTINE MAINTENANCE

Routine maintenance is preventive medicine. It is the single most important process that can be taken in avoiding repairs and extending the life of any automobile. By taking only a minute or so each day to check oil level, tire pressures and coolant level, you'll be saving yourself time and money in the long run.

Air Cleaner

The 1979–80 Chevettes have a removable filter element. It is easily replaced by removing the wing nut on top of the air cleaner and plac-

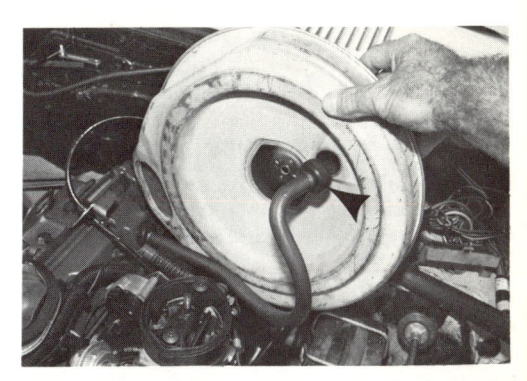

Lift off the old filter and disconnect the hose and grommet (arrow)

This shield keeps direct road dirt from hitting the filter element. Wipe it clean if you are not replacing the filter

The air cleaner wing nut screws off counterclockwise, don't overtighten it when putting it back on

The retaining bail snaps off. Use a screwdriver to pry it off, if it's stubborn

Check the rubber gasket that the air cleaner sits on. If it's in bad shape or missing, replace it

4 GENERAL INFORMATION AND MAINTENANCE

ing the new filter in the same position as the old one. GM recommends that the filter be replaced at 50,000 mile intervals when driving under normal conditions. When driving under dusty conditions the filter should be replaced more frequently.

The air cleaner on 1976–78 Chevettes is a welded, non-serviceable unit. GM recommends this filter be changed at 50,000 mile intervals.

To replace the unit:

1. Remove the wing nut from the mounting stud.
2. Pry the retaining bail wire from the air cleaner.

NOTE: *On 1979–80 models, simply remove the air cleaner lid, replace the old filter with a new one and replace the lid. On 1976–78 models, continue as follows.*

3. Disconnect the attaching hose and remove the air cleaner.
4. Position the new air cleaner over the carburetor, attach the hose, reconnect the bail wire, and screw the wing nut back on.

Positive Crankcase Ventilation Valve

PCV valve replacement is recommended at 30,000 miles or 2 year intervals. A clogged PCV system will cause poor idle and rough running. To replace the valve:

1. Pull the PCV valve from the valve cover, under the air cleaner.
2. Using a pair of pliers, release the valve retaining clip and remove the valve.
3. Install the new valve and insert it into the valve cover.
4. Inspect all PCV connecting hoses. Replace any cracked or deteriorated hoses.

The PCV valve is located in the valve cover (arrow)

Finally, remove the valve from the connecting hose. Some are retained by a clip which is released by squeezing with pliers

The valve pulls right out of its grommet in the valve cover

Evaporative Canister

The canister stores carburetor and fuel tank vapors while the engine is off, holding them to be drawn into the engine and burned when the engine is started. The filter mounted on the bottom of the canister requires replacement at 15,000 mile intervals. To replace the filter:

1. Loosen the screw retaining the canister in its bracket.
2. Lift the canister slightly out of the bracket.
3. Remove the old filter from the bottom of the canister.
4. Install the new filter by working it into the retainers on the bottom of the canister.
5. Lower the canister back into its bracket and tighten the screw.

GENERAL INFORMATION AND MAINTENANCE

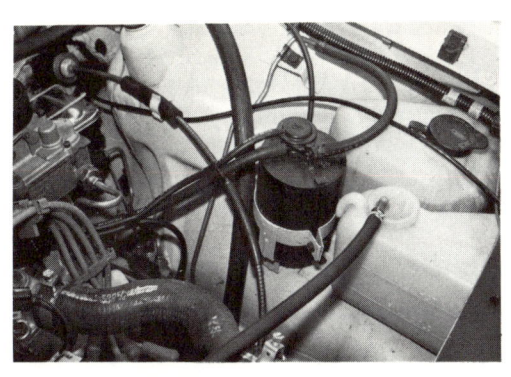

The evaporative canister is located at the front of the engine compartment on the driver's side

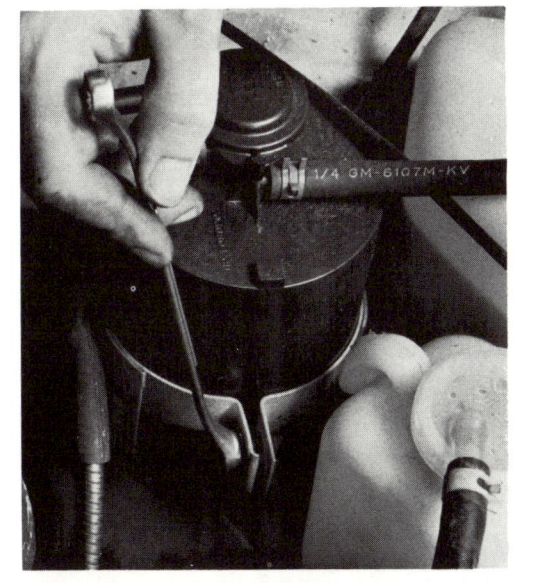

Loosen the bracket retaining screw enough so that you can slip the canister out

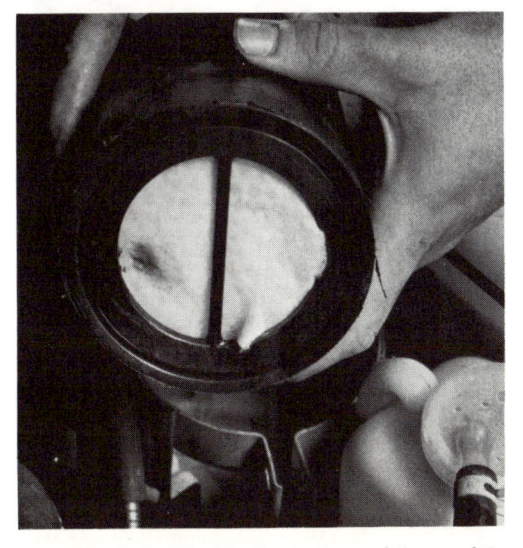

The filter is located in the bottom of the canister

Work the old filter out and discard it. The new filter goes in the same way

6. Check all connecting hoses and replace any that are suspect.

Belts

TENSION CHECKING, ADJUSTING, AND REPLACEMENT

Push in on the drive belt about midway between the crankshaft pulley and the alternator. Depending on its length, the belt should not deflect more than ¼–½ in. If the belt is frayed or cracked, replace it. Adjust belt tension as follows:

1. Loosen both nuts on the bracket.
2. When replacing the belt, pry the alternator toward the engine and slip the belt from the pulleys.
3. Carefully pry the alternator out with a bar, such as a ratchet handle or broom handle, and then tighten the alternator bracket nuts.

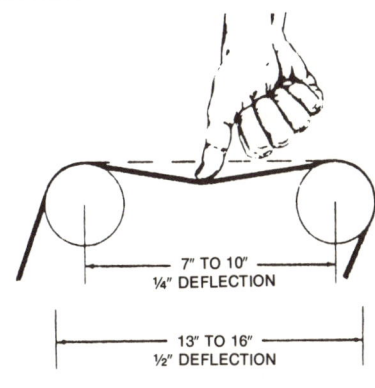

7" TO 10"
¼" DEFLECTION

13" TO 16"
½" DEFLECTION

Allowable fan belt deflection

GENERAL INFORMATION AND MAINTENANCE

pands into the atmosphere at a temperature of −21.7° F or lower. This will freeze any surface, including your eyes, that it contacts. In addition, the refrigerant decomposes into a poisonous gas in the presence of flame. Do not open or disconnect any part of the air conditioning system.

Fluid Level Checks
ENGINE OIL

The best time to check the engine oil is before operating the engine or after it has been sitting for at least 10 minutes in order to gain

The engine dipstick is located on the passenger side

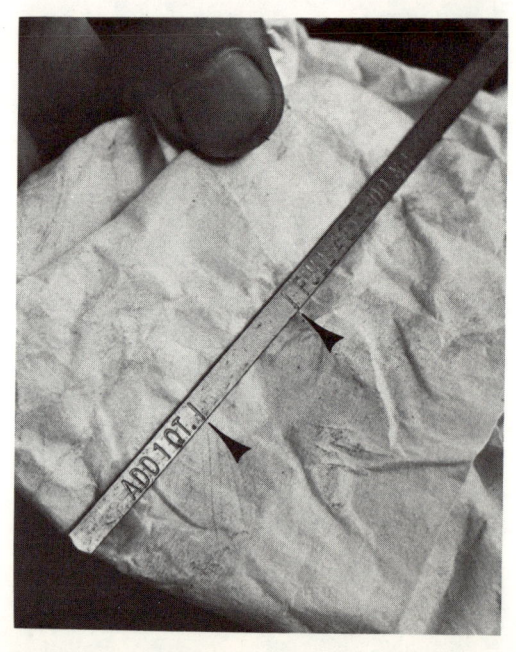

Loosen the bracket nuts to adjust the belt tension

4. Recheck the tension.

The alternator drive belt also operates the water pump. It might be good insurance to carry an extra belt in the trunk.

NOTE: *The optional air conditioning drive belt is adjusted in a similar fashion.*

Air Conditioning

The air conditioner should be turned on and allowed to run for a few minutes every two or three weeks during the winter. This will help the compressor seals stay lubricated and prevent drying and cracking.

This book contains no repair or maintenance procedures for the air conditioning system. It is recommended that any such repairs be left to the experts, whose personnel are well aware of the hazards and who have the proper equipment.

CAUTION: *The compressed refrigerant used in the air conditioning system ex-*

Add oil only when the level is even with or below the "Add 1 qt" mark

GENERAL INFORMATION AND MAINTENANCE 7

an accurate reading. This will allow the oil to drain back into the crankcase. To check the engine oil level, make sure that the vehicle is resting on a level surface, remove the oil dipstick, wipe it clean and reinsert the stick firmly for an accurate reading. The oil dipstick has two marks to indicate high and low oil level. If the oil is at or below the "add" mark on the dipstick, oil should be added as necessary. The oil level should be maintained in the safety margin, neither going above the "full" mark or below the "add" mark.

TRANSMISSION
Manual

Check the level of the lubricant in the transmission at 7,500 mile intervals or every 6 months. The lubricant should be maintained at the level of the filler plug. To check the level, remove the square-headed plug from the side of the transmission case. A slight amount of fluid may run out (indicating the transmission is full) or you can use your finger to determine if the gear lube is at the filler plug. If not, top it up with SAE 80 or 80–90 gear oil. Cars operated in Canada should use the SAE 80 all year.

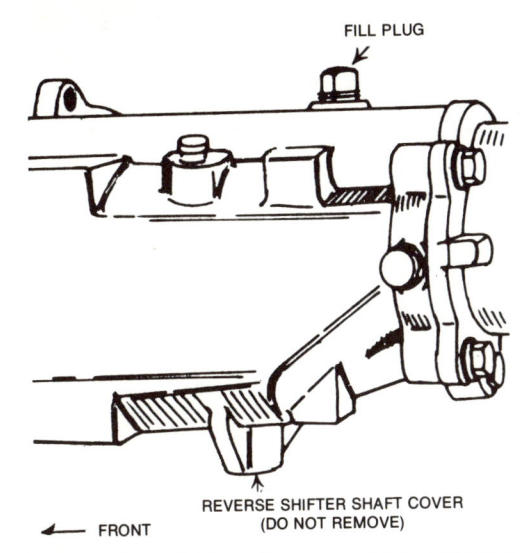

Bottom view of Chevette manual transmission. The fill plug is located on the driver's side of the transmission case

Automatic

Check the automatic transmission fluid level whenever you check the engine oil. It is even more important to check the fluid level when you are pulling a trailer or driving in a moun-

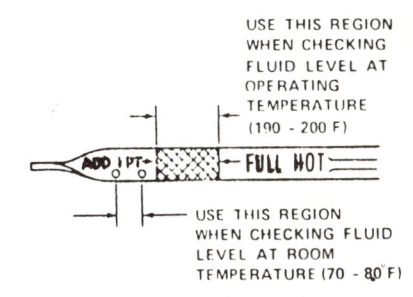

Automatic transmission dipstick markings

tainous area. Automatic transmission fluid that smells burned or has a dark brown appearance is a signal of impending problems.

Check the fluid level with the car parked on a level spot, shift lever in Park, and with the engine running and warmed up.

1. Remove the dipstick, which is located in the engine compartment on the passenger's side.
2. Carefully touch the end of the dipstick to determine whether the fluid is cool, warm, or hot.
3. Use a clean rag to wipe off the dipstick.
4. Fully reinsert the dipstick until the cap at the top is firmly seated.
5. Remove the dipstick and take your reading. If the fluid felt cool, the level should be about 3 mm–10 mm (⅛–⅜ in.) below the "Add" mark. There are two raised dots below the "Add" mark" to denote this range. If the fluid was warm, the fluid should be right around the "Add" mark. The level should be between the "Add" and "Full" marks if the fluid was hot to the touch.

NOTE: *One pint will raise the fluid level from "Add" to "Full" when the transmission is hot. Be careful not to overfill the transmission, as this is just as bad as running with the fluid low.*

If it is necessary to top up the transmission fluid use DEXRON® II automatic transmission fluid only.

BRAKE MASTER CYLINDER

The master cylinder is in the left rear side of the engine compartment, on the firewall. To check the fluid level as recommended at each engine oil change interval:

1. Clean off the area around the cap. Very small particles of dirt can cause serious difficulties in the brake system.
2. Pry the two wire retaining clips off the cap and to one side with a screwdriver. Take off the cover.
3. The proper level in each of the two res-

GENERAL INFORMATION AND MAINTENANCE

Master cylinder retaining clips (arrows)

After prying the retaining wires back, lift off the cover

ervoirs is within ¼ in. of the top. Add fluid as necessary.

4. Replace the cover and snap the retaining wire back in place.

NOTE: *Use only high-quality brake fluid specifically designated for disc brake systems. Ordinary fluid will boil during heavy braking, causing complete loss of braking power.*

ENGINE COOLANT

Since the cooling system is pressurized, the radiator cap should not be removed unless the engine has cooled. To do otherwise involves the risk of being scalded by steam. To check the coolant level; simply note the coolant level in relation to the level marks on the overflow canister.

If the coolant needs to be replenished, refer to the "Anti-Freeze" charts in the Appendix and to the "capacities" chart in this chapter to determine the proper amounts of anti-freeze and water to add to maintain the proper coolant mix.

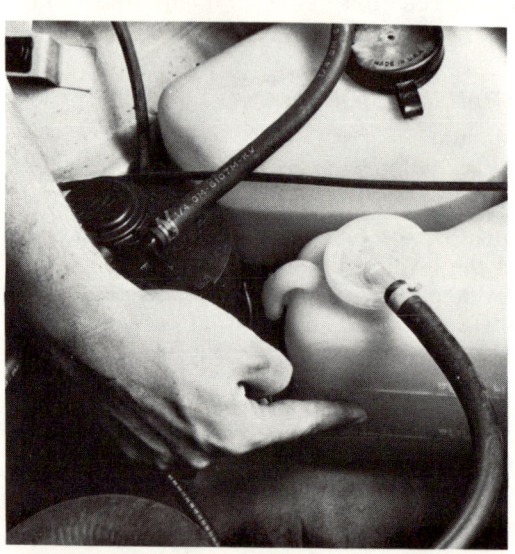

Coolant level should be at the lower mark when cold, higher mark when hot

NOTE: *Even in summer, the coolant mixture must provide 0° F protection. This is required to prevent rust and to ensure proper operation of the temperature warning light.*

If the coolant level is frequently low, refer to the cooling system section of Chapter 11.

REAR AXLE

It is recommended that the rear axle lubricant level be checked at each engine oil change interval. The proper lubricant is SAE 80 or 90 GL-5 gear lubricant. The filler plug is removed with a ⅜ in. drive ratchet and short extension. When the unit is cold, the level should be ½ in. below the filler plug hole; when it is hot, it should be even with the hole. Lubricant may be added by a suction gun.

STEERING GEAR

There is no filler plug on the steering gear box. The unit is factory filled. It should be

GENERAL INFORMATION AND MAINTENANCE

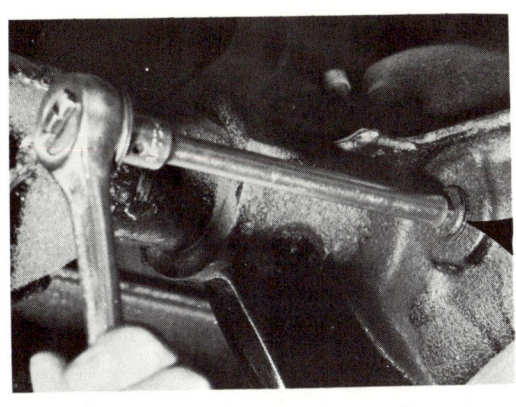

You'll need a 3/8 in. drive ratchet handle and an extension to remove the rear axle plug

checked for leakage every 36,000 miles. An oily film is not evidence of leakage. Leakage is the actual loss of grease.

BATTERY

Although the original equipment battery is a sealed unit and does not require added water, it does need periodic cleaning. Any accumulation of dirt or an acid film on the battery may permit current to flow from one terminal to the other, causing the battery to slowly discharge. Clean the battery regularly with diluted ammonia and rinse with clean water.

The sealed eye on top of the battery is the charge indicator. When the battery is fully charged the eye will be dark green. If the battery requires recharging, the eye will become a lighter green. When the indicator loses its color the battery must be replaced. Do not attempt to recharge a battery with a lightened indicator. It must be replaced.

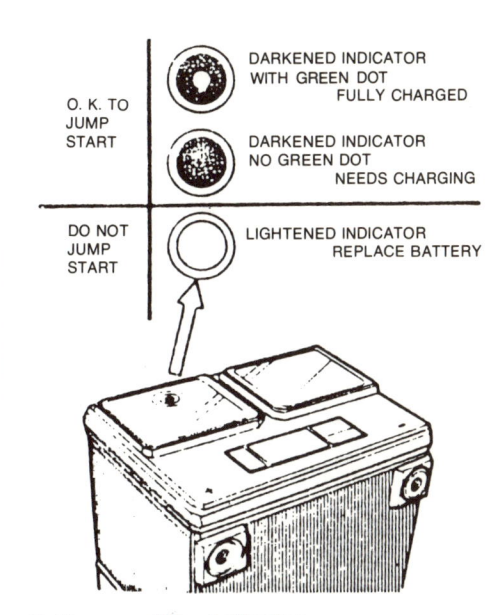

Battery condition indicator

TIRES

Proper tire pressures for standard size tires are given on a sticker on the edge of the driver's door. Tire pressures should be checked before driving, since pressure can increase as much as 6 psi due to heat. It is a good idea to have an accurate gauge on hand and to check tire pressures weekly. Not all the gauges on service station air pumps are reliable. Do not exceed the maximum pressures marked on the tire sidewall. All four tires should be of the same type; do not mix radial, bias, or bias-belted tires. Serious handling difficulties may result.

To obtain maximum tire wear, rotate the tires every 6,000 miles in one of the patterns

Capacities

Year	ENGINE No. Cyl Displacement liters	Crankcase Add ½ Qt For New Filter	TRANSMISSION Pts to Refill After Draining 4-Speed Manual	Automatic	Drive Axle (pts)	Gasoline Tank (gals)	COOLING SYSTEM (qts) With Heater	With A/C
1976–77	4—1.4	4	3	7	2.8	13	8.5	9
	4—1.6	4	3	7	2.8	13	8.5	9
1978	4—1.6	4	3	10	2	12.5	8.5	9
1979–80	4—1.6	4	3.4	10	1.75	12.5	9	9.25

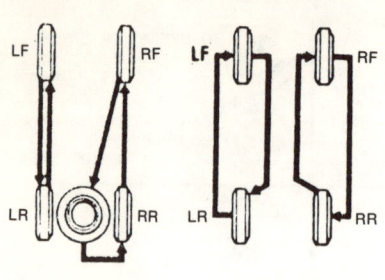

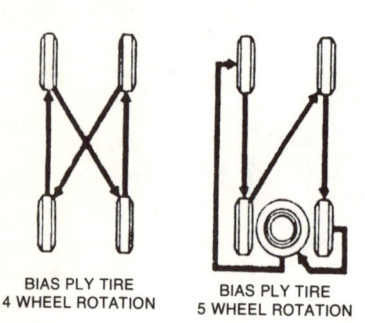

GENERAL INFORMATION AND MAINTENANCE

Correct rotation patterns for radial and bias/belted tires

The fuel filter is located behind the inlet fitting in the carburetor

Hold the fitting while loosening the nut

shown. The pattern to be used depends on the owner. The five-tire pattern results in all the tires being worn out at about the same time. This is good for new cars, especially if the owner intends to replace the worn-out original tires with a different size or type. The four-tire pattern is good for cars on which the original five tires have worn out and have been replaced with four new ones. If this pattern is used on a new car, the spare will be unused, requiring that only three new tires be purchased.

Fuel Filter

A paper filter element is located behind the carburetor fuel line inlet nut. The filter should be replaced every 12 months or 12,000 miles whichever occurs first. To replace the filter:

1. Place an absorbent rag beneath the fuel line connection to the carburetor to absorb any spills.
2. Unscrew the large nut while holding the fitting.
3. Remove the large filter retaining nut from the carburetor. There is a spring behind the filter. Remove the filter and spring.
4. Install the spring and the filter element.
5. Install the new gasket on the retaining nut and screw it into place. Do not overtighten; the threads are rather soft.
6. Install the fuel line.
7. Discard the gas-soaked rag safely.

GENERAL INFORMATION AND MAINTENANCE

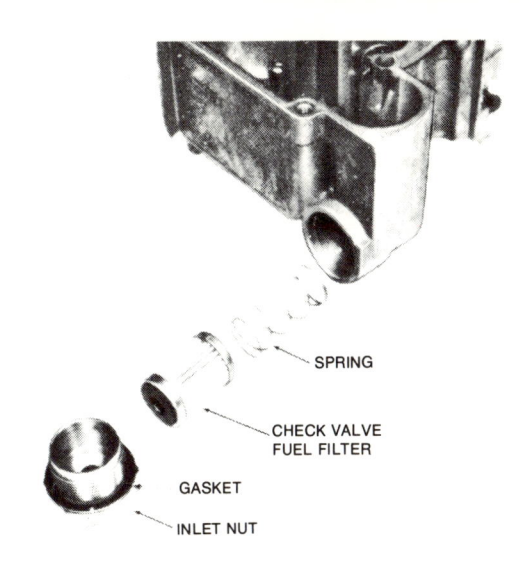

Filter assembly

(Labels: SPRING, CHECK VALVE FUEL FILTER, GASKET, INLET NUT)

Use these SAE viscosity grades

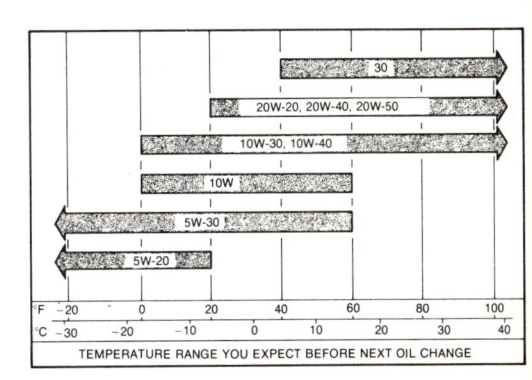

NOTICE: DO NOT USE SAE 5W-20 OILS FOR CONTINUOUS HIGH-SPEED DRIVING. 5W-30 OILS MAY BE USED IN 4-CYLINDER ENGINES UP TO 100°F (38°C)

LUBRICATION

Oil and Fuel Recommendations

All Chevette engines are designed to operate on 91 Research Octane Number fuel (regular). Unleaded fuels only are recommended. The manufacturer points out that fuels of the same octane number may vary in antiknock qualities, and cautions that ". . . continuous or excessive knocking may result in engine damage and constitutes misuse of the engine for which Chevrolet Division is not responsible under the terms of the New Vehicle Warranty."

Only oils labeled SE are approved under warranty. The manufacturer does not recommend the use of oil supplements on a regular basis, but does suggest that a Chevrolet dealer be consulted if a problem exists which can be solved by the temporary use of a specific additive. The accompanying illustration will be helpful in selecting the proper viscosity oil.

Oil Changes

Chevrolet recommends that the oil be changed every 6 months or 7500 miles, whichever comes first. However, this is only if the car is operated under "normal" conditions. Since many cars are operated beyond the "normal" conditions, the oil should be changed more frequently. It certainly won't do any harm. If your car is used under extreme conditions, such as dusty roads, trailer pulling, or short trips in cold climates, the oil should be changed at least every 3,000 miles or 3 months.

It is also recommended that the oil filter be changed at every oil change. By leaving the old filter in, you are leaving almost a quart of worn oil in the engine which will cause the fresh oil to break down faster than normal.

Always drain the oil when the engine is at operating temperature as the oil will flow easier and more contaminants will be removed. You'll need a draining pan capable of holding at least 5 quarts.

CHANGING YOUR ENGINE OIL

1. Run the engine until it reaches normal operating temperature.
2. Jack up the front of the car and support it on safety stands.

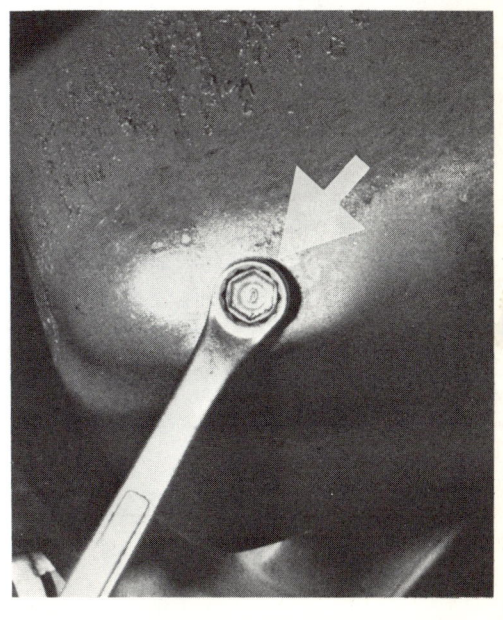

The oil drain plug is a 12 mm hex head bolt

12 GENERAL INFORMATION AND MAINTENANCE

Vehicle Maintenance Schedule

INTERVAL (Months or miles, whichever occurs first)	SERVICES

SECTION A—Lubrication and General Maintenance

Interval	Services
Every 12 months or 7500 miles (12,000 km)	Chassis lubrication Fluid levels check Engine oil change Oil filter change Tire rotation Rear axle lube change Wheel bearing repack
Every 12 months or 15,000 miles (24,000 km)	Cooling system check
Every 30,000 miles (48,000 km)	Manual steering gear check Clutch cross shaft lubrication
Every 60,000 miles (96,000 km)	Auto. transmission fluid change

SECTION B—Safety Maintenance

Interval	Services
Every 12 months or 7500 miles (12,000 km)	Owner safety checks Tire, wheel and disc brake check Exhaust system check Suspension and steering check Brake and power steering check
Every 12 months or 15,000 miles (24,000 km)	Drive belt check Drum brake and parking brake check Throttle linkage check Underbody flush and check Bumper check

SECTION C—Emission Control Maintenance

Interval	Services
At first 6 months or 7500 miles (12,000 km)- Then at 18 month/22,500 miles (36,000 km) Intervals	Thermo. controlled air cleaner check Carburetor choke check Engine idle speed adjustment Vacuum advance system, hoses check
Every 12 months or 15,000 miles (24,000 km)	Fuel filter replacement PCV system check PCV valve and filter replacement

GENERAL INFORMATION AND MAINTENANCE

Vehicle Maintenance Schedule (cont.)

INTERVAL (Months or miles, whichever occurs first)	SERVICES
Every 22,500 miles (36,000 km)	Spark plug wire check Idle stop solenoid and/or dashpot check Spark plug replacement Engine timing adjustment and Distributor check Carburetor vacuum break adjustment
Every 24 months or 30,000 miles (48,000 km)	Evaporative control system (ECS) check Fuel cap, tank and lines check
Every 50,000 miles	Air cleaner replacement

3. Slide a drain pan of at least 5 quarts capacity under the oil pan.

4. Loosen the drain plug. Turn the plug out by hand. By keeping an inward pressure on the plug as you unscrew it, oil won't escape past the threads and you can remove it without being burned by hot oil.

5. Allow the oil to drain completely and then install the drain plug. Don't overtighten the plug, or you'll be buying a new pan.

6. Using a strap wrench, remove the oil filter. Keep in mind that it's holding about one quart of dirty, hot oil.

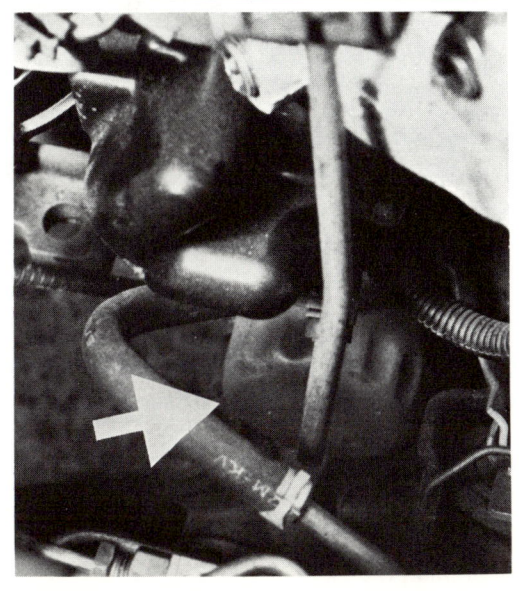

Bottom view of the oil filter. It will be easier to remove the filter from beneath the car

The oil filter is located on the driver's side of the engine

7. Empty the old filter into the drain pan and dispose of the filter.

8. Using a clean rag, wipe off the filter adapter on the engine block. Be sure that the rag doesn't leave any lint which could clog an oil passage.

9. Chevrolet recommends an AC PF-40 oil filter. Coat the rubber gasket on the filter with fresh oil. Spin it onto the engine *by hand;* when the gasket touches the adapter surface give it another ½–¾ turn. No more, or you'll squash the gasket and it will leak.

14   GENERAL INFORMATION AND MAINTENANCE

You'll need four quarts of oil and a filter for an oil change. Use the viscosity chart to select the proper oil for your climate

Lightly coat the filter gasket with fresh oil

Refill the engine through the cap in the valve cover

10. Refill the engine with four quarts of oil.

11. Start the car. If the oil pressure light does not turn off or the oil pressure gauge shows no pressure after a few seconds, shut off the engine and locate the problem.

12. If the oil pressure is OK and there are no leaks, shut the engine off and lower the car.

TRANSMISSION

Manual Transmission

The manufacturer states that the transmission lubricant need never be changed. However, persons buying a used vehicle or those subjecting their cars to heavy-duty use may wish to change the lubricant. This may be done by removing the drain plug and draining off the old lube. Dispose of this in the same manner as you would used oil. Reinstall the drain plug. Using a suction gun or squeeze bulb filler, fill the transmission to the level of the filler plug. Use SAE 80–90 or 90 GL-5 gear lubricant.

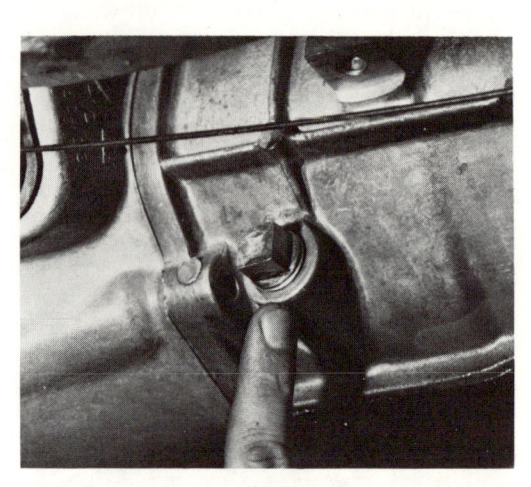

Manual transmission drain plug

Automatic Transmission

The automatic transmission oil pan should be drained, the screen cleaned, and fresh fluid added every 60,000 miles. If you're frequently pulling a trailer, you should perform this service every 15,000 miles.

1. Jack up the front of the car and support the transmission with a jack at the vibration damper.

2. Place a drain pan under the transmission.

GENERAL INFORMATION AND MAINTENANCE

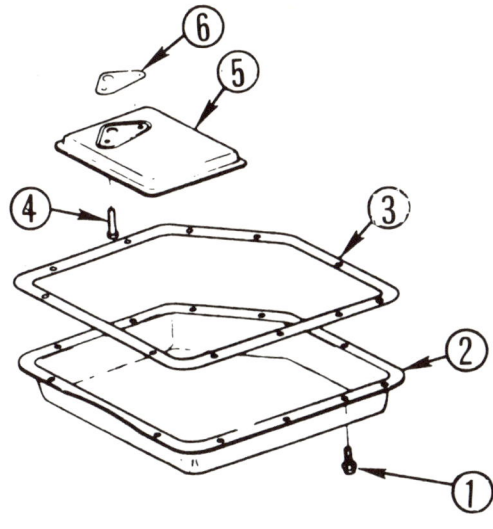

1. Oil pan bolt
2. Pan
3. Gasket
4. Filter screen bolt
5. Filter screen
6. Gasket

Automatic transmission oil pan and filter

3. Remove the oil pan retaining bolts at the front and sides of the pan.
4. Loosen the rear pan retaining bolts about four turns.
5. Using a screwdriver, pry the transmission pan loose and let the fluid drain into the drain pan. Be careful not to gouge the pan mating surface on the transmission.
6. Remove the remaining bolts and remove the oil pan and its gasket. Throw the old gasket away.
7. Drain off all the fluid from the pan.
8. Clean the pan with solvent and let it dry.
9. Remove the two screen-to-valve body bolts, screen, and gasket. Throw the gasket away.
10. Give the screen a good cleaning in solvent and let it dry.
11. Install a new gasket on the screen and replace the two bolts. Tighten the two bolts to 6–10 ft lbs (8–14 Nm).
12. Install a new gasket on the oil pan and install the oil pan. Tighten the bolts to 10–13 ft lbs (14–18 Nm).
13. Lower the car and add the correct amount of DEXRON® II automatic transmission fluid through the filler tube. (See capacities chart). A long neck funnel is handy for this operation.
14. Place the selector in Park, apply the parking brake, start the engine and let it idle normally.
15. Shift the selector through each transmission range, place it in Park, and then check the fluid level.
16. Add fluid as necessary.

REAR AXLE

The manufacturer states that the rear axle lubricant need never be changed on vehicles in normal use. It is recommended that the lubricant be changed every 7,500 miles on trailer towing vehicles. In addition, persons buying a used vehicle or those subjecting their cars to heavy-duty usage, may wish to change the lubricant. The proper lubricant is SAE 80 or 90 GL-5 gear lubricant. Positraction axles require a special Positraction lubricant. The lubricant should be level with the bottom of the filler hole. The positraction axle should be drained and refilled at the first 15,000 miles. After that, just check the axle as you would a standard axle.

Chassis Greasing

The proper grease to be used is water-resistant EP chassis lubricant. A hand grease gun is satisfactory.

NOTE: *Ball joints must not be lubricated at temperatures below 10° F.*

1. There are two steering linkage grease fittings, all reached from under the car. A grease gun with a flexible extension will allow you to reach all the fittings. Wipe off the fittings, install the gun, and pump in grease until it leaks out around the rubber seals. Wipe off the excess and the grease fitting.
2. There is a grease fitting above both upper ball joints and below both lower ball joints, four in all. Grease these as in Step 1.
3. Rub a little grease on the steering stops riveted to the lower control arms. Rub a little grease on the parking brake cable guides under the rear of the car.

BODY LUBRICATION AND MAINTENANCE

Door, Hood and Trunk Hinges

Use a heavy grease or silicone lubricant on the hinges to avoid binding conditions. After the initial application, exercise the hinge a few times to assure proper lubrication.

Door Locks

Apply graphite through the key slot. Insert the key and operate the lock several times to

16 GENERAL INFORMATION AND MAINTENANCE

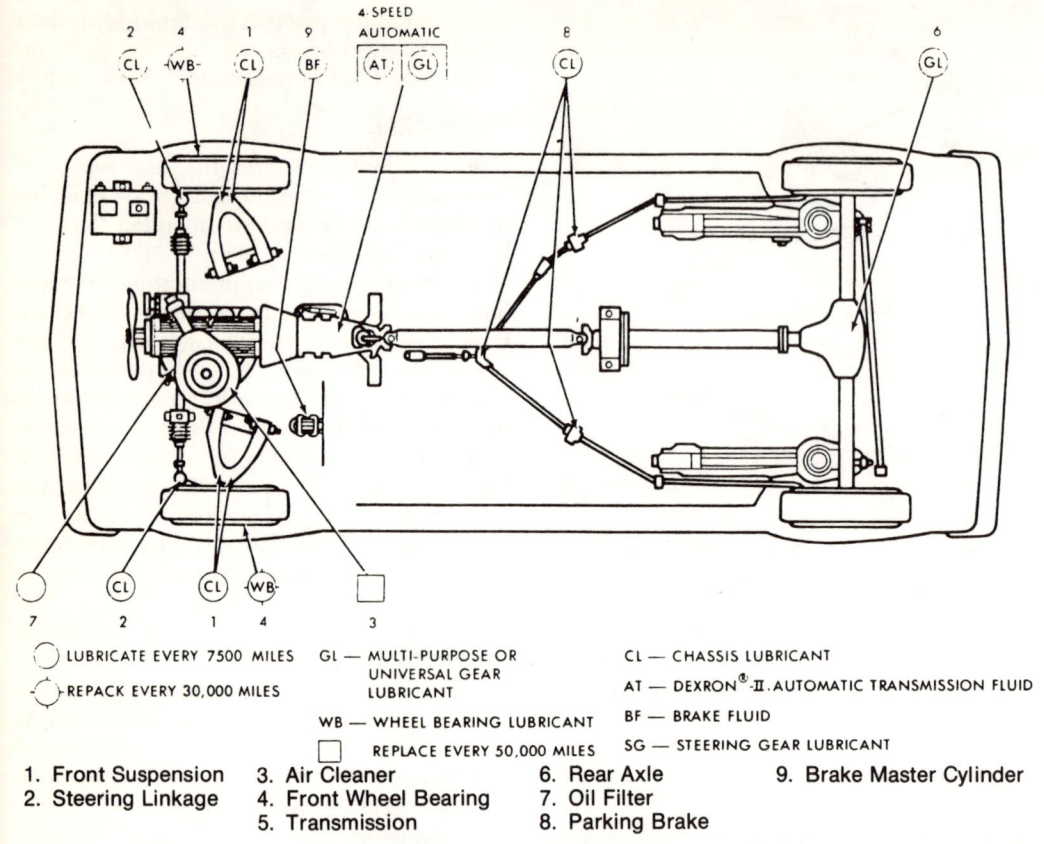

Chassis lubication diagram

○ LUBRICATE EVERY 7500 MILES
◇ REPACK EVERY 30,000 MILES
□ REPLACE EVERY 50,000 MILES

GL — MULTI-PURPOSE OR UNIVERSAL GEAR LUBRICANT
WB — WHEEL BEARING LUBRICANT
CL — CHASSIS LUBRICANT
AT — DEXRON®-II. AUTOMATIC TRANSMISSION FLUID
BF — BRAKE FLUID
SG — STEERING GEAR LUBRICANT

1. Front Suspension
2. Steering Linkage
3. Air Cleaner
4. Front Wheel Bearing
5. Transmission
6. Rear Axle
7. Oil Filter
8. Parking Brake
9. Brake Master Cylinder

make sure the graphite has worked into the mechanism.

Windshield Washers

Fill the windshield washer tank with a cleaning solution. Do not use antifreeze as it may cause damage to the paint.

PUSHING AND TOWING

Do not attempt to push start a Chevette, whether it's equipped with an automatic or manual transmission. Under certain conditions this may damage the catalytic converter or other parts of the car.

The car should not be towed to start, since there is a chance of the towed vehicle ramming the tow car. A Chevette may be towed with its rear wheels on the ground at speeds under 35 mph for distances up to 50 miles. If the car must be towed farther or faster, the driveshaft must be disconnected or the car must be towed on its front wheels.

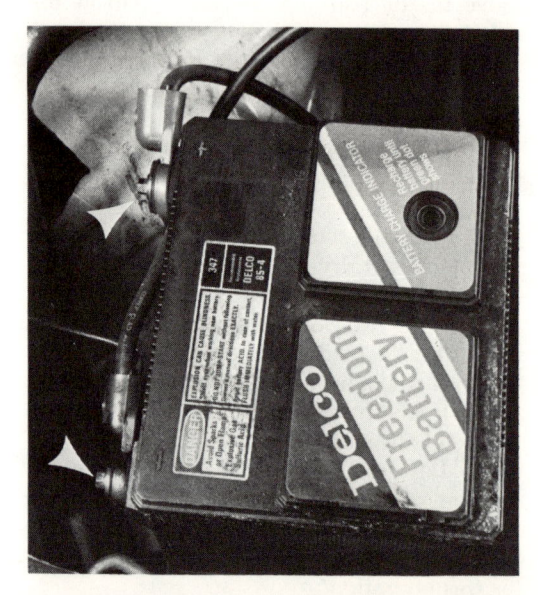

To jump start a side terminal battery, you'll need adapters (which are readily available) which attach under the retaining bolts (arrows)

Manual transmission Chevettes can be towed on all four wheels at freeway speeds

GENERAL INFORMATION AND MAINTENANCE 17

for extensive distances, provided that the transmission is overfilled by about a quart of gear oil and a sturdy tow bar is used.

NOTE: *Whenever the car is towed with all four wheels on the ground, the steering column must not be locked.*

JUMP STARTING

Jump starting is the only way to start a Chevette with a weak battery. The following method is recommended by the manufacturer:

NOTE: *Do not attempt this procedure on a frozen battery. It will very likely explode. If your Chevette is equipped with a Delco Freedom battery and the charge indicator is light, do not attempt to jump start the car.*

1. Turn off all electrical equipment. Place the automatic transmission in Park and the manual unit in neutral. Set the handbrake.

2. Make sure that the two vehicles are not contacting each other. It is a good idea to keep the engine running in the booster vehicle.

3. Remove all vent caps from both batteries and cover the openings with cloths.

4. Attach one end of a jumper cable to the positive (+) terminal of the booster battery. The red cable is normally used. Attach the other end to the positive (+) terminal of the discharged battery.

5. Attach one end of the other cable (the black one) to the negative (−) terminal of the booster battery. Attach the other end to a ground point on the engine of the car being started. An ideal point is the engine lift bracket located between two of the spark plugs. Do not connect it to the battery.

NOTE: *Be careful not to lean over the battery while making this last connection.*

6. If the engine will not start, disconnect the batteries as soon as possible. If this is not done, the two batteries will soon reach a state of equilibrium, possibly with both of them too weak to start an engine. This should be no problem if the engine of the booster vehicle is left running fast enough to keep up the charge.

7. Reverse the procedure exactly to remove the jumper cables. Discard the rags, because they may have acid on them.

NOTE: *To jump start a Maintenance Free® battery, you must first check the charge indicator on top of the battery. If the green dot is visible or the indicator is dark, you may jump the battery. If the indicator is light, under no circumstances should you jump the battery. The battery then must be replaced.*

JACKING AND HOISTING

The bumper jack supplied with the car should never be used for any service operation other than tire changing. NEVER get under the car while it is supported by a bumper jack. If the jack should slip or tip over, as bumper jacks often do, it would be exceedingly difficult to raise the car again while pinned underneath. Always block the wheels when changing tires.

The service operations in this book often require that one end or the other, or both, of the car be raised and supported safely. The best arrangement is a grease pit or a vehicle hoist. The illustrations show the contact points for various types of lift equipment. A hydraulic floor jack is also referred to. It is realized that these items are not often found in the home garage, but there are reasonable and safe substitutes. Small hydraulic, screw, or scissors jacks are satisfactory for raising the car. Heavy wooden blocks or adjustable jackstands should be used to support the car while it is being worked on.

Drive-on trestles, or ramps, are a handy and safe way to raise the car. These can be bought or constructed from suitable heavy timbers or steel.

In any case, it is always best to spend a little extra time to make sure that the car is lifted and supported safely.

NOTE: *Concrete blocks are not recommended. They may break if the load is not evenly distributed.*

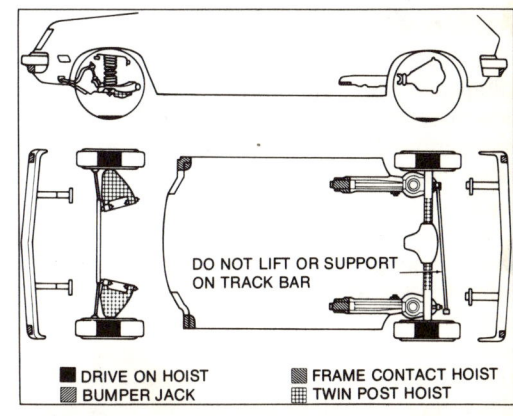

Jacking and hoisting points

Tune-Up

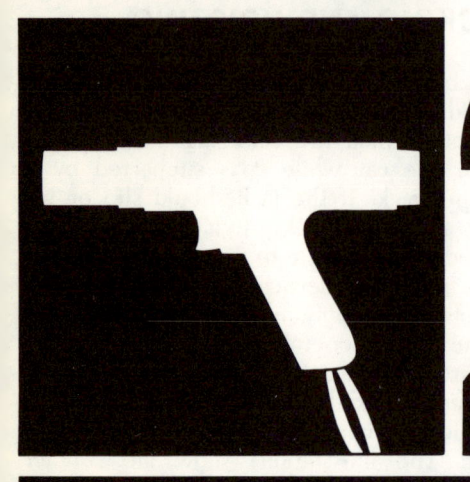

TUNE-UP PROCEDURES

Keeping a car in tune should be considered by the owner as routine maintenance. By tuning the car regularly you will not only be improving the power and performance of the automobile but at the same time you'll be increasing the life-span of the car. It will also greatly aid the car in meeting with federal specifications for emission control. The best pollution control device is a well tuned car.

Spark Plugs

Chevrolet recommends replacing the spark plugs at 22,500 mile intervals. They should, however, be removed and checked before that figure. Chapter 11 provides illustrations of correct and incorrect spark plug conditions and what causes them to burn incorrectly. This chart will enable you to locate any developing problems and make the necessary adjustments to possibly prevent a major repair.

1. Remove each spark plug wire by pulling on the rubber cap, not on the wire. The wires have a carbon core to suppress radio static, and this core is easily separated if the wire is roughly handled.
2. Wipe the wires clean with a cloth dampened in kerosene and wipe them dry. If the wires appear to be cracked, they should be replaced.
3. Blow or brush the dirt away from each of the spark plugs. Sometimes this is done by

Carefully pull the spark plug boot off. Don't yank on the wire

Tune-Up Specifications

When analyzing compression test results, look for uniformity among cylinders rather than specific pressures.

Year	ENGINE No. Cyl Displacement liters	HP	SPARK PLUGS Type	Gap (in.)	DISTRIBUTOR Point Dwell (deg)	Point Gap (in.)	IGNITION TIMING (deg) Man. Trans	IGNITION TIMING (deg) Auto Trans	Fuel Pump Pressure (psi)	IDLE SPEED (rpm) Man. Trans	IDLE SPEED (rpm) Auto Trans
1976–77	4—1.4	52 ①	R43TS	.035	Electronic		10B	10B	5–6.5	800 (1000)	800 (850)
	4—1.6	60 ②	R43TS	.035	Electronic		8B	10B	5–6.5	800 (1000)	800 (850)
1978	4—1.6	63 ③	R43TS	.035	Electronic		8B	8B	5–6.5	800 (800)	800 (800)
1979	4—1.6	④	R42TS	.035	Electronic		12B	18B(16B)	5–6.5	800(800)	750(750)
	4—1.6	⑤	R42TS	.035	Electronic		12B	18B(12B)	5–6.5	800(800)	750(750)
1980	4—1.6	④	R42TS	.035	Electronic		⑥	⑥	5–6.5	⑥	⑥
	4—1.6	⑤	R42TS	.035	Electronic		⑥	⑥	5–6.5	⑥	⑥

Figures in parenthesis are for California
B Before Top Dead Center
① 59 for 1977
② 62 for 1977
③ Optional H.O. engine rated at 68 bhp
④ VIN code E
⑤ VIN code O
⑥ See underhood specification sticker

NOTE: The underhood specifications sticker occasionally reflects tune-up specification changes made in production. Sticker information must be followed if it disagrees with data supplied here.

Part numbers in this chart are not recommendations by Chilton for any product by brand name.

TUNE-UP 19

TUNE-UP

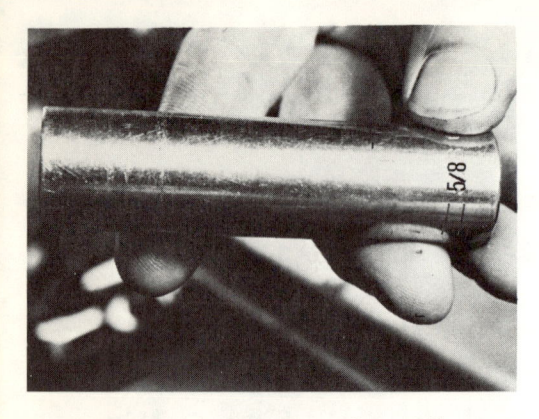

You'll need a ⅝ in. spark plug socket, not the more common ¹³/₁₆ in. variety

Turn the wrench counterclockwise to remove the spark plug

The plug can usually be unscrewed by hand once it's loosened

loosening the plugs and cranking the engine with the starter.

4. Remove each spark plug with a ⅝ in. spark plug socket. This size is common to most current Chevrolet engines. However, the spark plug socket supplied in most tool kits is the larger ¹³/₁₆ in. size. Be careful that the socket is all the way down on the plug to prevent it from slipping and cracking the porcelain insulator.

5. Refer to Chapter 11 for details on evaluating the condition of the plugs. In general, a tan or medium gray color on the business end of the plug indicates normal combustion conditions. The manufacturer states that the spark plug's useful life is about 22,500 miles. This being the case, it would be wise to replace the plugs if it has been more than 22,500 miles since the last tune-up or if the 22,500 mile interval will be reached before the next tune-up. Refer to the "Tune-Up Specifications" chart for the proper spark plug type.

6. If the plugs are to be reused, file the center and side electrodes with a small, fine file. Check the gap between the two electrodes with a spark plug gap gauge. The round wire type is the most accurate. If the gap is incorrect, use the adjusting device on the wire gauge to correct the error. Be careful not to bend the electrode too far, because excessive bending may cause it to weaken and possibly fall off into the engine. This would require cylinder head removal to reach the broken piece, and could result in cylinder wall and ring damage.

7. Clean the plug threads with a wire brush. Crank the engine with the starter to blow out any dirt particles from the cylinder head threads.

8. Screw the plugs in finger tight. Tighten them with the plug socket. If a torque wrench is available, tighten them to 15 ft lbs.

9. Reinstall the wires. If there is any

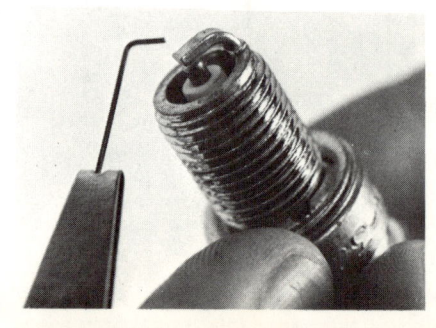

Use a round wire gauge to check spark plug gap

TUNE-UP

doubt as to their proper locations, refer to the "Firing Order" illustration in Chapter 3.

High Energy Ignition System

Standard on all Chevettes is the High Energy Ignition (HEI) system. This is a transistorized ignition system which eliminates the conventional system's points and condenser, thus eliminating a major part of the tune-up. The voltage delivered by this system is also far greater than the conventional system, enabling longer spark plug life as the hotter plug won't be as susceptible to fouling. There is no regular servicing of the distributor other than checking the distributor cap and rotor for burning and pitting. The plugs should be replaced every 22,500 miles. The system operates as follows:

The magnetic pick-up assembly located inside the distributor contains a permanent magnet, a pole piece with internal teeth, and a pick-up coil. When the teeth of the rotating

To remove the distributor cap, push down on the screw latches and release them by turning

All of the HEI system components are housed in the distributor, except the coil

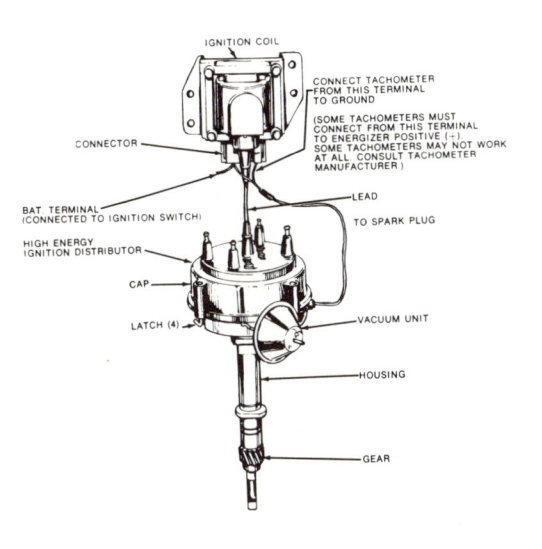

HEI system—This illustration is a representative schematic and does not depict actual component location

No regular maintenance is necessary with HEI, but an occasional check of cap and rotor condition is a good idea. Look for pitting and burning

22 TUNE-UP

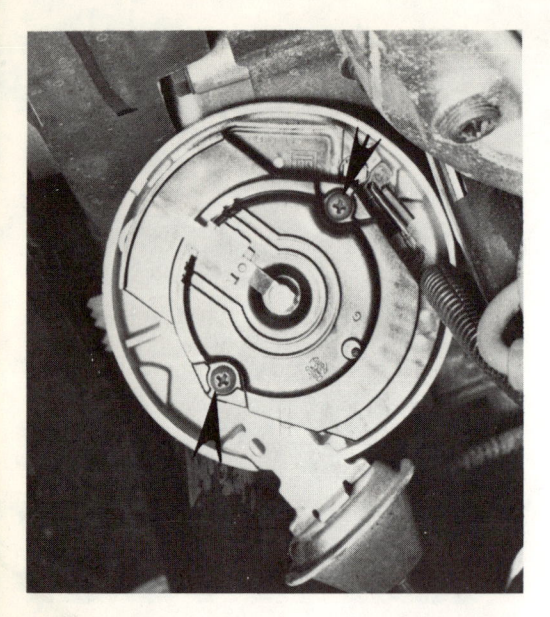

Unscrew the two phillips head screws (arrows) to remove the rotor

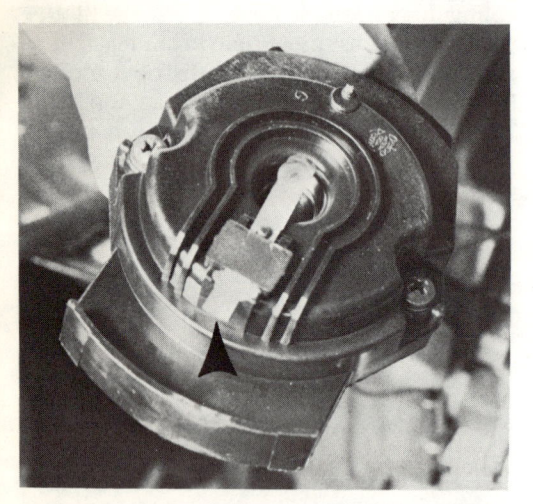

If the tip of the rotor is burned or pitted, replace it

timer core and pole piece align, an induced voltage in the pick-up coil signals the electronic module to open the coil primary circuit. As the primary current decreases, a high voltage is induced in the secondary windings of the ignition coil, directing a spark through the rotor and high voltage leads to fire the spark plugs. The dwell period is automatically controlled by the electronic module and is increased with increasing engine rpm. The HEI System features a longer spark duration which is instrumental in firing lean and EGR diluted fuel/air mixtures. The condenser (capacitor) located within the HEI distributor is provided for noise (static) suppression purposes only and is not a regularly replaced ignition system component.

HEI SYSTEM TACHOMETER HOOKUP

Connect the positive tachometer lead to the coil terminal that is connected to the distributor. Connect the negative lead to a good ground. Please note, however, that some tachometers must connect to the coil terminal and the battery positive terminal. Check the tachometer manufacturer's instructions.

CAUTION: *Never ground the coil terminal as the HEI electronic module could be damaged.*

Ignition Timing

1. Bring the engine to normal operating temperature. Stop the engine and connect a tachometer. Disconnect and plug the PCV hose at the vapor canister and the vacuum hose at the distributor vacuum advance unit.

NOTE: *Use an adapter to make timing light connections at the distributor No. 1 terminal.*

Start the engine and check curb idle speed. Adjust as necessary on cars without both automatic transmission and air conditioning by turning the idle solenoid in or out. On cars with both automatic transmission and air conditioning, make sure that the wire connected to the solenoid is green with a double white strip NOT a brown wire. Switch wires if necessary. With automatic transmission in Drive

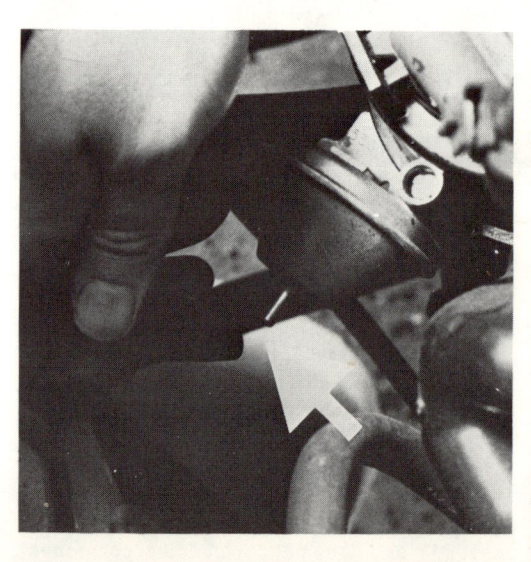

Disconnect and plug the distributor vacuum line

TUNE-UP 23

and air conditioning off, turn the ⅛ in. hex screw in the end of the solenoid in until fully bottomed. Turn the solenoid assembly to obtain 950 rpm and turn the hex screw out to obtain the necessary rpm. (See tune-up specifications chart.)

2. Stop the engine, clean the timing marks and mark them with chalk. Connect a timing light.

3. Start the engine and aim the timing light at the timing marks. If the marks align, stop the engine, reconnect the PCV and vacuum hoses, and remove the timing light.

4. If adjustment is necessary, loosen the distributor clamp and rotate the distributor to align the marks. Tighten the clamp and recheck the timing.

NOTE: *Air conditioned models require removal of the compressor, bracket, and belt to reach the distributor clamp.*

5. Reset the curb idle speed if necessary, stop the engine, and remove the tachometer and timing light. Reconnect the PCV and vacuum hoses.

VALVE LASH

The Chevette is equipped with a hydraulic valve system which requires no adjustment or maintenance.

Carburetor

IDLE SPEED ADJUSTMENT—THROUGH 1978

Two idle speeds are controlled by a solenoid on models without both automatic transmission and air conditioning. One is normal curb idle speed (solenoid energized). The other is base idle speed (solenoid de-energized), which is 200 rpm lower than curb idle speed and prevents dieseling when the ignition is turned off. On cars with air conditioning the solenoid is energized when the air conditioning is on to maintain curb idle speed.

1. With the engine at normal operating temperature, air cleaner on, choke open, and the air conditioner off, attach a tachometer to the engine. Apply the parking brake, block the rear wheels, disconnect and plug the PCV hose at the vapor cannister and the vacuum advance hose at the distributor.

2. For cars without automatic transmission and air conditioning, turn the idle solenoid in or out to obtain the curb idle speed stated in the tune-up specification chart, then disconnect the wire from the solenoid.

3. With the automatic transmission in

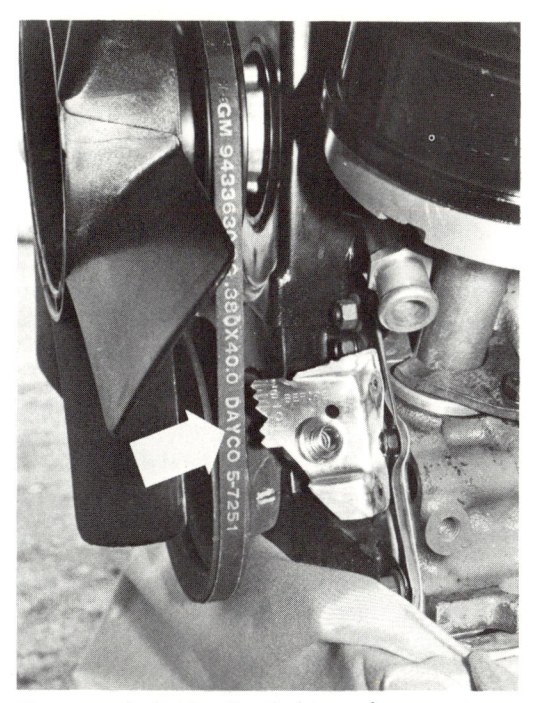

The arrow indicates the timing scale

The flash of the timing light will "stop" the timing marks which allows you to see if they align. Be careful that the timing light wires don't dangle into the fan or its belt

TUNE-UP

Drive or the manual transmission in Neutral, set the base idle speed to 200 rpm lower than the curb idle speed by turning the ⅛ in. hex screw located in the end of the solenoid. Reconnect the wire to the solenoid.

4. Cars with both automatic transmission and air conditioning must have a green wire with double white stripe connected to the idle solenoid, NOT a brown wire. Correct this if necessary.

5. With the air conditioning off and the automatic transmission in Drive, turn the ⅛ in. hex screw in the end of the solenoid until fully bottomed.

6. Turn the entire solenoid assembly to obtain 950 rpm.

7. Adjust the curb idle speed by turning the hex screw out to obtain the correct rpm. (See tune-up specifications chart.)

8. Check the ignition timing and adjust if necessary. Readjust the solenoid assembly and curb idle speed if necessary.

9. Stop the engine, remove the tachometer, and connect the PCV and vacuum hoses.

1979–80

Refer to the Vehicle Emission Control Information sticker on the vehicle for the latest specification information and idle speed adjustment procedure.

IDLE MIXTURE ADJUSTMENT

Carburetor idle mixture is preset at the factory and a plastic limiter cap is mounted on the idle mixture screw. The cap limits the mixture screw to approximately one turn leaner (clockwise) without breaking the cap. Idle mixture should be adjusted at major carburetor overhaul. Before suspecting the carburetor as the cause of poor performance or rough idle, check the ignition system thoroughly, including the distributor, timing, spark plugs and wires. Also be sure to check the air cleaner, evaporative emission system, PCV system, EGR valve and engine compression. Check the intake manifold, vacuum hoses and other connections for leaks and cracks.

NOTE: *A change has been made on some General Motors carburetors as of 1978 to limit the range of idle mixture adjustment on the rich side. In other words, backing out the adjustment screw will not make an appreciable difference. The new procedure requires the use of artificial enrichment through the addition of propane. Since it is not feasible to buy a tank of propane for one or two carburetor adjustments, the procedure for cars from 1978 on is not covered here.*

You'll need a tachometer and ⅛ in. allen wrench to adjust the idle speed. Leave the air cleaner on, it's removed here for clarity

TUNE-UP 25

The adjustment screw is at the center of the solenoid

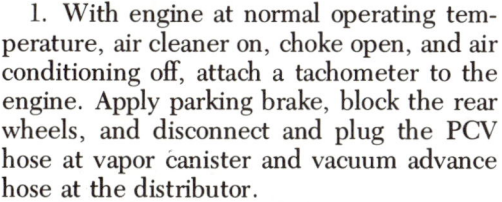

The arrow points to the idle mixture screw

1. With engine at normal operating temperature, air cleaner on, choke open, and air conditioning off, attach a tachometer to the engine. Apply parking brake, block the rear wheels, and disconnect and plug the PCV hose at vapor canister and vacuum advance hose at the distributor.
2. Start the engine and check ignition timing. Adjust timing as necessary. Replace vacuum advance hose.
3. Place automatic transmission in Drive or manual transmission in Neutral.
NOTE: *If the mixture screw is removed from the carburetor, gently seat it, then back it out 3 turns. Continue with Step 4.*
4. Remove the air cleaner, cut the tab off the limiter cap and remove the cap from the screw. Replace the air cleaner. Obtain the maximum idle speed by turning the mixture screw clockwise (leaner) or counterclockwise (richer).
5. Turn the idle speed solenoid in or out to obtain the higher idle speed stated on the underhood tune-up specifications sticker.
6. While turning the idle mixture screw

Cut the tab and remove the limiter cap

clockwise (leaner), watch the tachometer to obtain the lower idle speed stated on the underhood specifications sticker.

7. Stop engine, remove the tachometer, and replace the PCV and vacuum advance hoses.

Engine and Engine Rebuilding 3

ENGINE ELECTRICAL

HEI Distributor

All Chevette models are equipped with High Energy Ignition (HEI). This is a pulse triggered, transistor-controlled, inductive discharge ignition system that uses no breaker points. The HEI distributor contains a pick-up assembly and an electronic module which perform the function normally done by breaker points. The unit automatically controls the dwell period, stretching it with the increased speed of the engine. No dwell adjustment is necessary. Centrifugal and vacuum advance mechanisms are basically the same as those in breaker point distributors. The capacitor in the distributor only serves to reduce radio noise. The ignition coil is mounted externally of the distributor.

Distributor mounting is at the front of the engine on the left-side.

REMOVAL AND INSTALLATION

1. If the car is air conditioned: disconnect the electrical lead at the air conditioning compressor, remove the compressor mounting through bolt and two adjusting bolts. Remove the two bolts and remove the upper compressor mounting bracket. Raise the car

HEI connections are difficult to reach on the Chevette. The distributor is fairly accessible (except on models with A/C), but the ignition coil is hidden under the intake manifold.

ENGINE AND ENGINE REBUILDING

The arrow points to the distributor hold-down bolt

and remove the two bolts securing the lower compressor mounting bracket. Pull the bracket outward for clearance and lower the car.

2. Remove the air cleaner.
3. Remove the distributor cap and place it out of the way.
4. Remove the ignition coil cover by prying on the flat located on the front edge of the cover.
5. Remove the coil mounting bracket bolts.
6. Disconnect the electrical connector with red and brown wires that go from the coil to the distributor.
7. Remove the fuel pump, gasket, and push rod, making a note of which direction the push rod is installed. It's important that the push rod be installed in exactly the same direction as removed.
8. Scribe a mark on the engine in line with the rotor. Note the approximate position of the distributor housing in relation to the engine.
9. Remove the distributor hold down bolt and clamp.
10. Remove the distributor.
11. Install the distributor in reverse order of removal, making sure that the distributor is fully seated.

INSTALLATION—ENGINE DISTURBED

1. Remove the No. 1 spark plug and place a finger over the spark plug hole. Turn the engine until compression is felt in the No.1 cylinder.
2. Install the distributor with the distributor body scribe mark aligned with the mark on the engine and with the rotor pointing toward the distributor cap No. 1 spark plug tower.
3. Install the hold-down clamp and nut, but do not tighten them securely.
4. Install the distributor cap by aligning the tab in the cap with the notch in the housing and securing the four latches.
5. Connect the wiring harness connector to the terminals on the side of the cap. The connector will attach one way only. Reconnect the vacuum advance line.
6. Check and adjust the ignition timing. Securely tighten the distributor hold-down clamp.

Firing Order

To avoid confusion replace spark plug wires one at a time.

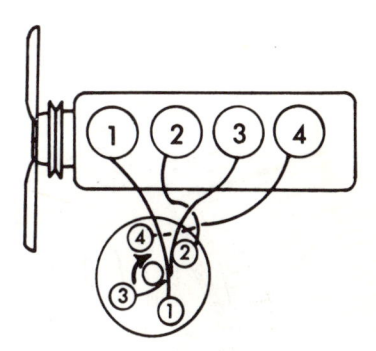

Alternator

A Delcotron 10-S1 series alternator is used. This unit also contains a solid state, integrated circuit voltage regulator. The alternator is nonadjustable and requires no periodic maintenance.

ALTERNATOR PRECAUTIONS

The following are a few precautions to observe in servicing the Delcotron (AC) generator and the regulator.

1. When installing a battery, be certain that the ground polarity of the battery and the ground polarity of the generator and regulator are the same.
2. When connecting a booster battery, be sure to connect the correct battery terminals together.
3. When hooking up a charger, connect the correct leads to the battery terminals.

28 ENGINE AND ENGINE REBUILDING

Alternator and Regulator Specifications

	ALTERNATOR			REGULATOR	
Year	Manufacturer	Output (amps)	Manufacturer	Type	Volts @ 85°
1976–80	Delco Remy	32	Delco Remy	Integral	13.8–14.8

4. Never operate the car on an open circuit. Be sure all battery, alternator and generator connections are tight.
5. Do not short across or ground any of the terminals on the generator or regulator.
6. Never polarize an AC system.
7. Do not use test lamps of more than 12 volts for checking diode continuity.
8. Avoid long soldering times when replacing diodes or transistors, as prolonged heat will damage them. Always use a heat sink.
9. Always disconnect the battery ground terminal when servicing any AC system. This will prevent accidentally reversing polarity.
10. Always disconnect the battery and AC generator if electric arc welding equipment is being used on the car.
11. Never "jump" a battery for starting purposes with more than 12 volts.

ALTERNATOR REMOVAL AND INSTALLATION

1. Disconnect the negative battery cable.
2. Disconnect the alternator wiring.
3. Remove the adjustment brace bolt and remove the drive belt.
4. Support the alternator, remove the alternator mounting bolt, and remove the alternator.

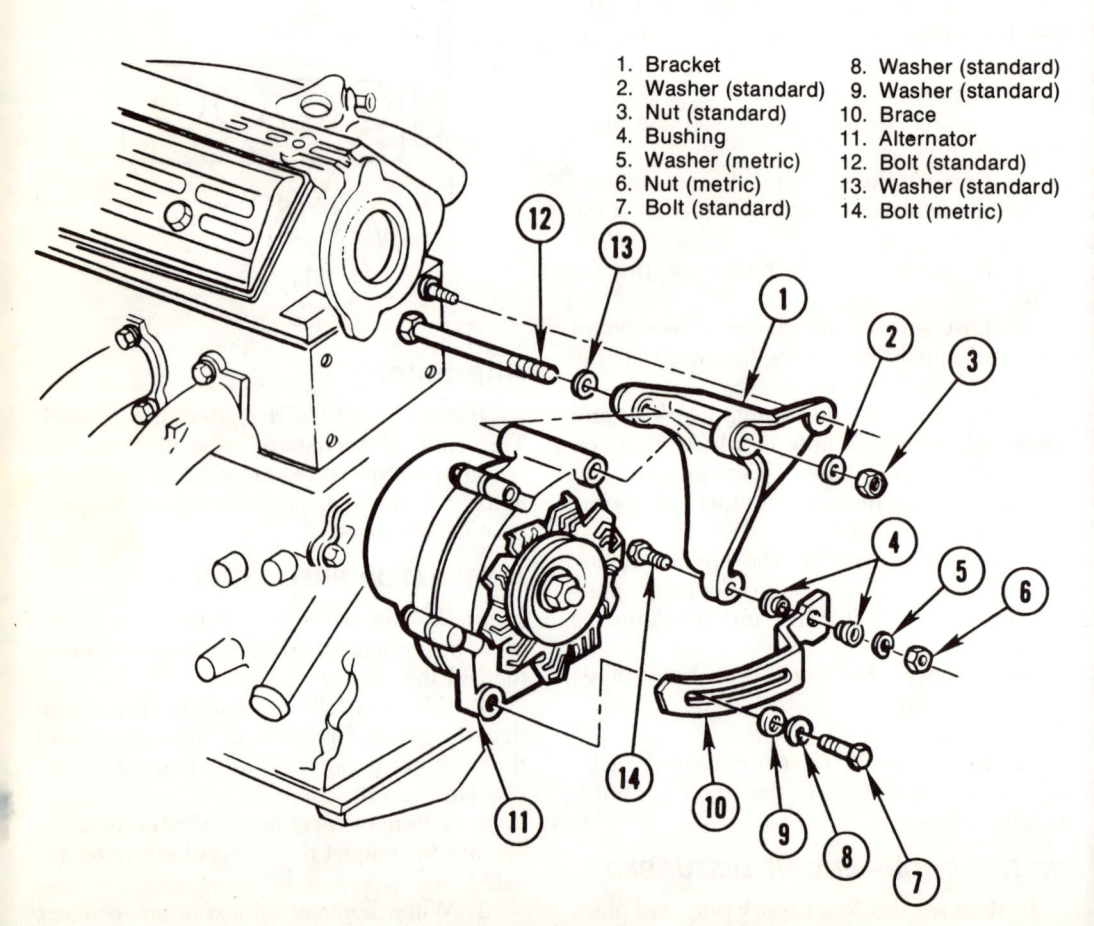

1. Bracket
2. Washer (standard)
3. Nut (standard)
4. Bushing
5. Washer (metric)
6. Nut (metric)
7. Bolt (standard)
8. Washer (standard)
9. Washer (standard)
10. Brace
11. Alternator
12. Bolt (standard)
13. Washer (standard)
14. Bolt (metric)

Alternator mounting

ENGINE AND ENGINE REBUILDING

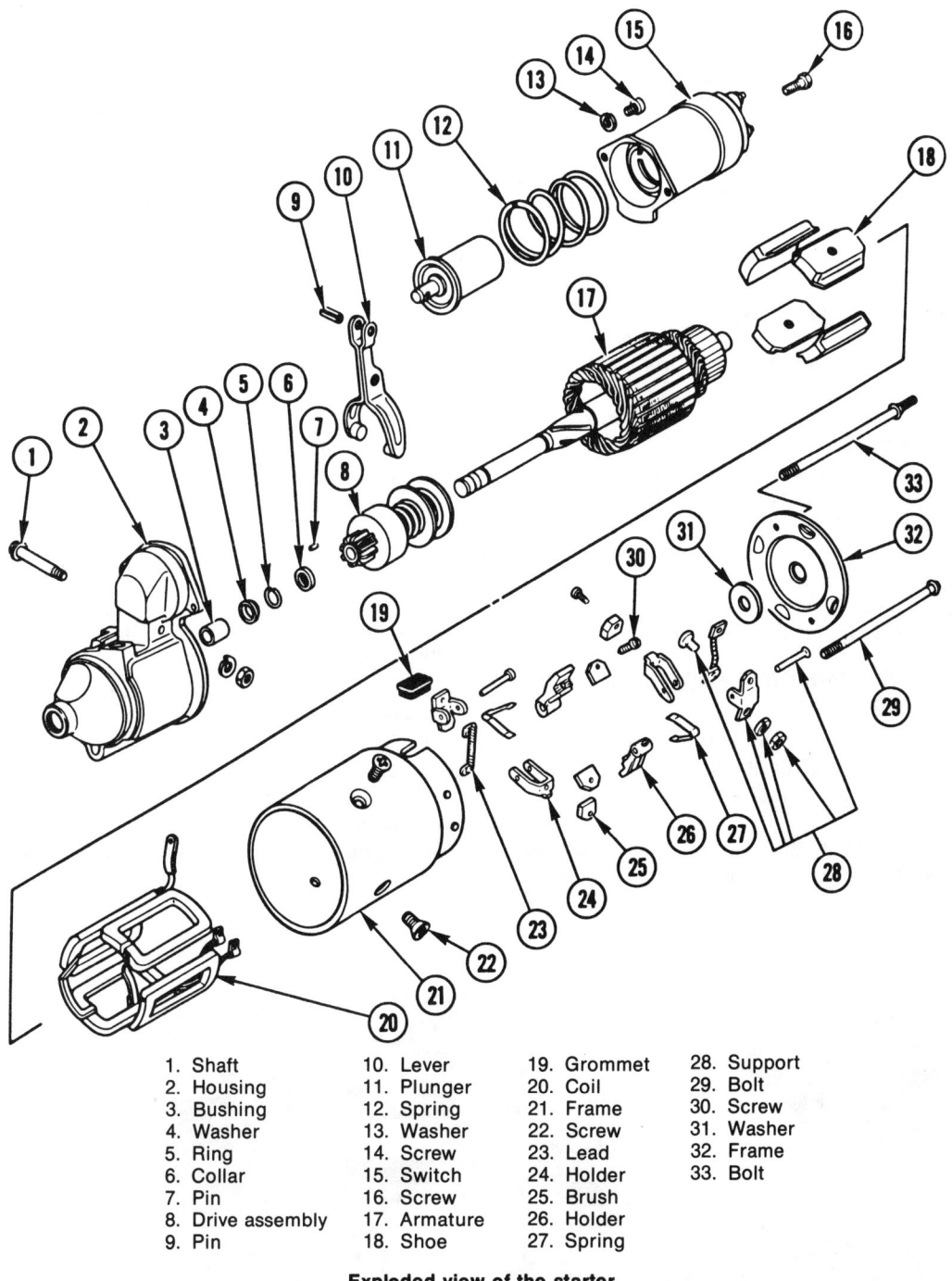

1. Shaft	10. Lever	19. Grommet	28. Support
2. Housing	11. Plunger	20. Coil	29. Bolt
3. Bushing	12. Spring	21. Frame	30. Screw
4. Washer	13. Washer	22. Screw	31. Washer
5. Ring	14. Screw	23. Lead	32. Frame
6. Collar	15. Switch	24. Holder	33. Bolt
7. Pin	16. Screw	25. Brush	
8. Drive assembly	17. Armature	26. Holder	
9. Pin	18. Shoe	27. Spring	

Exploded view of the starter

5. Installation is the reverse of removal. Be sure to adjust drive belt tension.

Regulator

The regulator is a micro circuit unit built in to the alternator. The unit requires no voltage adjustment.

Starter

Engine cranking is accomplished by a solenoid-actuated starter motor powered by the vehicle battery. The motor is a Delco-Remy unit similar to previous Chevrolet starters. No periodic lubrication of the motor or solenoid is necessary.

ENGINE AND ENGINE REBUILDING

STARTER REMOVAL AND INSTALLATION

Cars Without Power Brakes

1. Disconnect the negative battery cable and remove the air cleaner.
2. Disconnect the electrical connector from the oil pressure sending unit and remove the sending unit.

NOTE: *The oil pressure sending unit has a harness lock. To disconnect the electrical connector, lift the tab on the collar of the lock and remove the lock assembly.*

3. Disconnect the wires from the starter solenoid.
4. Remove the brace screw from the bottom of the starter housing.
5. Remove the two starter-to-flywheel housing mounting screws.
6. Hold the starter with both hands and tip it past the engine mount bracket, then upward between the intake manifold and wheel arch.
7. Installation is the reverse of removal.

Cars With Power Brakes (Without Air Conditioning)

1. Disconnect the battery negative cable and remove the air cleaner.
2. Remove the distributor cap and place it aside.
3. Remove the fuel line from the fuel pump to the carburetor.
4. Disconnect the electrical connector from the ignition coil. Remove the three coil bracket retaining screws and remove the coil with bracket.
5. Disconnect the vacuum hose to the distributor vacuum advance unit.
6. Disconnect the electrical connector from the oil pressure sending unit and remove the sending unit. See the preceding "Note" concerning the oil pressure sender harness lock.
7. Disconnect the wires from the starter solenoid.
8. Remove the brace screw from the bottom of the starter housing.
9. Remove the two starter-to-flywheel housing mounting screws.
10. Hold the starter with both hands and remove it by sliding it toward the front of the car.
11. Installation is the reverse of removal.

Cars With Power Brakes And Air Conditioning

1. Disconnect the negative battery cable and remove the air cleaner.
2. Remove the upper starter-to-flywheel housing mounting screw.
3. Remove the two steering column lever cover screws.
4. Remove the mast jacket lower bracket screw.

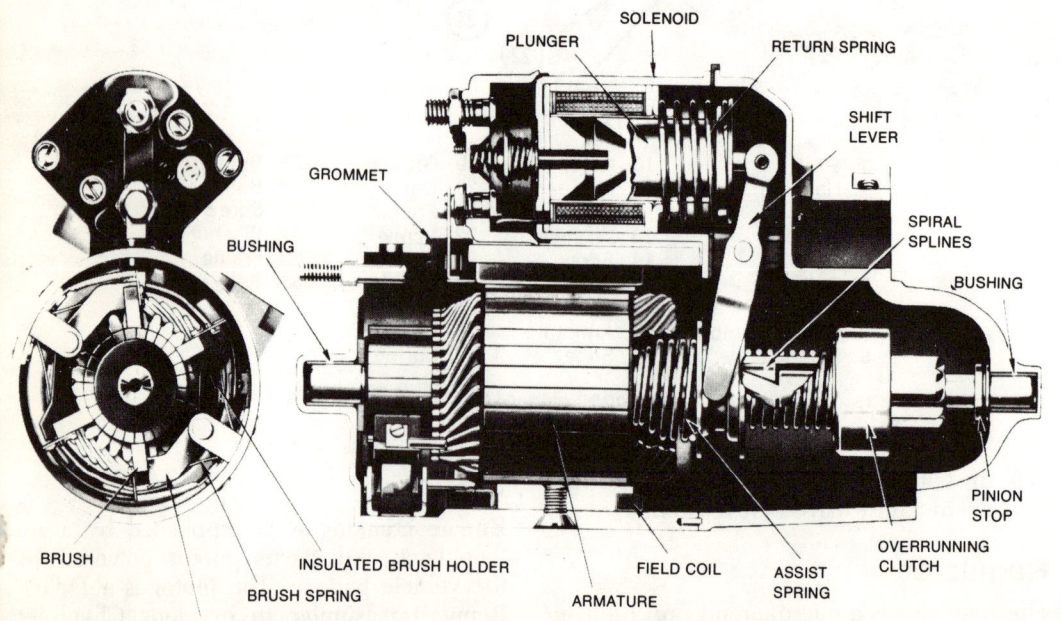

Cross section view of the starter motor

ENGINE AND ENGINE REBUILDING

5. Remove the upper steering column mounting bracket.
6. Disconnect the four electrical connectors from the steering column.
7. Raise the car.
8. Disconnect the flexible coupling (rag joint) and push it aside.
9. Disconnect the wires from the starter solenoid.
10. Remove the brace screw from the bottom of the starter housing.
11. Remove the lower starter-to-flywheel housing mounting screw.
12. To gain clearance, raise the engine ½ in. with a jack placed under the left-side of the engine.
13. Remove the starter by lowering it through the opening at the bottom of the engine.
14. Installation is the reverse of removal.

STARTER DRIVE REMOVAL AND INSTALLATION

1. Disconnect the field coil connector(s) from the starter solenoid terminal and remove the starter through-bolts.
2. Remove the commutator end frame, field frame assembly, and the armature from the drive housing.
3. Remove the starter drive by sliding the two-piece thrust collar off the armature shaft. Install a ½ in. pipe coupling or other suitable cylinder onto the shaft to butt against the edge of the retainer. Using a hammer, tap the coupling to force the retainer toward the armature end of the snap-ring.
4. Use pliers to remove the snap-ring from the groove in the shaft. If the snap-ring becomes distorted, use a new one upon assembly. Remove the retainer and starter drive from the armature.

Inspect all parts, replacing where necessary. Do not use grease dissolving solvent when cleaning starter parts—the drive mechanism and internal electrical insulation will be damaged.

To install:
5. Apply silicone lubricant to the drive end of the armature and slide the drive assembly onto the armature with the pinion outward. Install the retainer on the armature with its cupped surface facing away from the pinion.
6. Install the snap-ring on the shaft by standing the armature on a wood surface (commutator end down), placing the snap-ring on the end of the shaft held in position with a wood block, and tapping the wood block with a hammer. Slide the snap-ring into its groove on the shaft. Place the thrust collar on the shaft with its shoulder against the snap-ring.
7. With the armature on a flat surface, place the retainer and thrust collar next to the snap-ring. Using pliers on both sides of the shaft at the same time, grip the retainer and thrust collar and squeeze until the snap-ring is forced into the retainer.
8. Apply silicone lubricant to the drive housing bushing. With the thrust collar in place against the snap-ring and retainer, slide the armature and starter drive assembly into the drive housing. Engage the solenoid shift lever with the drive assembly.
9. Place the field frame over the armature and apply sealing compound between the frame and the solenoid case. Using care to avoid damage to the brushes, position the field frame against the drive housing.
10. Use silicone lubricant to lubricate the commutator end frame bushing. Install the leather washer onto the armature shaft and slide the commutator end frame onto the armature shaft.
11. Install the through-bolts and reconnect the field coil connector(s) to the starter solenoid terminal.

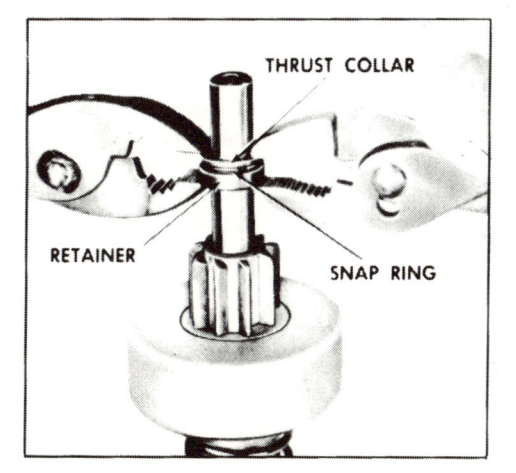

Forcing the snap-ring into the retainer

Battery

REMOVAL AND INSTALLATION

To remove the battery simply remove the hold down bolts and loosen and remove the cable ends at the battery.

Make sure the carrier is in sound condition and is capable of holding the battery firmly

ENGINE AND ENGINE REBUILDING

General Engine Specifications

Year	Engine No. Cyl Displacement (cu in.) liters	Carburetor Type	Horsepower @ rpm	Torque @ rpm (ft lbs)	Compression Ratio	Oil Pressure @ 2000 rpm
1976–77	4—1.4 (85)	1 bbl	52① @ 5300	67 @ 3400	8.5 : 1	39–46
	4—1.6 (98)	1 bbl	60② @ 5300	77 @ 3200	8.5 : 1	39–46
1978	4—1.6 (98)	1 bbl	63 @ 4800	82 @ 3200	8.6 : 1	34–42
	4—1.6 HO (98)	1 bbl	68 @ 5000	84 @ 3200	8.6 : 1	34–42
1979–80	4—1.6 (98)	2 bbl	70 @ 5200	82 @ 2400	8.6 : 1	55
	4—1.6 HO (98)	2 bbl	74 @ 5200	88 @ 2800	8.6 : 1	55

① 57 for 1977
② 63 for 1977
Bore and stroke for all 1.4 engines is 82 x 66.2 mm
Bore and stroke for all 1.6 engines is 82 x 75.7 mm

and keeping it level. To prevent the battery from shaking in its carrier, the hold-down bolts should be relatively tight, not tight enough, however, to place a severe strain on the battery case or cover.

Be sure to replace the battery terminals on the proper posts.

ENGINE MECHANICAL

All Chevettes are powered by a 1.4 or 1.6 liter, in line four cylinder, overhead camshaft engine. These engines are either 85 or 98 cu. in., respectively.

The cylinder block is made of cast iron. Each cylinder has individual intake and exhaust ports. The valve lifters are mounted in the head, next to their respective valves and are operated by lobes on the camshaft.

The camshaft is belt driven and housed on the top of the cylinder head. It is supported by five bearings in a "cam carrier". Bearing inserts are not used.

The crankshaft is also supported by five main bearings. It is lubricated through oil holes which lead from the main oil supply on the left side of the block. Number five bearing is the end thrust bearing.

The pistons are made of a cast aluminum alloy and incorporate the use of two compression rings and one oil control ring.

The crankshaft also drives, by way of a gear, the distributor and the oil pump. A cam on the shaft of the distributor drives the fuel pump.

Understanding the Engine

The basic piston engine is a metal block containing a series of chambers. The upper engine block is usually an iron or aluminum alloy casting, consisting of outer walls, which form hollow jackets around the cylinder walls. The lower block provides a number of rigid mounting points for the bearings which hold the crankshaft in place, and is known as the crankcase. The hollow jackets of the upper block add to the rigidity of the engine and contain the liquid coolant which carries the heat away from the cylinders and other engine parts. The block of an air cooled engine consists of a crankcase which provides for the rigid mounting of the crankshaft and for studs which hold the cylinders in place. In a water–cooled engine, only the cylinder head is bolted to the top of the block. The water pump is mounted directly to the block.

The crankshaft is a long, iron or steel shaft mounted rigidly in the bottom of the crankcase, at a number of points (usually 4–7). The crankshaft is free to turn and contains a number of counterweighted crankpins (one for each cylinder) that are offset several inches from the center of the crankshaft and turn in a circle as the crankshaft turns. The crankpins are centered under each cylinder.

ENGINE AND ENGINE REBUILDING

Pistons with circular rings to seal the small space between the pistons and wall of the cylinders are connected to the crankpins by steel connecting rods. The rods connect the pistons at their upper ends with the crankpins at their lower ends.

When the crankshaft spins, the pistons move up and down in the cylinders, varying the volume of each cylinder, depending on the position of the piston. Two openings in each cylinder head (above the cylinders) allow the intake of the air/fuel mixture and the exhaust of burned gasses. The volume of the combustion chamber must be variable for the engine to compress the fuel charge before combustion, to make use of the expansion of the burning gasses and to exhaust the burned gasses and take in a fresh fuel mixture. As the pistons are forced downward by the expansion of burning fuel, the connection rods convert the reciprocating (up and down) motion of the pistons into rotary (turning) motion of the crankshaft. A round flywheel at the rear of the crankshaft provides a large, stable mass to smooth out the rotation.

The cylinder heads form tight covers for the tops of the cylinders and contain machined chambers into which the fuel mixture is forced as it is compressed by the pistons reaching the upper limit of their travel. Each combustion chamber contains one intake valve, one exhaust valve and one spark plug per cylinder. The spark plugs are screwed into holes in the cylinder head so that the tips protrude into the combustion chambers. The valve in each opening in the cylinder head is opened and closed by the action of the camshaft. The camshaft is driven by the crankshaft through a chain or belt at ½ crankshaft speed (the camshaft gear is twice the size of the crankshaft gear). The valves are operated either through rocker arms and pushrods (overhead valve engine) or directly by the camshaft (overhead cam engine).

Lubrication oil is stored in a pan at the bottom of the engine and is force fed to all parts of the engine by a gear type pump, driven from the crankshaft. The oil lubricates the entire engine and also seals the piston rings, giving good compression.

ENGINE REMOVAL AND INSTALLATION

1. Remove the hood from the car.
CAUTION: *Do not discharge the air conditioning compressor or disconnect any air conditioning lines. Damage to the air conditioning system or personal injury could result.*

2. Disconnect the positive and negative battery cables.
3. Remove the battery cable clips from the right frame rail.
4. Drain the cooling system. Disconnect the radiator hoses from the engine and the heater hoses at the heater.
5. Disconnect the engine wiring harness at the firewall connector.
6. Remove the radiator upper support and remove the radiator and engine fan.
7. Remove the air cleaner assembly.
8. Disconnect the following items:
   a. Fuel line at the rubber hose along the left frame rail. Plug the line.
   b. Automatic transmission throttle valve linkage.
   c. Accelerator cable.
9. On air conditioned cars, remove the compressor from its mount and lay it aside.
10. Raise the car.
11. Disconnect the exhaust pipe at the exhaust manifold.
12. Remove the flywheel dust cover on manual transmission cars or the torque converter underpan on automatic transmission cars.
13. On automatic transmission cars, remove the torque converter-to-flywheel bolts.
14. Remove the converter housing or flywheel housing-to-engine retaining bolts and lower the car.
15. Position a floor jack or other suitable support under the transmission.
16. Remove the safety straps from the front engine mounts and remove the mount nuts.
17. Install the engine lifting apparatus.
18. Remove the engine by pulling forward to clear the transmission while lifting slowly. Check to make sure that all necessary disconnections have been made and that proper clearance exists with surrounding components. Remove the lifting apparatus.
19. On vehicles with synchromesh transmission: loosen the clutch cover-to-flywheel bolts alternately a turn at a time, to prevent distortion of the clutch cover, until the spring pressure is released.
20. Remove the flywheel from the crankshaft.

Installation

1. Install the flywheel on the crankshaft.
2. On synchromesh transmission equipped vehicles install the clutch disc and pressure plate as outlined in Chapter 6.

ENGINE AND ENGINE REBUILDING

Valve Specifications

Year	Engine No. Cyl Displacement liters	Seat Angle (deg)	Face Angle (deg)	Spring Test Pressure (Nm @ mm)	Spring Installed Height (mm)	STEM TO GUIDE Clearance mm (in.) Intake	STEM TO GUIDE Clearance mm (in.) Exhaust	STEM Diameter mm (in.) Intake	STEM Diameter mm (in.) Exhaust
1976–80	4—1.4	46	45	284 @ 32 (68 @ 1.26 lbs @ in.)	32 (1.26 in.)	.015–.045① (.0006–.0017 in.)	.035–.065② (.0014–.0025 in.)	7.97 (.3138 in.)	7.95 (.3130 in.)
	4—1.6	46	45	284 @ 32 (68 @ 1.26 lbs @ in.)	32 (1.26 in.)	.015–.045① (.0006–.0017 in.)	.035–.065② (.0014–.0025 in.)	7.97 (.3138 in.)	7.95 (.3130 in.)

① 1976—.0018–.0021
② 1976—.0026–.0029

Crankshaft and Connecting Rod Specifications

All measurements are given in inches

Year	Engine No. Cyl Displacement liters	CRANKSHAFT Main Brg Journal Dia	CRANKSHAFT Main Brg Oil Clearance	Shaft End-Play	Thrust on No.	CONNECTING ROD Journal Diameter	CONNECTING ROD Oil Clearance	Side Clearance
'76	4—1.4	2.0075–2.0085	.0009–.0025	.004–.008	4	1.809–1.810	.0014–.0030	.004–.012
	4—1.6	2.0075–2.0085	.0009–.0025	.004–.008	4	1.809–1.810	.0014–.0030	.004–.012
'77	4—1.4	2.0078–2.0088	.0009–.0026	.004–.008	4	1.809–1.810	.0014–.0031	.004–.012
'77–'80	4—1.6	2.0078–2.0088	.0009–.0026	.004–.008	4	1.809–1.810	.0014–.0031	.004–.012

ENGINE AND ENGINE REBUILDING

Ring Side Clearance

All measurements are given in mm except engine displacement, inches are given in parentheses

Year	Engine No. Cyl Displacement liters	Top Compression	Bottom Compression	Oil Control
1976–80	4—1.4	.305–.686 (.0012–.0027 in.)	.305–.813 (.0012–.0032 in.)	.000–.127 (.0000–.0050 in.)
	4—1.6	.305–.686 (.0012–.0027 in.)	.305–.813 (.0012–.0032 in.)	.000–.127 (.0000–.0050 in.)

Ring Gap

All measurements are given in mm except engine displacement, inches are given in parentheses

Year	Engine No. Cyl Displacement liters	Top Compression	Bottom Compression	Oil Control
1976–80	4—1.4, 1.6	.229–.483 (.009–.019 in.)	.203–.452 (.008–.018 in.)	.381–1.397 (.015–.055 in.)

Piston Clearance

All measurements are in mm except engine displacement, inches are given in parentheses

Year	Engine No. Cyl Displacement liters	Piston to Bore Clearance (mm)
1976–80	4—1.4	.020–.040 (.0008–.0016 in.)①
	4—1.6	.020–.040 (.0008–.0016 in.)①

① Measured 48 mm (1½ in.) from top of piston

Torque Specifications

All readings in Nm, ft lbs given in parentheses

Year	Engine No. Cyl Displacement liters	Cylinder Head Bolts	Rod Bearing Bolts	Main Bearing Bolts	Crankshaft Pulley or Damper Bolt	Flywheel to Crankshaft Bolts	MANIFOLD Intake	Exhaust
1976–80	4—1.4, 1.6	95–100 (70–80)	46–54 (34–40)	54–75 (40–52)	90–115 (65–85)	54–75 (40–52)	18–24 (13–18)	①

① Center bolts—18–24 (13–18); end bolts—26–34 (19–25)

36 ENGINE AND ENGINE REBUILDING

3. Install the guide pins in the engine block.
4. Install the engine in the vehicle by aligning the engine with the transmission housing.
5. Install the front engine mount nuts and safety straps.
6. Raise the car.
7. Install the engine-to-transmission housing bolts.
8. On automatic transmission cars, install the torque converter to the flywheel.
9. Install the flywheel dust cover or torque converter underpan as applicable.
10. Install the exhaust pipe to the exhaust manifold and lower the car.

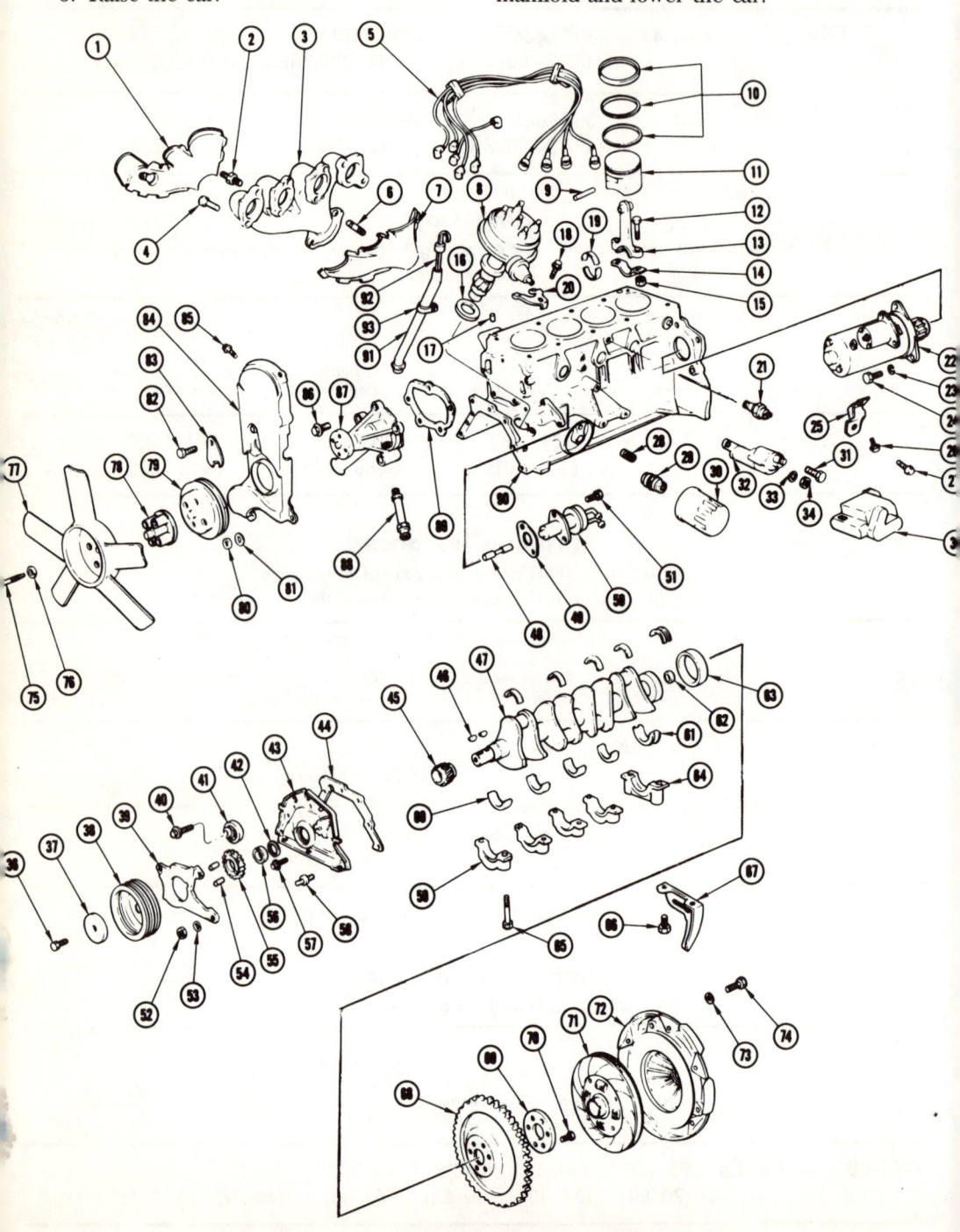

Exploded view of the cylinder head, oil pan, and related parts

ENGINE AND ENGINE REBUILDING

11. Install the air conditioning compressor if necessary, and adjust drive belt tension.
12. Connect the following items:
    a. Fuel line at the rubber hose along the left frame rail.
    b. Automatic transmission throttle valve linkage.
    c. Accelerator cable.
13. Install the air cleaner.
14. Install the engine fan, radiator, and radiator upper support.
15. Connect the engine wiring harness at the firewall connector.
16. Connect the radiator and heater hoses and fill the cooling system.
17. Install the battery cable clips along the right frame rail.
18. Install the engine hood.
19. Connect the battery cables, start the engine and check for leaks.

Valve System

Valve operation is accomplished by rocker arms bridging hydraulic lash adjusters and the valve stems depressed by the camshaft.

Periodic adjustment of the hydraulic valve lash adjusters is not necessary. Cleanliness should be exercised when handling the valve lash adjusters. Before installation of lash adjusters, check the lash adjuster hole in the cylinder head to make sure that it is free of foreign matter and fill the lash adjusters with oil.

Cylinder Head

REMOVAL

NOTE: *In order to complete the rocker arm removal a special tool (#J-25477) is necessary.*

1. Disconnect battery negative cable.
2. Remove the accessory drive belts.
3. Remove the engine fan.
4. Remove the timing belt upper cover retaining screws and nuts and remove the cover.
5. Loosen the idler pulley and remove the timing belt from the camshaft drive sprocket.
6. Remove the air cleaner and silencer assembly.
7. Drain the cooling system. Disconnect the upper radiator hose at the thermostat and the heater hose at the intake manifold.
8. Remove the accelerator cable support bracket.

---

1. Stove
2. Stud
3. Manifold
4. Bolt
5. Wires
6. Stud
7. Stove
8. Distributor
9. Piston pin
10. Piston ring
11. Piston
12. Bolt
13. Rod
14. Cap
15. Nut
16. Gasket
17. Pin
18. Bolt
19. Connecting rod bearing
20. Clamp
21. Switch
22. Motor and switch
23. Washer
24. Bolt
25. Brace
26. Bolt
27. Bolt
28. Valve
29. Connector
30. Element
31. Bolt
32. Coil
33. Washer
34. Nut
35. Shield
36. Bolt
37. Washer
38. Pulley
39. Cover
40. Bolt
41. Pulley
42. Seal
43. Cover
44. Gasket
45. Gear
46. Key
47. Crankshaft
48. Fuel pump pushrod
49. Gasket
50. Fuel pump
51. Bolt
52. Nut
53. Washer
54. Pin
55. Sprocket
56. Spacer
57. Bolt
58. Stud
59. Cap
60. Bearing
61. Bearing
62. Bearing
63. Seal
64. Cap
65. Bolt
66. Bolt
67. Deflector
68. Flywheel
69. Retainer
70. Bolt
71. Plate
72. Clutch cover and pressure plate
73. Lockwasher
74. Bolt
75. Bolt
76. Lockwasher
77. Fan
78. Spacer
79. Pulley
80. Nut
81. Washer
82. Bolt
83. Cover
84. Cover
85. Bolt
86. Bolt
87. Water pump
88. Nipple
89. Gasket
90. Engine Cylinder Block
91. Tube
92. Gauge
93. Clamp

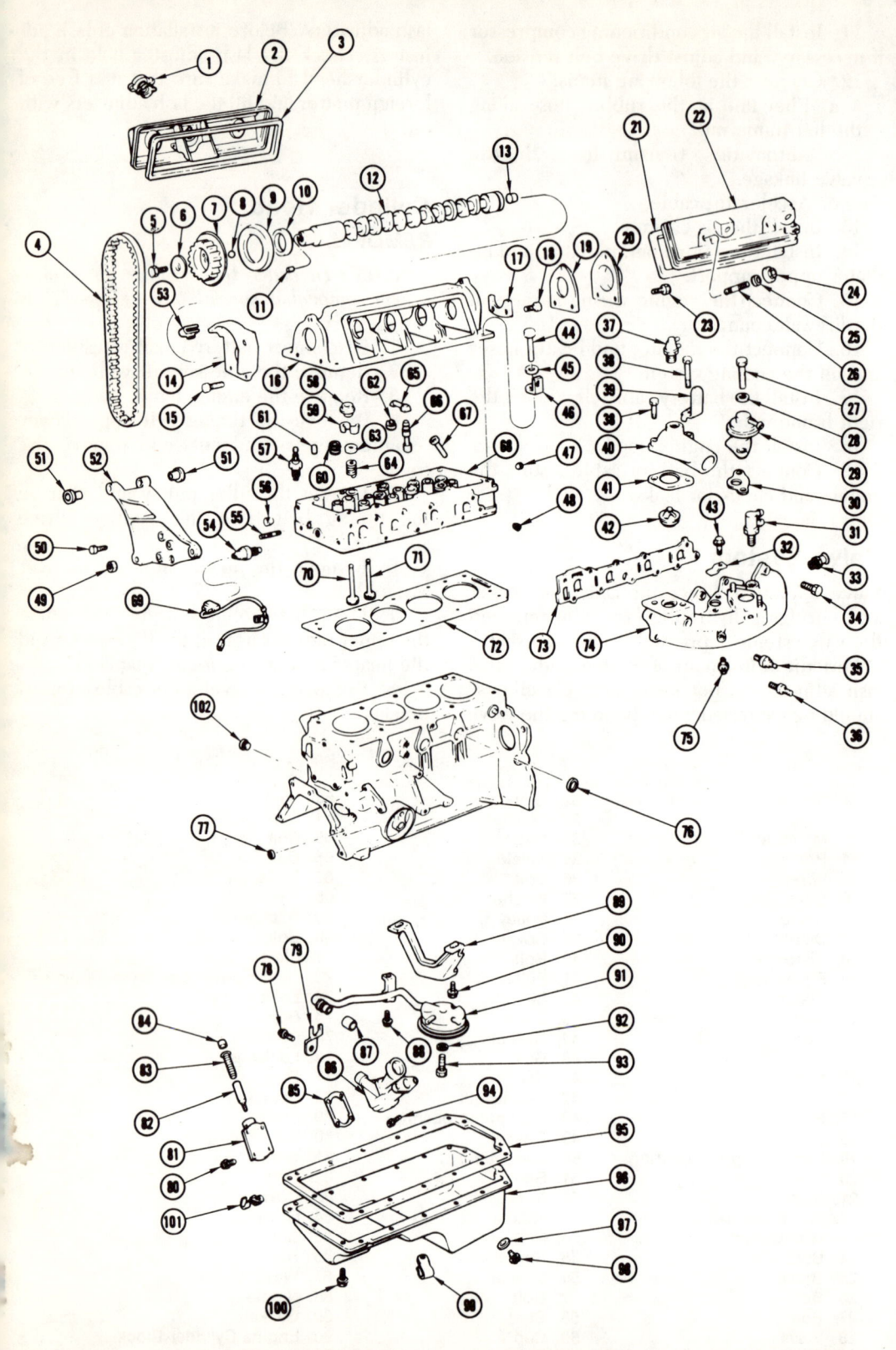

38 ENGINE AND ENGINE REBUILDING

Exploded view of the cylinder block and related parts

ENGINE AND ENGINE REBUILDING

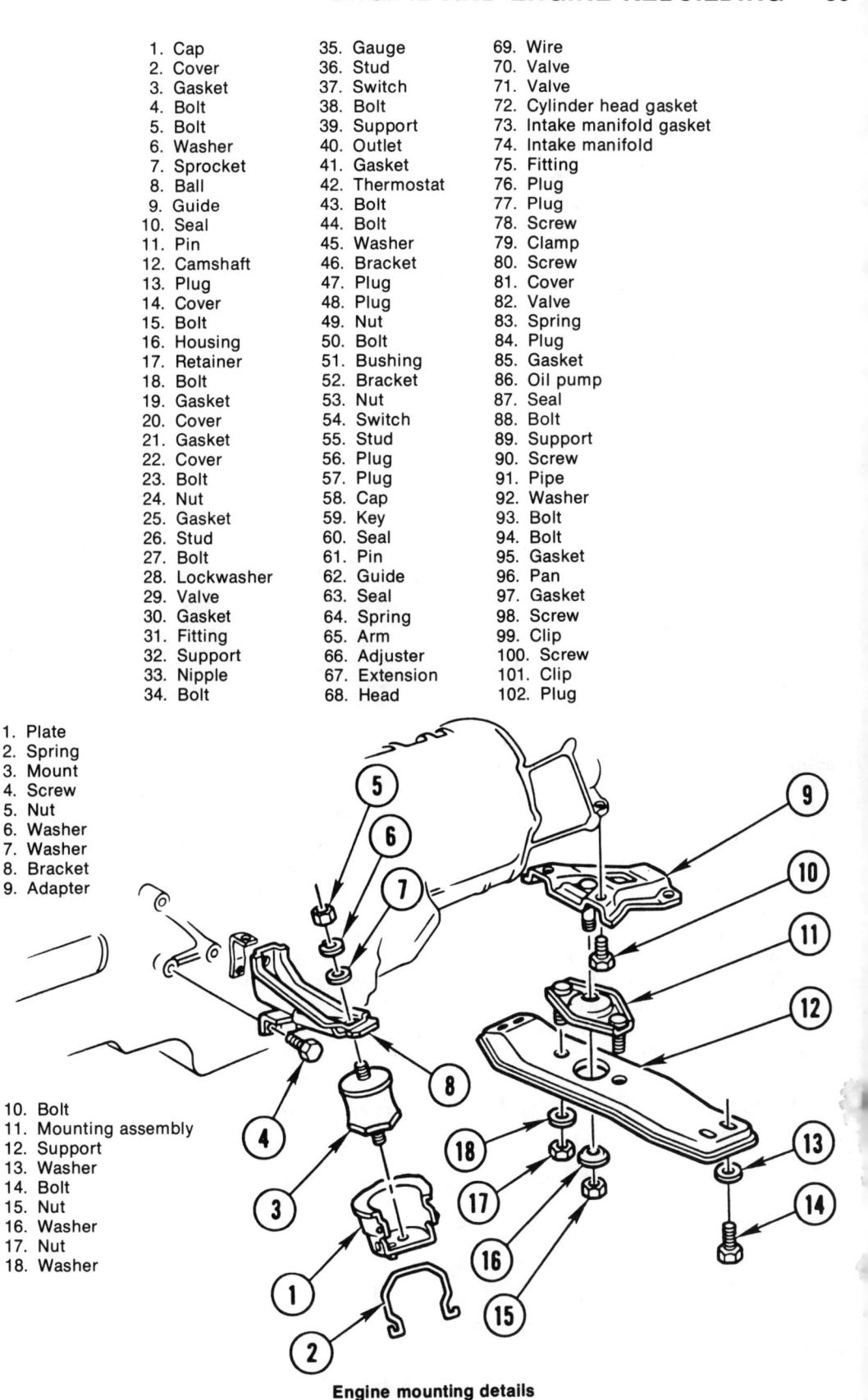

1. Cap	35. Gauge	69. Wire
2. Cover	36. Stud	70. Valve
3. Gasket	37. Switch	71. Valve
4. Bolt	38. Bolt	72. Cylinder head gasket
5. Bolt	39. Support	73. Intake manifold gasket
6. Washer	40. Outlet	74. Intake manifold
7. Sprocket	41. Gasket	75. Fitting
8. Ball	42. Thermostat	76. Plug
9. Guide	43. Bolt	77. Plug
10. Seal	44. Bolt	78. Screw
11. Pin	45. Washer	79. Clamp
12. Camshaft	46. Bracket	80. Screw
13. Plug	47. Plug	81. Cover
14. Cover	48. Plug	82. Valve
15. Bolt	49. Nut	83. Spring
16. Housing	50. Bolt	84. Plug
17. Retainer	51. Bushing	85. Gasket
18. Bolt	52. Bracket	86. Oil pump
19. Gasket	53. Nut	87. Seal
20. Cover	54. Switch	88. Bolt
21. Gasket	55. Stud	89. Support
22. Cover	56. Plug	90. Screw
23. Bolt	57. Plug	91. Pipe
24. Nut	58. Cap	92. Washer
25. Gasket	59. Key	93. Bolt
26. Stud	60. Seal	94. Bolt
27. Bolt	61. Pin	95. Gasket
28. Lockwasher	62. Guide	96. Pan
29. Valve	63. Seal	97. Gasket
30. Gasket	64. Spring	98. Screw
31. Fitting	65. Arm	99. Clip
32. Support	66. Adjuster	100. Screw
33. Nipple	67. Extension	101. Clip
34. Bolt	68. Head	102. Plug

1. Plate
2. Spring
3. Mount
4. Screw
5. Nut
6. Washer
7. Washer
8. Bracket
9. Adapter
10. Bolt
11. Mounting assembly
12. Support
13. Washer
14. Bolt
15. Nut
16. Washer
17. Nut
18. Washer

Engine mounting details

40 ENGINE AND ENGINE REBUILDING

Timing belt cover retaining screws

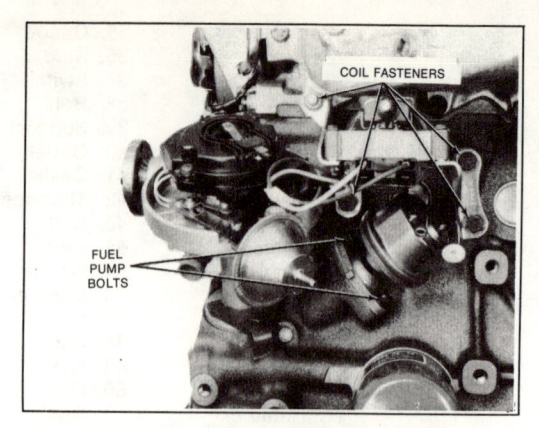

Location of the coil bracket fasteners

Depressing valve springs

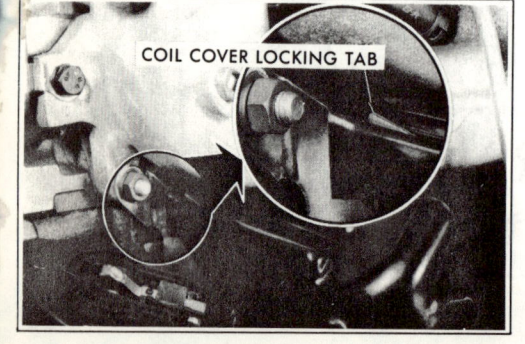

Coil cover locking tab location

9. Remove the spark plug wires from the cam cover.
10. Disconnect the electrical connections at:
    a. Idle solenoid
    b. Choke
    c. Temperature sending unit
    d. Alternator
11. Raise the car and disconnect the exhaust pipe at the manifold.
12. Lower the car and remove the bolt holding the dipstick tube bracket to the exhaust manifold.
13. Disconnect the fuel line at the carburetor.
14. Remove the coil cover and disconnect the secondary voltage wire from the coil.
15. Remove the coil bracket fasteners and lay the coil aside.
16. Remove the cam cover as follows:
    a. Remove the PCV valve.
    b. Remove the heat stove assembly.
    c. Remove the spark plug wiring harness from cam cover.
17. Remove the rocker arms by depressing the valve spring with tool #J-25477. Place the rocker arms and guides in a rack so they may be installed in the same location.
18. Remove the nut and gasket assemblies from the studs in the camshaft carrier. Remove the studs and cam carrier. It may be necessary to use a sharp wedge to separate the carrier from the cylinder head. Be careful not to damge the mating surfaces.
19. Remove the cylinder head and manifold assembly.

INSTALLATION

1. Install the cylinder head gasket over the dowel pins with the note "This Side Up" facing up.
2. Replace the cylinder head and manifold.
3. Replace the cam carrier. Apply a thin, continuous coat of Loctite #75® (or equivalent) to both surfaces (head and cam carrier). Wipe the excess sealer from the cylinder head. Coat the threads of the cylinder head bolts with sealing compound and install bolts

ENGINE AND ENGINE REBUILDING

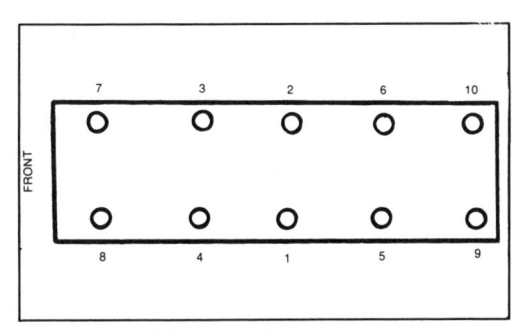

Cylinder head bolt torquing sequence

finger tight. Tighten bolts to 100 N·m (75 lb ft) in the proper sequence.

4. Install cam cover attaching studs.
5. Install rocker arms and apply Moly-coat® or equivalent.
6. Replace camshaft cover gasket. Clean surfaces on camshaft cover and cam carrier with degreaser. Place a 1/8 in. bead of RTV sealer all around the cam cover sealing area. Install covers and torque retaining nut assemblies to 1.6 N·m (15 lb in.) while the sealer is still wet.
7. Install accelerator support.
8. Install spark plug wiring harness and heat stove assembly.
9. Install PCV valve.
10. Install coil bracket bolt. Torque to 20 N·m (15 lb ft)
11. Connect fuel line to carburetor.
12. Replace dipstick tube bracket to manifold.
13. Raise vehicle and attach exhaust pipe to manifold.
14. Lower vehicle and make the electrical connections at:
    a. Idle solenoid
    b. Choke
    c. Temperature sending switch
    d. Generator
15. Connect spark plug wires.
16. Connect air cleaner and silencer assembly.
17. Connect upper radiator hose and heater hose at the inlet manifold.
18. Replace engine coolant.
19. Replace timing belt.

VALVE STEM OIL SEAL AND VALVE SPRING REPLACEMENT

NOTE: *A special valve spring compressor is necessary for this procedure.*

1. Remove the rocker arm from the valve to be serviced.
2. Remove the spark plug from the cylinder to be serviced.
3. Install an air hose adapter in the spark plug hole and apply air pressure to hold the valve in place.
4. Using the spring compressor, compress the valve spring, remove the rocker arm guide, valve locks, caps, and valve spring.
5. Remove the valve stem oil seal.
6. Install the new valve stem oil seal.
7. Compress the valve spring and cap and install the valve locks and rocker arm guide.
8. Release the compressor while making sure that the locks seat correctly in the upper groove of the valve stem. Grease can be used to hold the locks while releasing the compressor.
9. Remove the air hose adapter, install the spark plug, and install the rocker arm.

VALVE GUIDES

Valves with oversize stems are available. Remove the cylinder head and remove the camshaft from the cylinder head. Remove the valves and ream the valve guides with an appropriate oversize reamer.

Intake Manifold

REMOVAL

1. Disconnect negative battery cable.
2. Drain cooling system.
3. Remove air cleaner.
4. Disconnect upper radiator and heater hoses at intake manifold.
5. Remove the EGR valve, located on the intake manifold.
6. Disconnect all electrical wiring vacuum hoses and the accelerator linkage from the carburetor. Remove the fuel line from the carburetor.
7. If vehicle is equipped with air conditioning, perform the following operations before continuing.
    a. Remove radiator upper support.
    b. Remove the generator and A/C drive belts, including the two A/C adjusting bolts.
    c. Remove fan blade and pulley.
    d. Remove timing belt cover.
    e. Move the compressor so it is out of the way. CAUTION: DO NOT DISCONNECT ANY OF THE TUBING IN THE AIR CONDITIONING SYSTEM AS PERSONAL INJURY MAY RESULT.
    f. Raise the vehicle and remove the lower A/C compressor bracket.

ENGINE AND ENGINE REBUILDING

g. Lower the vehicle and remove the upper A/C compressor bracket.
8. Remove the coil and set aside.
9. Remove the intake manifold bolts and remove manifold.

INSTALLATION

NOTE: *If a new intake manifold is being installed, transfer the following parts from the old one.*
- Thermostat and housing
- Carburetor
- Vacuum fittings and plugs

1. With the new gasket, and gasket surface well cleaned, install the new manifold.
2. Install manifold bolts and torque to 20 N•m (15 lb ft)
3. Remount the coil.
4. For vehicles equipped with air conditioning, the following steps must be completed before continuing.
   a. Install the upper A/C compressor bracket.
   b. Raise the vehicle and install the lower A/C compressor bracket.
   c. Lower the vehicle and install the A/C compressor.
   d. Install the timing bolt cover.
   e. Install the pulley and fan blades.
   f. Install the A/C drive belt, two adjusting bolts and adjust as necessary.
   g. Install the generator drive belt and adjust as necessary.
   h. Install the radiator upper support.
5. Connect all electrical wiring, vacuum hoses and accelerator linkage to the carburetor. Install the fuel line to the carburetor.
6. Install the EGR valve. Torque to 13–18 ft lbs.
7. Connect the upper radiator and heater hoses to intake manifold.
8. Refill the cooling system.
9. Install the air cleaner.
10. Connect the battery cable, start the engine and check for leaks.

Exhaust Manifold

REMOVAL

1. Remove the negative battery cable.
2. Raise the vehicle and disconnect the exhaust pipe from the manifold.
3. Lower the vehicle and remove the carburetor heat tube.
4. On California models, remove the pulse air injection tubing.
5. Remove the exhaust manifold bolts and manifold.

INSTALLATION

1. Install the manifold and manifold bolts. Install the inner upper bolts first as these are guide bolts.
NOTE: *Exhaust manifold center bolts must be torqued to 20 N·m (15 ft lbs). The end legs must be torqued to 30 N·m (22 ft lbs).*
2. On California models, install the pulse air injection tubing.
3. Install the carburetor heat tube.
4. Raise the vehicle and connect the exhaust pipe to the manifold.
5. Lower the vehicle and connect the battery cable. Start the engine and check for leaks.

Timing Cover, Belt and Camshaft

TIMING BELT COVER REMOVAL AND INSTALLATION

Upper Front Cover

1. Disconnect the negative battery cable.
2. Remove the engine accessory drive belts.
3. Remove the engine fan.
4. Remove the cover retaining screws and nuts, and remove the cover.

To install the cover:
5. Align the screw slots on the upper and lower parts of the cover.
6. Install the cover retaining screws and nuts. Torque the nuts to 80–105 in. lbs.
7. Install the engine fan.
8. Install the engine accessory drive belts.
9. Connect the negative battery cable.

Lower Front Cover

1. Disconnect the negative battery cable.
2. Remove the crankshaft pulley.
3. Remove the upper front timing belt cover.
4. Remove the one cover-to-block retaining nut.
5. To install the cover, align the cover with the studs on the engine block.
6. Install the lower front cover retaining nut and torque to 80–105 in. lbs.
7. Install the upper front timing belt cover.
8. Install the crankshaft pulley. Torque the retaining bolt to 65–85 ft lbs.
9. Connect the negative battery cable.

ENGINE AND ENGINE REBUILDING

Upper Rear Cover

1. Disconnect the negative battery cable.
2. Remove the upper and lower front cover, the timing belt, and the camshaft timing sprocket.
3. Remove the three screws retaining the camshaft sprocket cover to the camshaft carrier.
4. Inspect the condition of the cam seal.
5. Position and align a new gasket over the end of the camshaft and against the camshaft carrier.
6. Install the three camshaft sprocket cover retaining screws.
7. Install the camshaft sprocket, timing belt, and upper and lower front covers.
8. Connect the negative battery cable.

Timing Belt Sprockets

REMOVAL

CAUTION: *Do not discharge the air conditioner compressor or disconnect any air conditioning lines. Damage to the air conditioning system or personal injury could result.*

NOTE: *A belt tension gauge is necessary for the completion of this procedure.*

1. Rotate the engine so the timing mark on the crankshaft pulley is at 0°, #1 cylinder is at Top Dead Center. With #1 cylinder at TDC, a ⅛ in. drill rod may be inserted through a hole in the timing belt upper rear cover into a hole in the camshaft drive sprocket. This is provided to verify camshaft timing and to facilitate installation of the belt.

Mark the location of the rotor in No. 1 spark plug firing position on the distributor housing

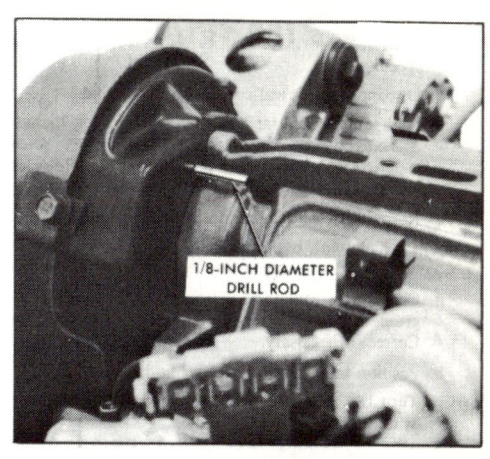

A ⅛ in. drill rod should go through the hole in the rear of the upper rear timing belt cover and the hole in the camshaft sprocket

2. Remove timing belt lower cover.
3. Loosen the idler pulley retaining bolt and allow idler to rotate clockwise.
4. Remove the timing belt from camshaft and crankshaft sprockets.
5. Remove the distributor cap and mark the location of the rotor at #1 cylinder firing position. For vehicles equipped with A/C, remove the A/C compressor and the lower compressor bracket. DO NOT disconnect any lines!
6. Remove timing belt sprocket bolt and washer.
7. Remove camshaft sprocket.
8. Remove crankshaft sprocket.

INSTALLATION

1. Place crankshaft sprocket on end of crankshaft. Be sure that the locating tabs face outward.
2. Align the dowel in the camshaft sprocket with the locating hole in the end of the camshaft.
3. Apply Loctite® sealer or equivalent to the threads of the bolt and install bolt and washer. Torque to 100 N·m (75 ft lbs)
4. Install belt on camshaft and crankshaft sprockets.
5. Using a ¼ in. allen wrench, rotate the idler pulley counterclockwise on its attaching bolt until all the slack is taken out of the belt. Tighten the bolt.
6. To facilitate the installation of the timing belt, #1 cylinder should be at TDC. If necessary, rotate the crankshaft clockwise a minimum of one revolution. Stop when #1 cylinder reaches TDC. DO NOT reverse direction.

44 ENGINE AND ENGINE REBUILDING

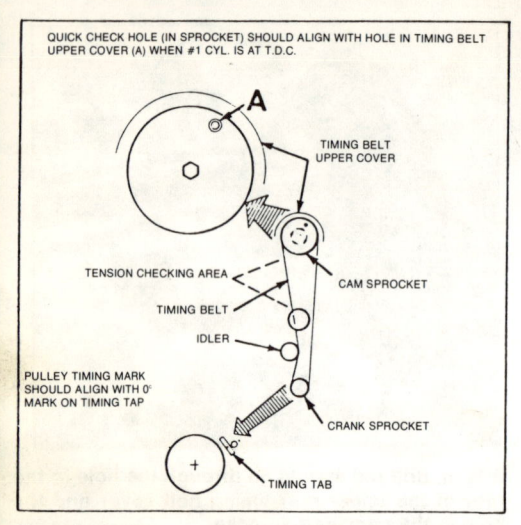

Camshaft alignment and timing belt tension check

BELT SIZE	ACCEPTABLE OPERATING RANGE	ADJUSTMENT SPECIFICATION
19mm	222 – 356N (50–80 LB.)	311±31N (70±7 LB.)

Timing belt adjustment specifications

7. Install a belt tension gauge between the camshaft sprocket and the idler pulley on the slack side. (see illus.)
8. Adjust to the proper tension by loosening the idler attaching bolt. Using the ¼ in. allen wrench, rotate the idler pulley until the proper tension is attained. Torque the attaching bolt to 20 N·m (15 ft lbs).
9. Install the timing belt lower cover and front cover.
10. Replace the distributor cap.
11. For vehicles with A/C, replace the lower compressor bracket and the A/C compressor.
12. Attach the negative battery cable.

Crankcase Front Cover
REMOVAL AND INSTALLATION

NOTE: *A special oil seal alignment tool is required for this procedure.*

1. Disconnect the negative battery cable.
2. Remove the upper and lower front timing belt covers, crankshaft pulley, idler pulley, timing belt, and the crankshaft timing sprocket.
3. Remove the three oil pan bolts and the cover attaching bolts.
4. Remove the old cover, gasket and the front portion of the oil pan gasket.

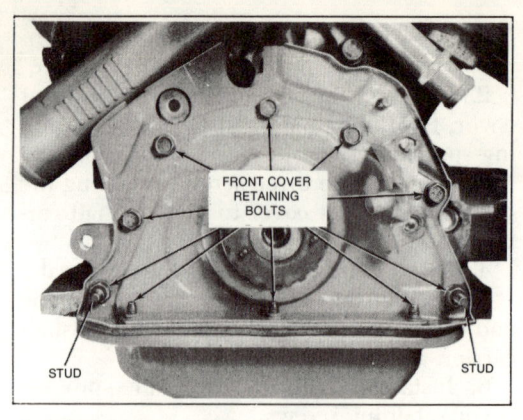

Crankcase front cover retaining bolts

5. Inspect the crankshaft front oil seal and replace if necessary.
To install:
6. Replace the crankcase cover gasket, cut the front portion of the oil pan gasket, and apply RTV sealer or its equivalent to the cut-off portion of the oil pan gasket.
7. Using the special oil seal alignment tool, install the front cover. Torque the cover bolts to 75–110 in. lbs.
8. Install the crankshaft timing sprocket, timing belt, idler and crankshaft pulleys. Adjust timing belt tension using all parts of Step 19 in "Timing Belt and Sprockets Removal and Installation." Install the upper and lower front timing belt covers.
9. Connect the negative battery cable.

Camshaft
REMOVAL AND INSTALLATION

NOTE: *A special valve spring compressor is necessary for this procedure. Also, if replacing camshaft or rocker arms, prelube new parts with Molykote or its equivalent.*

1. Disconnect the negative battery cable.
2. Remove engine accessory drive belts.
3. Remove the engine fan and pulley.
4. Remove the upper and lower front timing belt covers.
5. Loosen the idler pulley and remove the timing belt from the camshaft sprocket.
6. Remove the camshaft sprocket attaching bolt and washer and remove the camshaft sprocket.
7. Remove the camshaft covers. Using the special valve spring compressor, remove the valve rocker arms and guides. Keep the rocker arms and guides in order so that they can be installed in their original locations.

ENGINE AND ENGINE REBUILDING

8. Remove any components necessary to gain working clearance.

NOTE: *The heater assembly will probably have to be removed from the firewall to gain working clearance.*

9. Remove the camshaft carrier rear cover.
10. Remove the camshaft thrust plate bolts. Slide the camshaft slightly to the rear and remove the thrust plate.
11. Remove the engine mount nuts and wire retainers.
12. Using a floor jack, raise the engine.
13. Remove the camshaft from the camshaft carrier.

To install:

14. Install the camshaft into the camshaft carrier.
15. Lower the engine.
16. Install the engine mount nuts and attach the retaining wires.
17. Slide the camshaft to the rear and install thrust plate. Slide the camshaft forward.
18. Position and align a new gasket over the end of the camshaft, against the camshaft carrier. Using RTV sealer, install the camshaft carrier rear cover.
19. Position and align a new gasket over the end of the camshaft, against the camshaft carrier, and install the upper rear timing belt cover.
20. Install any components which were removed to gain working clearance.
21. Install the valve rocker arms and guides in their original locations using the special valve spring compressor. Install the camshaft covers.
22. Align the dowel in the camshaft sprocket with the hole in the end of the camshaft and install the sprocket.
23. Apply Loctite® sealer or its equivalent to the sprocket retaining bolt threads and install the bolt and washer. Torque the sprocket retaining bolt to 65-85 ft lbs.
24. Turn the crankshaft counterclockwise to bring the #1 cylinder to top dead center. Check to make sure the distributor rotor is in firing position for #1 cylinder. Place a ⅛ in drill rod through the cam sprocket quick check hole into the hole in the upper timing belt cover. If the holes do not line up, loosen the timing belt and rotate the camshaft until it is properly aligned.
25. Adjust timing belt tension as outlined in "Timing Belt and Sprocket Removal and Installation".
26. Install the upper and lower front timing belt covers.
27. Install the engine fan and pulley.
28. Install the engine accessory drive belts.
29. Connect the negative battery cable.

Piston Installation

Removal and installation procedures for the pistons and connecting rods are covered in the engine rebuilding section at the end of the chapter.

Install piston and connecting rod assemblies into their original cylinders. Lubricate the connecting rod bearings and install them in the connecting rods and bearing caps. Lightly oil the pistons, rings, and cylinder walls, and cover the connecting rod bolts with pieces of plastic tubing. Make sure of correct ring gap positioning and install the

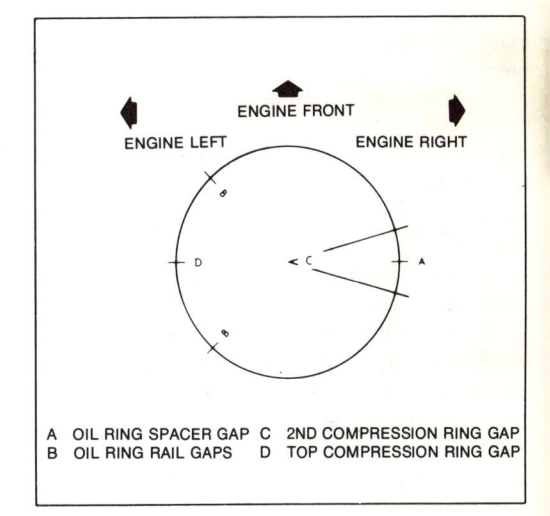

A OIL RING SPACER GAP   C 2ND COMPRESSION RING GAP
B OIL RING RAIL GAPS   D TOP COMPRESSION RING GAP

Piston ring gap positioning

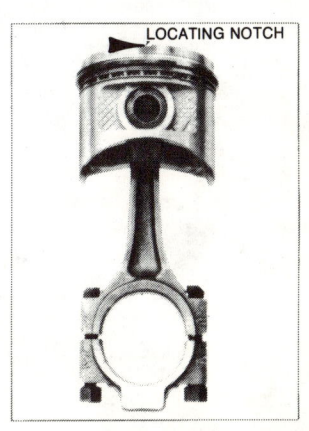

The piston notch must face toward the front of the engine

ENGINE AND ENGINE REBUILDING

piston and rod assemblies with the notch on the piston crown facing to the front of the engine. Use a piston ring compressor and a wooden hammer handle on installation. The numbers on the connecting rods and bearing caps must be on the same side when installing used pistons and connecting rods. Install the connecting rod bearing caps after removing the pieces of plastic tubing from the bolts. Torque the bolts to 34–40 ft lbs.

LUBRICATION

Oil Pan

REMOVAL

NOTE: *A special lifting tool is necessary for this procedure. This tool can be fabricated from channel iron; pattern it after the tool shown in the illustration.*

1. Remove the heater housing assembly from the firewall and rest it on top of the engine.
2. Drain the cooling system.
3. Remove upper radiator support. On A/C equipped vehicles, remove the upper half of the fan shroud.
4. Remove radiator hoses and radiator.

NOTE: *If equipped with automatic transmission, disconnect the cooler lines from the radiator.*

5. If equipped with A/C, remove the condenser to radiator support attaching nuts and remove condenser from support. Lay it on top of the engine.
6. Remove the engine mount retaining nuts and clips.

Engine lift tool for oil pan removal

7. Disconnect the fuel line from the charcoal cannister.
8. Raise the vehicle and drain the engine oil.
9. Remove the exhaust pipe bolts at the manifold.
10. Remove the body to cross member braces.
11. On manual transmission equipped vehicles, remove the rack and pinion-to-front crossmember attaching bolts. Pull the unit down and out of the way.
12. Remove the stabilizer from the body.
13. Install tool J-26436 and raise the engine.
14. Remove the oil pan bolts.
15. With the oil pan lowered down from the block, remove the oil pump suction pipe. On 1976–77 models remove the screen. On newer models, the screen is attached to the pick-up tube.
16. Remove the oil pan through the front of the car. On vehicles equipped with manual transmission, lower the oil pan about 1 inch, rotate the front of the pan to the right and the rear to the left. Tilt the pan 45° and remove it.

INSTALLATION

NOTE: *Some 1978–80 engines have RTV sealer in between the block and the oil pan. These can be identified by a smooth sealing surface on the oil pan rather than having a raised bead. These units MUST be reassembled using RTV sealer. The use of a gasket may allow an oil leak to develop.*

Conversely, if the oil pan has a raised bead, a gasket MUST be used for reinstallation. The use of RTV sealer in this case may cause an oil leak to develop.

Before installing an oil pan using RTV, it is necessary to remove all old RTV which is loose or will interfere with the installation. All old RTV need not be removed. The new sealer may be placed on top of the remaining RTV.

1. Install a new oil pump suction pipe and screen seal in the oil pump.
2. Lay the suction pipe and screen in the oil pan.
3. Clean the mating surfaces of the block and oil pan as necessary. Apply RTV or a gasket to the oil pan.
4. Tilt the pan and install it under the block.
5. Attach the oil pan bolts. Torque to 6

ENGINE AND ENGINE REBUILDING

N·m (55 in. lb). On oil pans using RTV sealer, the bolts must be attached while the sealer is still wet.

6. Replace the rack and pinion-to-front crossmember.
7. Attach the exhaust pipe to the manifold.
8. Lower the engine on to the engine mounts and remove the lifting tool. Attach the mounting nuts and clips.
9. Install the heater core housing.
10. Connect the fuel line to the charcoal cannister.
11. If equipped with A/C, install the condenser assembly and attach the radiator support.
12. Install the radiator and attach the hoses.
13. If equipped with automatic transmission, connect the cooler lines to the radiator.
14. Install the upper radiator support.
15. On A/C equipped models, install the upper half of the fan shroud.
16. Refill the cooling system.
17. Refill the crankcase with oil.
18. Start the engine and check for leaks.

Oil Pump Removal and Installation

1976–77

1. Remove the ignition coil attaching bolts and lay the coil aside.
2. Raise the car and remove the fuel pump, pushrod, and gasket.
3. Lower the car and remove the distributor. On air conditioned cars, remove the compressor mounting bolts and lay it aside. Do not disconnect any refrigerant lines.
4. Raise the car and remove the oil pan.
5. Remove the oil pump pipe and screen assembly clamp and remove the bolts attaching the pipe and screen assembly to the cylinder and case.
6. Remove the pipe and screen assembly from the oil pump.
7. Remove the pick-up tube seal from the oil pump.
8. Remove the oil pump attaching bolts and remove the oil pump.

To install:

9. Install the oil pump. Torque the oil pump bolts to 45–60 in. lbs.

NOTE: *Make certain that the pilot on the oil pump engages the case.*

10. Install the pick-up tube seal in the oil pump.

11. Install the pick-up pipe and screen assembly in the oil pump and install the pick-up pipe and screen clamp. Torque the clamp bolt to 70–95 in. lbs. Torque the pick-up tube and screen mounting bolt to 19–25 ft lbs.
12. Install the oil pan.
13. Lower the car and install the distributor.
14. Raise the car and install the fuel pump with gasket and pushrod.
15. Lower the car and install the ignition coil. Torque the coil bracket attaching bolts to 13–18 ft lbs.

1978–80

REMOVAL

1. Remove the coil attaching bracket bolts and set the coil aside.
2. Raise the vehicle and remove the fuel pump and push rod.
3. Lower the vehicle and remove the distributor.
4. On A/C equipped vehicles, remove the A/C compressor and set it aside. Do not remove any of the lines from the compressor.
5. Raise the vehicle and remove the oil pan.
6. Remove the oil pump.
7. Remove the oil pump cover bolts.
8. Remove the cover and gasket.
9. Remove the pump gear assembly.
10. Remove the pressure regulator valve and connecting parts.
11. If necessary, remove the pick-up tube from the pump and replace it with a new tube and "O" ring seal. Do not separate the screen from the tube as they are one unit.

Clean the parts of the pump with solvent and allow to dry. Inspect the body of the pump for cracks and inspect the gears of the pump for damage or excessive wear. Also check the inside of the pump for any wear that would permit oil to leak past the ends of the gears. Check the pick-up tube and screen for any damage. If the gears or body of pump are damaged, replace the entire oil pump assembly.

INSTALLATION

1. Install the pressure regulator valve and connecting parts.
2. Install the pump gear assemblies.
3. Replace the cover and torque the bolts to 9 N·m (85 in. lbs.)
4. Install the oil pump and attaching screws.

48 ENGINE AND ENGINE REBUILDING

5. Install the oil pan.
6. Replace the distributor.
7. Raise the vehicle and install the fuel pump gasket, fuel pump and push rod assembly.
8. Lower the vehicle and install the coil attaching bracket bolts. Torque to 20 N•m (15 ft lb)

Rear Main Oil Seal Replacement

1. Remove the engine from the car and place it in a stand.
2. Remove the oil pan.
3. Remove the rear main bearing cap.
4. Clean the bearing cap and case.
5. Check the crankshaft seal for excessive wear, etc.
6. Install a new crankshaft seal. Make sure that it is properly seated against the rear main bearing seal bulkhead.
7. Apply RTV sealer or its equivalent to the bearing cap horizontal split line.
8. With the sealer still wet, install the rear main bearing cap. On 1976–77 models, tighten the cap bolts to 40–52 ft lbs.

On 1978 and later models, tighten the cap bolts to 10–12 ft lbs then tap the crankshaft, first rearward then forward, and tighten the bolts to 50 ft lbs.

9. Apply RTV sealer or its equivalent in the vertical grooves of the rear main bearing cap.
10. Remove any excess sealer and install the oil pan. Torque the oil pan bolts to 45–60 in. lbs.
11. Install the engine in the car.

ENGINE COOLING

The cooling system is a standard, pressurized (15 psi) system. A permanently lubricated, impeller-type water pump is used to force water through the engine and keep the engine operating at its most efficient temperatures at all speeds and driving conditions. Some models use a heavy duty radiator with a fan shroud. All Chevette radiators are of the cross-flow type. The water flows horizontally from the left side of the tank to the output hoses on the right side. A plastic recovery tank is provided for coolant expansion. The coolant level is checked by observing the level in the reservoir at normal operating temperatures. Never add coolant to the radiator but instead add it to the plastic reservoir tank. A 50/50 mixture of ethylene glycol base coolant will protect the engine to −20° F.

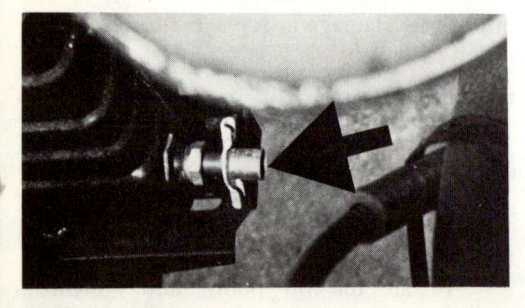

Radiator hoses are retained by screw clamps

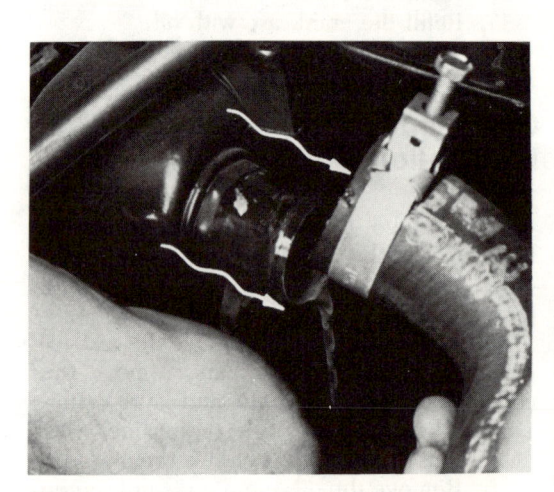

Remove the hoses by twisting and pulling simultaneously

Radiator petcock

ENGINE AND ENGINE REBUILDING

RADIATOR REMOVAL AND INSTALLATION

CAUTION: *Do not remove the radiator cap while the engine is still hot as the hot steam may cause personal injury.*

1. Drain the radiator.
2. Disconnect the upper and lower radiator hoses and the coolant recovery reservoir hose.
3. Remove the radiator baffle or shroud. Remove the baffle by removing the four baffle-to-radiator support screws. Remove the shroud by removing the two upper screws and the two middle screws. Remove the upper radiator shroud. Remove the lower shroud from its mounting clips.
4. Disconnect and plug the transmission cooler lines if necessary.
5. Remove the radiator upper mounting panel or brackets and lift the radiator out of the lower brackets.
6. To install, reverse the removal procedure.

WATER PUMP REMOVAL AND INSTALLATION

1. Disconnect the battery negative cable, and remove engine drive belt(s).
2. Remove the engine fan, spacer (air conditioned models), and the pulley.
CAUTION: *A bent or damaged fan assembly should always be replaced. Do not attempt repairs as fan balance is critical. If unbalanced, the fan could fail and break apart while in use.*
3. Remove the timing belt front cover by removing the two upper bolts, center bolt, and two lower nuts.
4. Drain the coolant from the engine.
5. Remove the lower radiator hose and the heater hose at the water pump.
6. Turn the crankshaft pulley so that the mark on the pulley is aligned with the "0" mark on the timing scale and that a 1/8 in. drill bit can be inserted through the timing belt upper cover and cam gear.
7. Remove the idler pulley and pull the timing belt off the gear. Don't disturb crankshaft position.
8. Remove the water pump retaining bolts and remove the pump and gasket from the engine.
9. Clean all the old gasket material from the cylinder case.
10. With a new gasket in place on the water pump, position the water pump in place on the cylinder case and install the water pump retaining bolts.
11. Install the timing belt onto the cam gear.
12. Apply sealer to the idler pulley attaching bolt and install the bolt and the idler pulley. Turn the idler pulley counterclockwise on its mounting bolt to remove the slack in the timing belt.
13. Use a tension gauge to adjust timing belt tension. Check belt tension midway between the tensioner and the cam sprocket on the idler pulley side. Correct belt tension is 55 lbs. Torque the idler pulley mounting bolt to 13–18 ft lbs.
14. Remove the 1/8 in. drill bit from the upper timing belt cover and cam gear.
15. Install the lower radiator hose and the heater hose to the water pump.
16. Install the timing belt front cover.
17. Install the water pump pulley, spacer (if equipped), and engine fan.

It's necessary to first remove the idler pulley to remove the water pump

The thermostat housing is retained by two bolts (arrows)

ENGINE AND ENGINE REBUILDING

18. Install the engine drive belt(s).
19. Refill the cooling system.
20. Connect the battery negative cable.
21. Start the engine and check for leaks.

THERMOSTAT REMOVAL AND INSTALLATION

1. Drain the radiator.
2. Remove the thermostat housing bolts and remove the housing with upper hose attached, gasket, and thermostat.
3. Install the thermostat. Use a new gasket on the thermostat housing and install the thermostat housing bolts.

Install the new thermostat with the spring down

4. Install the upper radiator hose at the water outlet.
5. Fill the cooling system.

ENGINE AND ENGINE REBUILDING

ENGINE REBUILDING

Most procedures involved in rebuilding an engine are fairly standard, regardless of the type of engine involved. This section is a guide to accepted rebuilding procedures. Examples of standard rebuilding practices are illustrated and should be used along with specific details concerning your particular engine, found earlier in this chapter.

The procedures given here are those used by any competent rebuilder. Obviously some of the procedures cannot be performed by the do-it-yourself mechanic, but are provided so that you will be familiar with the services that should be offered by rebuilding or machine shops. As an example, in most instances, it is more profitable for the home mechanic to remove the cylinder heads, buy the necessary parts (new valves, seals, keepers, keys, etc.) and deliver these to a machine shop for the necessary work. In this way you will save the money to remove and install the cylinder head and the mark-up on parts.

On the other hand, most of the work involved in rebuilding the lower end is well within the scope of the do-it-yourself mechanic. Only work such as hot-tanking, actually boring the block or Magnafluxing (invisible crack detection) need be sent to a machine shop.

Tools

The tools required for basic engine rebuilding should, with a few exceptions, be those included in a mechanic's tool kit. An accurate torque wrench, and a dial indicator (reading in thousandths) mounted on a universal base should be available. Special tools, where required, are available from the major tool suppliers. The services of a competent automotive machine shop must also be readily available.

Precautions

Aluminum has become increasingly popular for use in engines, due to its low weight and excellent heat transfer characteristics. The following precautions must be observed when handling aluminum (or any other) engine parts:

—Never hot-tank aluminum parts.
—Remove all aluminum parts (identification tags, etc.) from engine parts before hot-tanking (otherwise they will be removed during the process).
—Always coat threads lightly with engine oil or anti-seize compounds before installation, to prevent seizure.
—Never over-torque bolts or spark plugs in aluminum threads. Should stripping occur, threads can be restored using any of a number of thread repair kits available (see next section).

Inspection Techniques

Magnaflux and Zyglo are inspection techniques used to locate material flaws, such as stress cracks. Magnaflux is a magnetic process, applicable only to ferrous materials. The Zyglo process coats the material with a fluorescent dye penetrant, and any material may be tested using Zyglo. Specific checks of suspected surface cracks may be made at lower cost and more readily using spot check dye. The dye is sprayed onto the suspected area, wiped off, and the area is then sprayed with a developer. Cracks then will show up brightly.

Overhaul

The section is divided into two parts. The first, Cylinder Head Reconditioning, assumes that the cylinder head is removed from the engine, all manifolds are removed, and the cylinder head is on a workbench. The camshaft should be removed from overhead cam cylinder heads. The second section, Cylinder Block Reconditioning, covers the block, pistons, connecting rods and crankshaft. It is assumed that the engine is mounted on a work stand, and the cylinder head and all accessories are removed.

Procedures are identified as follows:

Unmarked—Basic procedures that must be performed in order to successfully complete the rebuilding process.

Starred (*)—Procedures that should be performed to ensure maximum performance and engine life.

Double starred (**)—Procedures that may be performed to increase engine performance and reliability.

When assembling the engine, any parts that will be in frictional contact must be pre-lubricated, to provide protection on initial start-up. Any product specifically formulated for this purpose may be used. NOTE: *Do not use engine oil.* Where semi-permanent (locked but removable) installation of bolts or nuts is desired, threads should be cleaned and located with Loctite® or a similar product (non-hardening).

52 ENGINE AND ENGINE REBUILDING

Repairing Damaged Threads

Several methods of repairing damaged threads are available. Heli-Coil® (shown here), Keenserts® and Microdot® are among the most widely used. All involve basically the same principle—drilling out stripped threads, tapping the hole and installing a pre-wound insert—making welding, plugging and oversize fasteners unnecessary.

Two types of thread repair inserts are usually supplied—a standard type for most Inch Coarse, Inch Fine, Metric Coarse and Metric Fine thread sizes and a spark plug type to fit most spark plug port sizes. Consult the individual manufacturer's catalog to determine exact applications. Typical thread repair kits will contain a selection of pre-wound threaded inserts, a tap (corresponding to the outside diameter threads of the insert) and an installation tool. Spark plug inserts usually differ because they require a tap equipped with pilot threads and a combined reamer/tap section. Most manufacturers also supply blister-packed thread repair inserts separately in addition to a master kit containing a variety of taps and inserts plus installation tools.

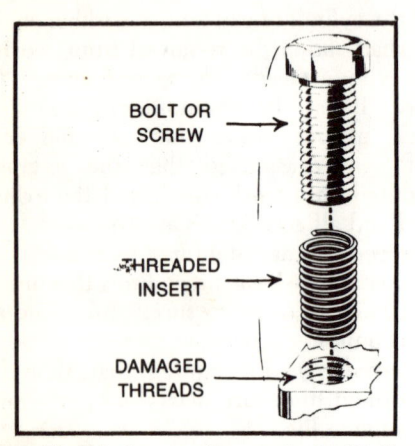

Before effecting a repair to a threaded hole, remove any snapped, broken or damaged bolts or studs. Penetrating oil can be used to free frozen threads; the offending item can be removed with locking pliers or with a screw or stud extractor. After the hole is clear, the thread can be repaired, as follows:

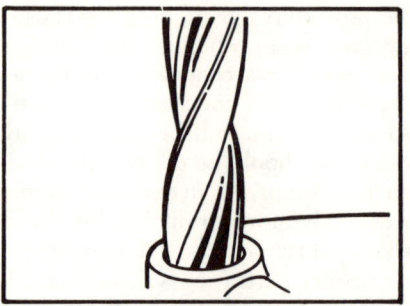

Drill out the damaged threads with specified drill. Drill completely through the hole or to the bottom of a blind hole

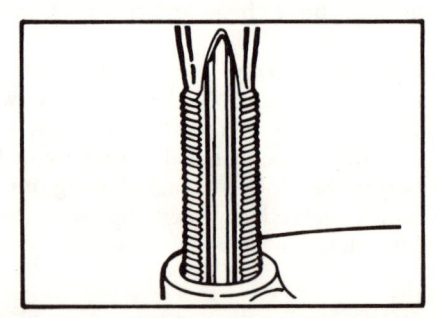

With the tap supplied, tap the hole to receive the thread insert. Keep the tap well oiled and back it out frequently to avoid clogging the threads

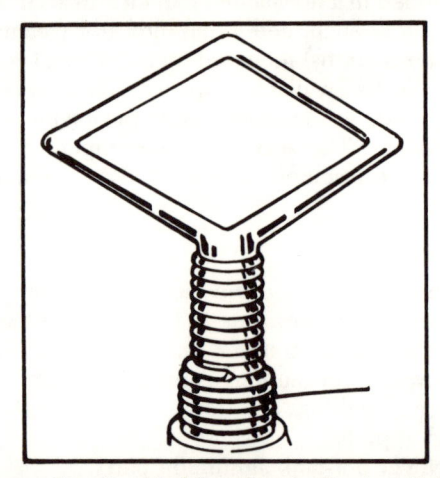

Damaged bolt holes can be repaired with thread repair inserts

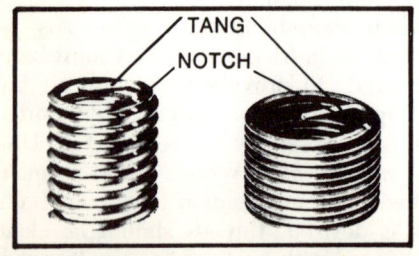

Standard thread repair insert (left) and spark plug thread insert (right)

Screw the threaded insert onto the installation tool until the tang engages the slot. Screw the insert into the tapped hole until it is ¼–½ turn below the top surface. After installation break off the tang with a hammer and punch

ENGINE AND ENGINE REBUILDING 53

Standard Torque Specifications and Fastener Markings

The Newton-metre has been designated the world standard for measuring torque and will gradually replace the foot-pound and kilogram-meter. In the absence of specific torques, the following chart can be used as a guide to the maximum safe torque of a particular size/grade of fastener.

- There is no torque difference for fine or coarse threads.
- Torque values are based on clean, dry threads. Reduce the value by 10% if threads are oiled prior to assembly.
- The torque required for aluminum components or fasteners is considerably less.

U. S. BOLTS

SAE Grade Number	1 or 2			5			6 or 7		
Bolt Markings Manufacturer's marks may vary—number of lines always 2 less than the grade number.									
Usage	Frequent			Frequent			Infrequent		
Bolt Size (inches)—(Thread)	Maximum Torque			Maximum Torque			Maximum Torque		
	Ft-Lb	kgm	Nm	Ft-Lb	kgm	Nm	Ft-Lb	kgm	Nm
¼—20	5	0.7	6.8	8	1.1	10.8	10	1.4	13.5
—28	6	0.8	8.1	10	1.4	13.6			
5⁄16—18	11	1.5	14.9	17	2.3	23.0	19	2.6	25.8
—24	13	1.8	17.6	19	2.6	25.7			
⅜—16	18	2.5	24.4	31	4.3	42.0	34	4.7	46.0
—24	20	2.75	27.1	35	4.8	47.5			
7⁄16—14	28	3.8	37.0	49	6.8	66.4	55	7.6	74.5
—20	30	4.2	40.7	55	7.6	74.5			
½—13	39	5.4	52.8	75	10.4	101.7	85	11.75	115.2
—20	41	5.7	55.6	85	11.7	115.2			
9⁄16—12	51	7.0	69.2	110	15.2	149.1	120	16.6	162.7
—18	55	7.6	74.5	120	16.6	162.7			
⅝—11	83	11.5	112.5	150	20.7	203.3	167	23.0	226.5
—18	95	13.1	128.8	170	23.5	230.5			
¾—10	105	14.5	142.3	270	37.3	366.0	280	38.7	379.6
—16	115	15.9	155.9	295	40.8	400.0			
⅞—9	160	22.1	216.9	395	54.6	535.5	440	60.9	596.5
—14	175	24.2	237.2	435	60.1	589.7			
1—8	236	32.5	318.6	590	81.6	799.9	660	91.3	894.8
—14	250	34.6	338.9	660	91.3	849.8			

54 ENGINE AND ENGINE REBUILDING

METRIC BOLTS

NOTE: *Metric bolts are marked with a number indicating the relative strength of the bolt. These numbers have nothing to do with size.*

Description	Torque ft-lbs (Nm)			
Thread size x pitch (mm)	Head mark—4		Head mark—7	
6 x 1.0	2.2–2.9	(3.0–3.9)	3.6–5.8	(4.9–7.8)
8 x 1.25	5.8–8.7	(7.9–12)	9.4–14	(13–19)
10 x 1.25	12–17	(16–23)	20–29	(27–39)
12 x 1.25	21–32	(29–43)	35–53	(47–72)
14 x 1.5	35–52	(48–70)	57–85	(77–110)
16 x 1.5	51–77	(67–100)	90–120	(130–160)
18 x 1.5	74–110	(100–150)	130–170	(180–230)
20 x 1.5	110–140	(150–190)	190–240	(160–320)
22 x 1.5	150–190	(200–260)	250–320	(340–430)
24 x 1.5	190–240	(260–320)	310–410	(420–550)

NOTE: *This engine rebuilding section is a guide to accepted rebuilding procedures. Typical examples of standard rebuilding procedures are illustrated. Use these procedures along with the detailed instructions earlier in this chapter, concerning your particular engine.*

Cylinder Head Reconditioning

Procedure	Method
Remove the cylinder head:	See the engine service procedures earlier in this chapter for details concerning specific engines.
Identify the valves:	Invert the cylinder head, and number the valve faces front to rear, using a permanent felt-tip marker.
Remove the camshaft:	See the engine service procedures earlier in this chapter for details concerning specific engines.
Remove the valves and springs:	Using an appropriate valve spring compressor (depending on the configuration of the cylinder head), compress the valve springs. Lift out the keepers with needlenose pliers, release the compressor, and remove the valve, spring, and spring retainer. See the engine service procedures earlier in this chapter for details concerning specific engines.
Check the valve stem-to-guide clearance:	Clean the valve stem with lacquer thinner or a similar solvent to remove all gum and varnish. Clean the valve guides using solvent and an expanding wire-type valve guide cleaner. Mount a dial indicator so that the stem is at 90° to the valve stem, as close to the valve guide as possible. Move the valve off its seat, and measure the valve guide-to-stem clearance by rocking the stem back and forth to actuate the dial indicator. Measure the valve stems using a micrometer, and compare to specifications, to determine whether stem or guide wear is responsible for excessive clearance. **NOTE:** *Consult the Specifications tables earlier in this chapter.*

Check the valve stem-to-guide clearance

ENGINE AND ENGINE REBUILDING 55

Cylinder Head Reconditioning

Procedure	Method
De-carbon the cylinder head and valves: Remove the carbon from the cylinder head with a wire brush and electric drill	Chip carbon away from the valve heads, combustion chambers, and ports, using a chisel made of hardwood. Remove the remaining deposits with a stiff wire brush. NOTE: *Be sure that the deposits are actually removed, rather than burnished.*
Hot-tank the cylinder head (cast iron heads only): CAUTION: *Do not hot-tank aluminum parts.*	Have the cylinder head hot-tanked to remove grease, corrosion, and scale from the water passages. NOTE: *In the case of overhead cam cylinder heads, consult the operator to determine whether the camshaft bearings will be damaged by the caustic solution.*
Degrease the remaining cylinder head parts:	Clean the remaining cylinder head parts in an engine cleaning solvent. Do not remove the protective coating from the springs.
Check the cylinder head for warpage: 1 & 3 CHECK DIAGONALLY 2 CHECK ACROSS CENTER Check the cylinder head for warpage	Place a straight-edge across the gasket surface of the cylinder head. Using feeler gauges, determine the clearance at the center of the straight-edge. If warpage exceeds .003" in a 6" span, or .006" over the total length, the cylinder head must be resurfaced. NOTE: *If warpage exceeds the manufacturer's maximum tolerance for material removal, the cylinder head must be replaced.* When milling the cylinder heads of V-type engines, the intake manifold mounting position is altered, and must be corrected by milling the manifold flange a proportionate amount.
*Knurl the valve guides: Cut-away view of a knurled valve guide	*Valve guides which are not excessively worn or distorted may, in some cases, be knurled rather than replaced. Knurling is a process in which metal is displaced and raised, thereby reducing clearance. Knurling also provides excellent oil control. The possibility of knurling rather than replacing valve guides should be discussed with a machinist.
Replace the valve guides: NOTE: *Valve guides should only be replaced if damaged or if an oversize valve stem is not available.*	See the engine service procedures earlier in this chapter for details concerning specific engines. Depending on the type of cylinder head, valve guides may be pressed, hammered, or shrunk in. In cases where the guides are shrunk into the head, replacement should be left to an equipped machine shop. In other

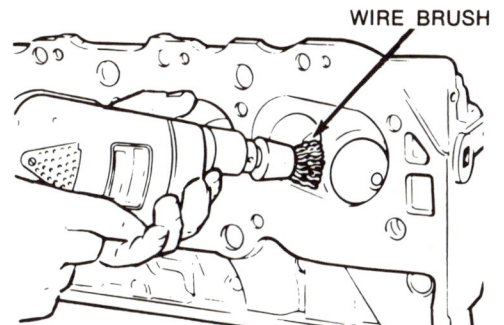

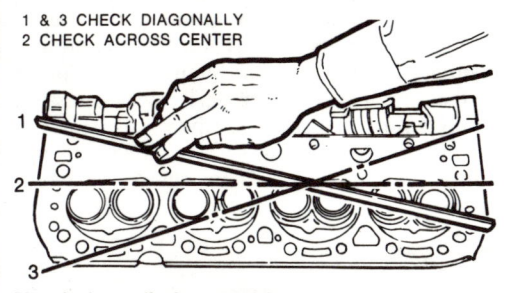

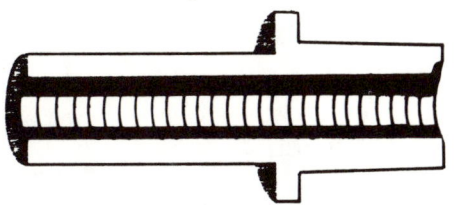

ENGINE AND ENGINE REBUILDING

Cylinder Head Reconditioning

Procedure	Method
A—VALVE GUIDE I.D. B—LARGER THAN THE VALVE GUIDE O.D. WASHERS A—VALVE GUIDE I.D. B—LARGER THAN THE VALVE GUIDE O.D. **Valve guide installation tool using washers for installation**	cases, the guides are replaced using a stepped drift (see illustration). Determine the height above the boss that the guide must extend, and obtain a stack of washers, their I.D. similar to the guide's O.D., of that height. Place the stack of washers on the guide, and insert the guide into the boss. NOTE: *Valve guides are often tapered or beveled for installation.* Using the stepped installation tool (see illustration), press or tap the guides into position. Ream the guides according to the size of the valve stem.
Replace valve seat inserts:	Replacement of valve seat inserts which are worn beyond resurfacing or broken, if feasible, must be done by a machine shop.
Resurface (grind) the valve face: FOR DIMENSIONS, REFER TO SPECIFICATIONS CHECK FOR BENT STEM DIAMETER VALVE FACE ANGLE 1/32" MINIMUM THIS LINE PARALLEL WITH VALVE HEAD **Critical valve dimensions**	Using a valve grinder, resurface the valves according to specifications given earlier in this chapter. CAUTION: *Valve face angle is not always identical to valve seat angle.* A minimum margin of 1/32" should remain after grinding the valve. The valve stem top should also be squared and resurfaced, by placing the stem in the V-block of the grinder, and turning it while pressing lightly against the grinding wheel. NOTE: *Do not grind sodium filled exhaust valves on a machine. These should be hand lapped.* **Valve grinding by machine**

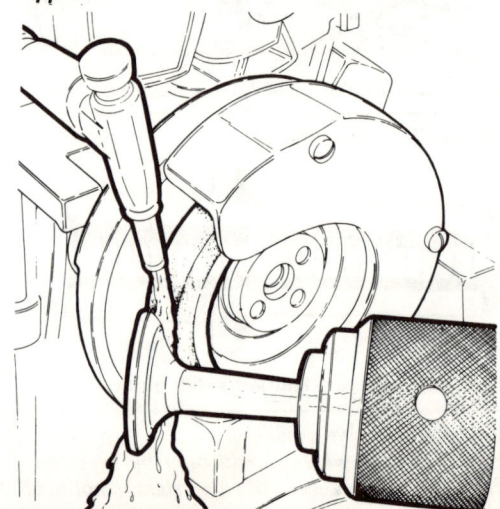

ENGINE AND ENGINE REBUILDING

Cylinder Head Reconditioning

Procedure	Method
Resurface the valve seats using reamers or grinder: *Valve seat width and centering* *Reaming the valve seat with a hand reamer*	Select a reamer of the correct seat angle, slightly larger than the diameter of the valve seat, and assemble it with a pilot of the correct size. Install the pilot into the valve guide, and using steady pressure, turn the reamer clockwise. **CAUTION:** *Do not turn the reamer counterclockwise.* Remove only as much material as necessary to clean the seat. Check the concentricity of the seat (following). If the dye method is not used, coat the valve face with Prussian blue dye, install and rotate it on the valve seat. Using the dye marked area as a centering guide, center and narrow the valve seat to specifications with correction cutters. **NOTE:** *When no specifications are available, minimum seat width for exhaust valves should be 5/64", intake valves 1/16".* After making correction cuts, check the position of the valve seat on the valve face using Prussian blue dye. To resurface the seat with a power grinder, select a pilot of the correct size and coarse stone of the proper angle. Lubricate the pilot and move the stone on and off the valve seat at 2 cycles per second, until all flaws are gone. Finish the seat with a fine stone. If necessary the seat can be corrected or narrowed using correction stones.
Check the valve seat concentricity: *Check the valve seat concentricity with a dial gauge*	Coat the valve face with Prussian blue dye, install the valve, and rotate it on the valve seat. If the entire seat becomes coated, and the valve is known to be concentric, the seat is concentric. * Install the dial gauge pilot into the guide, and rest of the arm on the valve seat. Zero the gauge, and rotate the arm around the seat. Run-out should not exceed .002".

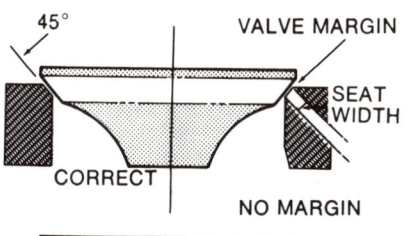

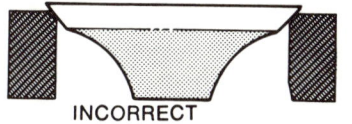

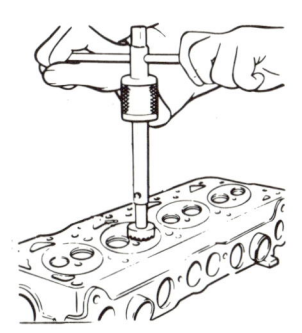

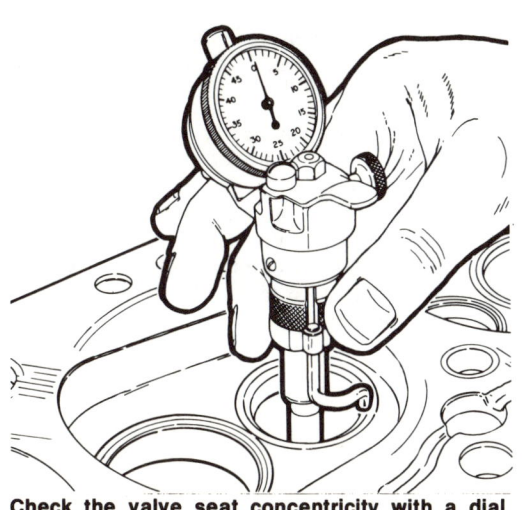

58 ENGINE AND ENGINE REBUILDING

Cylinder Head Reconditioning

Procedure	Method
*Lap the valves: NOTE: *Valve lapping is done to ensure efficient sealing of resurfaced valves and seats.* *Lapping the valves by hand* *Home-made valve lapping tool*	Invert the cyclinder head, lightly lubricate the valve stems, and install the valves in the head as numbered. Coat valve seats with fine grinding compound, and attach the lapping tool suction cup to a valve head. NOTE: *Moisten the suction cup.* Rotate the tool between the palms, changing position and lifting the tool often to prevent grooving. Lap the valve until a smooth, polished seat is evident. Remove the valve and tool, and rinse away all traces of grinding compound. **Fasten a suction cup to a piece of drill rod, and mount the rod in a hand drill. Proceed as above, using the hand drill as a lapping tool. CAUTION: *Due to the higher speeds involved when using the hand drill, care must be exercised to avoid grooving the seat.* Lift the tool and change direction of rotation often.
Check the valve springs: *Check the valve spring free length and squareness* *Check the valve spring test pressure*	Place the spring on a flat surface next to a square. Measure the height of the spring, and rotate it against the edge of the square to measure distortion. If spring height varies (by comparison) by more than $1/16''$ or if distortion exceeds $1/16''$, replace the spring. **In addition to evaluating the spring as above, test the spring pressure at the installed and compressed (installed height minus valve lift) height using a valve spring tester. Springs used on small displacement engines (up to 3 liters) should be $\mp$ 1 lb of all other springs in either position. A tolerance of $\mp$ 5 lbs is permissible on larger engines.

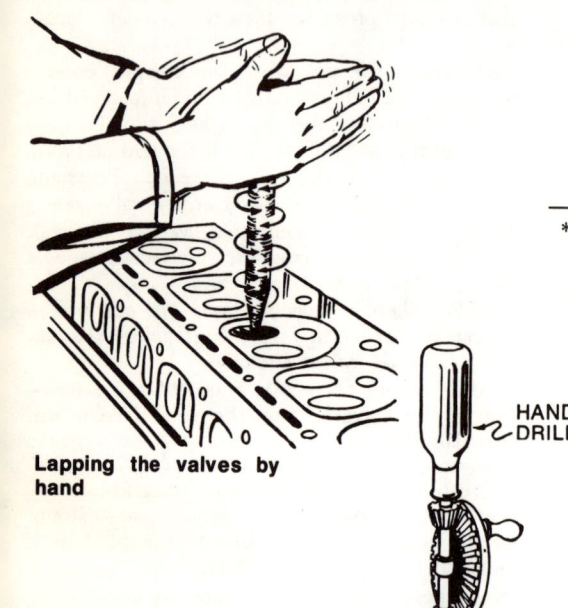

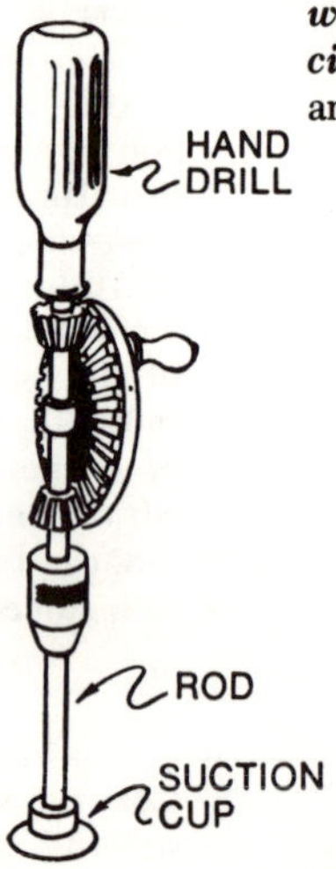

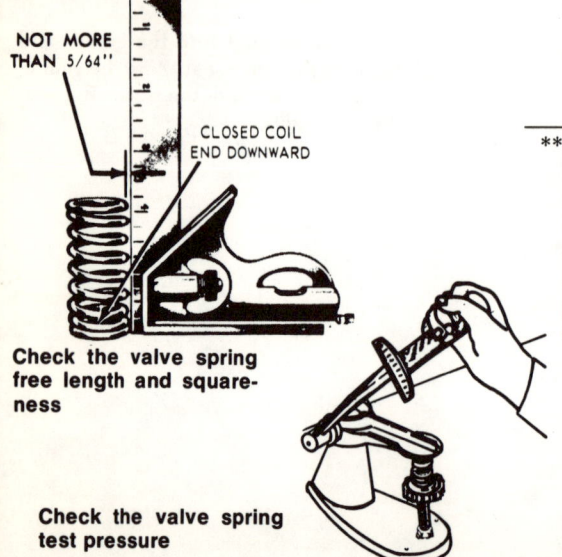

ENGINE AND ENGINE REBUILDING 59

Cylinder Head Reconditioning

Procedure	Method
*Install valve stem seals: RETAINER SPRING VALVE SEAL **Install valve stem seals**	*Due to the pressure differential that exists at the ends of the intake valve guides (atmospheric pressure above, manifold vacuum below), oil is drawn through the valve guides into the intake port. This has been alleviated somewhat since the addition of positive crankcase ventilation, which lowers the pressure above the guides. Several types of valve stem seals are available to reduce blow-by. Certain seals simply slip over the stem and guide boss, while others require that the boss be machined. Recently, Teflon guide seals have become popular. Consult a parts supplier or machinist concerning availability and suggested usages. NOTE: *When installing seals, ensure that a small amount of oil is able to pass the seal to lubricate the valve guides; otherwise, excessive wear may result.*
Install the valves:	See the engine service procedures earlier in this chapter for details concerning specific engines. Lubricate the valve stems, and install the valves in the cylinder head as numbered. Lubricate and position the seals (if used) and the valve springs. Install the spring retainers, compress the springs, and insert the keys using needlenose pliers or a tool designed for this purpose. NOTE: *Retain the keys with wheel bearing grease during installation.*
Check valve spring installed height: **Valve spring installed height (A)**	Measure the distance between the spring pad the lower edge of the spring retainer, and compare to specifications. If the installed height is incorrect, add shim washers between the spring pad and the spring. CAUTION: *Use only washers designed for this purpose.* GRIND OUT THIS PORTION **Measure the valve spring installed height (A) with a modified steel rule**
Clean and inspect the camshaft:	Degrease the camshaft, using solvent, and clean out all oil holes. Visually inspect cam lobes and bearing journals for excessive wear. If a lobe is questionable, check all lobes as indicated below. If a journal or lobe is worn, the camshaft must be reground or replaced.

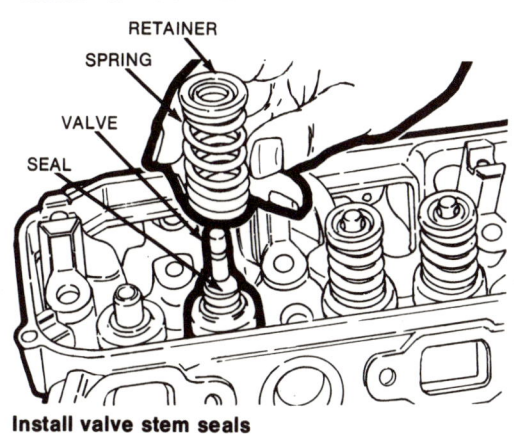

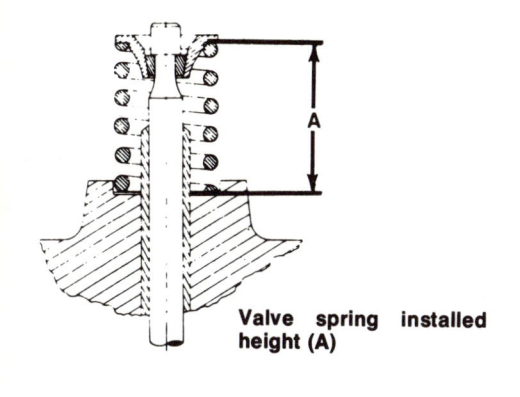

ENGINE AND ENGINE REBUILDING

Cylinder Head Reconditioning

Procedure	Method
	NOTE: *If a journal is worn, there is a good chance that the bushings are worn.* If lobes and journals appear intact, place the front and rear journals in V-blocks, and rest a dial indicator on the center journal. Rotate the camshaft to check straightness. If deviation exceeds .001″, replace the camshaft.

*Check the camshaft lobes with a micrometer, by measuring the lobes from the nose to base and again at 90° (see illustration). The lift is determined by subtracting the second measurement from the first. If all exhaust lobes and all intake lobes are not identical, the camshaft must be reground or replaced.

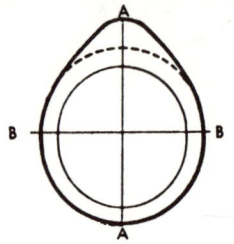

Check the camshaft for straightness

Camshaft lobe measurement

Install the camshaft:	See the engine service procedures earlier in this chapter for details concerning specific engines.
Install the rocker arms:	See the engine service procedures earlier in this chapter for details concerning specific engines.

Cylinder Block Reconditioning

Procedure	Method
Checking the main bearing clearance:	Invert engine, and remove cap from the bearing to be checked. Using a clean, dry rag, thoroughly clean all oil from crankshaft journal and bearing insert. NOTE: *Plastigage® is soluble in oil; therefore, oil on the journal or bearing could result in erroneous readings.* Place a piece of Plastigage along the full length of journal, reinstall cap, and torque to specifications. NOTE: *Specifications are given in the engine specifications earlier in this chapter.* Remove bearing cap, and determine bearing clearance by comparing width of Plastigage to the scale on Plastigage envelope. Journal taper is determined by comparing width of the Plastigage strip near its ends. Rotate crankshaft 90° and retest, to determine journal eccentricity. NOTE: *Do not rotate crankshaft with Plastigage installed.* If bearing insert and journal appear in-

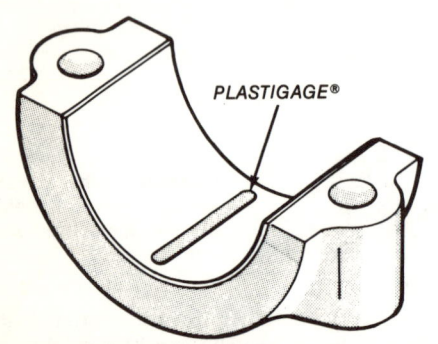

Plastigage® installed on the lower bearing shell

ENGINE AND ENGINE REBUILDING 61

Cylinder Block Reconditioning

Procedure	Method
Measure Plastigage® to determine main bearing clearance	tact, and are within tolerances, no further main bearing service is required. If bearing or journal appear defective, cause of failure should be determined before replacement.
	*Remove crankshaft from block (see below). Measure the main bearing journals at each end twice (90° apart) using a micrometer, to determine diameter, journal taper and eccentricity. If journals are within tolerances, reinstall bearing caps at their specified torque. Using a telescope gauge and micrometer, measure bearing I.D. parallel to piston axis and at 30° on each side of piston axis. Subtract journal O.D. from bearing I.D. to determine oil clearance. If crankshaft journals appear defective, or do not meet tolerances, there is no need to measure bearings; for the crankshaft will require grinding and/or undersize bearings will be required. If bearing appears defective, cause for failure should be determined prior to replacement.
Check the connecting rod bearing clearance:	Connecting rod bearing clearance is checked in the same manner as main bearing clearance, using Plastigage. Before removing the crankshaft, connecting rod side clearance also should be measured and recorded.
	*Checking connecting rod bearing clearance, using a micrometer, is identical to checking main bearing clearance. If no other service is required, the piston and rod assemblies need not be removed.
Remove the crankshaft:	Using a punch, mark the corresponding main bearing caps and saddles according to position (i.e., one punch on the front main cap and saddle, two on the second, three on the third, etc.). Using number stamps, identify the corresponding connecting rods and caps, according to cylinder (if no numbers are present). Remove the main and connecting rod caps, and replace sleeves of plastic tubing or vacuum hose over the connecting rod bolts, to protect the journals as the crankshaft is removed. Lift the crankshaft out of the block.
Match the connecting rod to the cylinder with a number stamp	**Match the connecting rod and cap with scribe marks**

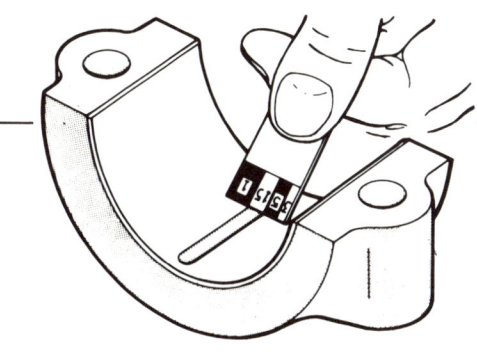

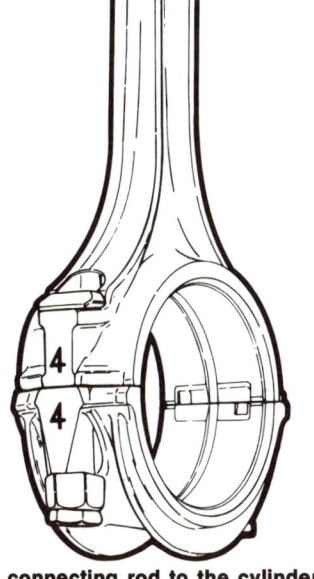

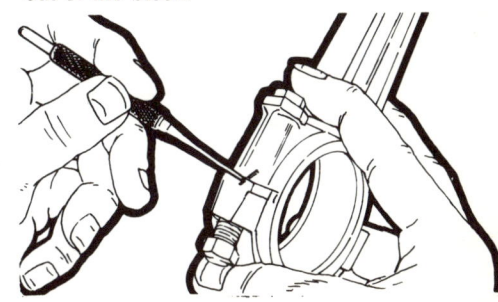

ENGINE AND ENGINE REBUILDING

Cylinder Block Reconditioning

Procedure	Method
Remove the ridge from the top of the cylinder: *Cylinder bore ridge*	In order to facilitate removal of the piston and connecting rod, the ridge at the top of the cylinder (unworn area; see illustration) must be removed. Place the piston at the bottom of the bore, and cover it with a rag. Cut the ridge away using a ridge reamer, exercising extreme care to avoid cutting too deeply. Remove the rag, and remove cuttings that remain on the piston. **CAUTION:** *If the ridge is not removed, and new rings are installed, damage to rings will result.*
Remove the piston and connecting rod: *Push the piston out with a hammer handle*	Invert the engine, and push the pistons and connecting rods out of the cylinders. If necessary, tap the connecting rod boss with a wooden hammer handle, to force the piston out. **CAUTION:** *Do not attempt to force the piston past the cylinder ridge* (see above).
Service the crankshaft:	Ensure that all oil holes and passages in the crankshaft are open and free of sludge. If necessary, have the crankshaft ground to the largest possible undersize.
	** Have the crankshaft Magnafluxed, to locate stress cracks. Consult a machinist concerning additional service procedures, such as surface hardening (e.g., nitriding, Tuftriding) to improve wear characteristics, cross drilling and chamfering the oil holes to improve lubrication, and balancing.
Removing freeze plugs:	Drill a small hole in the middle of the freeze plugs. Thread a large sheet metal screw into the hole and remove the plug with a slide hammer.
Remove the oil gallery plugs:	Threaded plugs should be removed using an appropriate (usually square) wrench. To remove soft, pressed in plugs, drill a hole in the plug, and thread in a sheet metal screw. Pull the plug out by the screw using pliers.
Hot-tank the block: **NOTE:** *Do not hot-tank aluminum parts.*	Have the block hot-tanked to remove grease, corrosion, and scale from the water jackets. **NOTE:** *Consult the operator to determine whether the camshaft bearings will be damaged during the hot-tank process.*

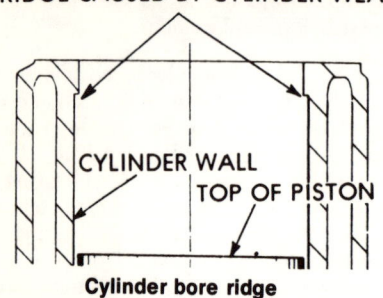

ENGINE AND ENGINE REBUILDING

Cylinder Block Reconditioning

Procedure	Method

Check the block for cracks:	Visually inspect the block for cracks or chips. The most common locations are as follows:
	    Adjacent to freeze plugs.
	    Between the cylinders and water jackets.
	    Adjacent to the main bearing saddles.
	    At the extreme bottom of the cylinders.
	Check only suspected cracks using spot check dye (see introduction). If a crack is located, consult a machinist concerning possible repairs.

	** Magnaflux the block to locate hidden cracks. If cracks are located, consult a machinist about feasibility of repair.
Install the oil gallery plugs and freeze plugs:	Coat freeze plugs with sealer and tap into position using a piece of pipe, slightly smaller than the plug, as a driver. To ensure retention, stake the edges of the plugs. Coat threaded oil gallery plugs with sealer and install. Drive replacement soft plugs into block using a large drift as a driver.
	* Rather than reinstalling lead plugs, drill and tap the holes, and install threaded plugs.
Check the bore diameter and surface:	Visually inspect the cylinder bores for roughness, scoring, or scuffing. If evident, the cylinder bore must be bored or honed oversize to eliminate imperfections, and the smallest possible oversize piston used. The new pistons should be given to the machinist with the block, so that the cylinders can be bored or honed exactly to the piston size (plus clearance). If no flaws are evident, measure the bore diameter using a telescope gauge and micrometer, or dial gauge, parallel and perpendicular to the engine centerline, at the top (below the ridge) and bottom of the bore. Subtract the bottom measurements from the top to determine taper, and the parallel to the centerline measurements from the perpendicular measurements to determine eccentricity. If the measurements are not within specifications, the cylinder must be bored or honed, and an oversize piston installed. If the measurements are within specifications the cylinder may

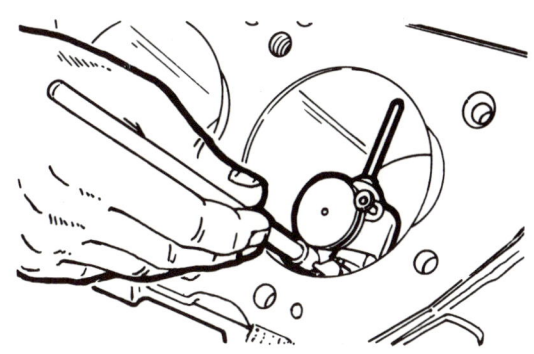

Measure the cylinder bore with a dial gauge

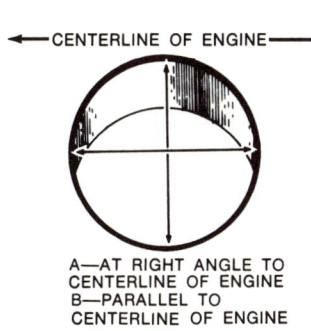

Cylinder bore measuring points
A—AT RIGHT ANGLE TO CENTERLINE OF ENGINE
B—PARALLEL TO CENTERLINE OF ENGINE

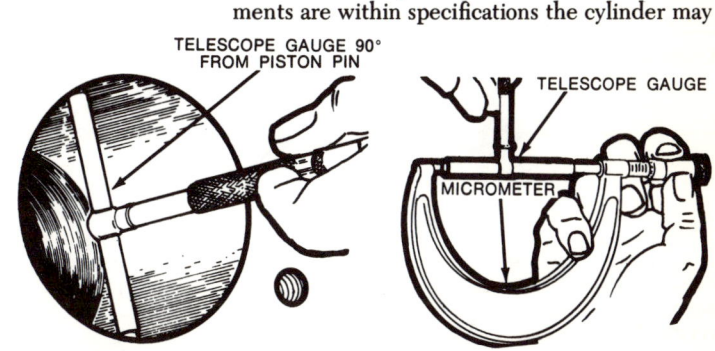

Measure the cylinder bore with a telescope gauge

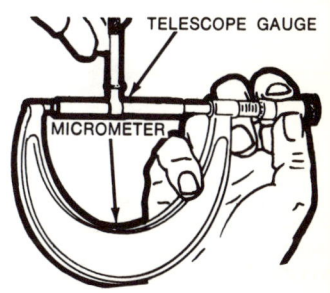

Measure the telescope gauge with a micrometer to determine the cylinder bore

Cylinder Block Reconditioning

Procedure	Method
	be used as is, with only finish honing (see below). **NOTE:** *Prior to submitting the block for boring, perform the following operation(s).*
Check the cylinder block bearing alignment: **Check the main bearing saddle alignment**	Remove the upper bearing inserts. Place a straightedge in the bearing saddles along the centerline of the crankshaft. If clearance exists between the straightedge and the center saddle, the block must be alignbored.
*Check the deck height:	The deck height is the distance from the crankshaft centerline to the block deck. To measure, invert the engine, and install the crankshaft, retaining it with the center maincap. Measure the distance from the crankshaft journal to the block deck, parallel to the cylinder centerline. Measure the diameter of the end (front and rear) main journals, parallel to the centerline of the cylinders, divide the diameter in half, and subtract it from the previous measurement. The results of the front and rear measurements should be identical. If the difference exceeds .005″, the deck height should be corrected. **NOTE:** *Block deck height and warpage should be corrected at the same time.*
Check the block deck for warpage:	Using a straightedge and feeler gauges, check the block deck for warpage in the same manner that the cylinder head is checked (see Cylinder Head Reconditioning). If warpage exceeds specifications, have the deck resurfaced. **NOTE:** *In certain cases a specification for total material removal (cylinder head and block deck) is provided. This specification must not be exceeded.*
Clean and inspect the pistons and connecting rods: RING EXPANDER **Remove the piston rings**	Using a ring expander, remove the rings from the piston. Remove the retaining rings (if so equipped) and remove piston pin. **NOTE:** *If the piston pin must be pressed out, determine the proper method and use the proper tools; otherwise the piston will distort.* Clean the ring grooves using an appropriate tool, exercising care to avoid cutting too deeply. Thoroughly clean all carbon and varnish from the piston with solvent. **CAUTION:** *Do not use a wire brush or caustic solvent on pistons.* Inspect the pistons for scuffing, scoring, cracks, pitting, or excessive ringsgroove wear. If wear is evident, the piston must be replaced. Check the connecting rod length by measuring

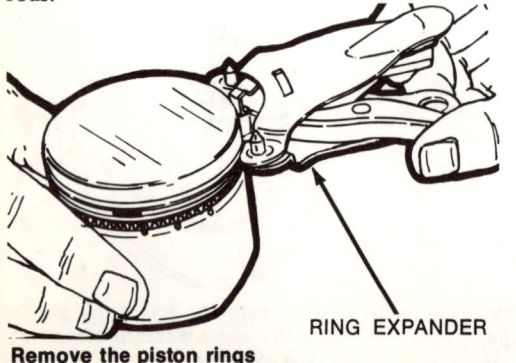

ENGINE AND ENGINE REBUILDING

Cylinder Block Reconditioning

Procedure	Method
Clean the piston ring grooves	the rod from the inside of the large end to the inside of the small end using calipers (see illustration). All connecting rods should be equal length. Replace any rod that differs from the others in the engine.
Check the connecting rod length (arrow)	* Have the connecting rod alignment checked in an alignment fixture by a machinist. Replace any twisted or bent rods. * Magnaflux the connecting rods to locate stress cracks. If cracks are found, replace the connecting rod.
Fit the pistons to the cylinders: *Measure the piston prior to fitting*	Using a telescope gauge and micrometer, or a dial gauge, measure the cylinder bore diameter perpendicular to the piston pin, 2½" below the deck. Measure the piston perpendicular to its pin on the skirt. The difference between the two measurements is the piston clearance. If the clearance is within specifications or slightly below (after boring or honing), finish honing is all that is required. If the clearance is excessive, try to obtain a slightly larger piston to bring clearance within specifications. Where this is not possible, obtain the first oversize piston, and hone (of if necessary, bore) the cylinder to size.
Assemble the pistons and connecting rods: *Install the piston pin lock-rings (if used)*	Inspect piston pin, connecting rod small end bushing, and piston bore for galling, scoring, or excessive wear. If evident, replace defective part(s). Measure the I.D. of the piston boss and connecting rod small end, and the O.D. of the piston pin. If within specifications, assemble piston pin and rod. **CAUTION:** *If piston pin must be pressed in, determine the proper method and use the proper tools; otherwise the piston will distort.* Install the lock rings; ensure that they seat properly. If the parts are not within specifications, determine the service method for the type of engine. In some cases, piston and pin are serviced as an assembly when either is defective. Others specify reaming the piston and connecting rods for an oversize pin. If the connecting rod bushing is worn, it may in many cases be replaced. Reaming the piston and replacing the rod bushing are machine shop operations.

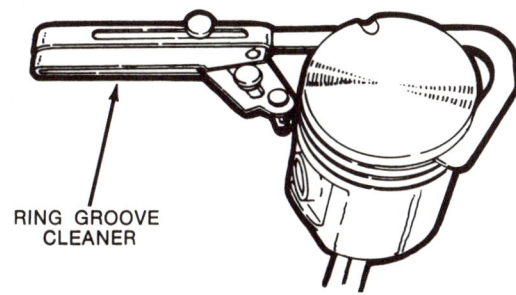

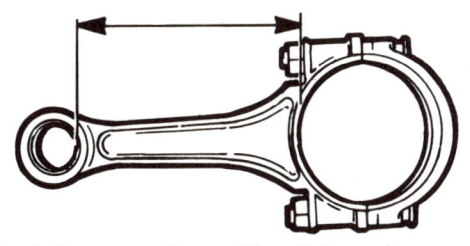

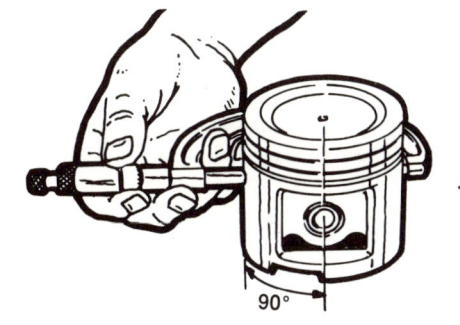

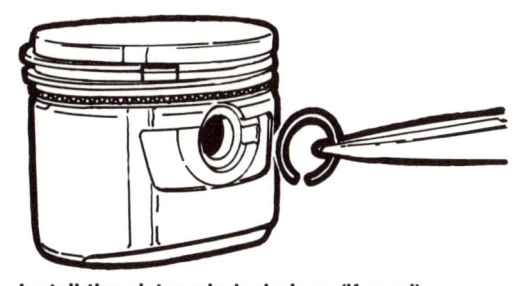

ENGINE AND ENGINE REBUILDING

Cylinder Block Reconditioning

Procedure	Method
Finish hone the cylinders: *[Illustration: Cross hatch pattern, 50°-60°]*	Chuck a flexible drive hone into a power drill, and insert it into the cylinder. Start the hone, and move it up and down in the cylinder at a rate which will produce approximately a 60° cross-hatch pattern. NOTE: *Do not extend the hone below the cylinder bore.* After developing the pattern, remove the hone and recheck piston fit. Wash the cylinders with a detergent and water solution to remove abrasive dust, dry, and wipe several times with a rag soaked in engine oil.
Check piston ring end-gap: *[Illustration]* Check the piston ring end gap	Compress the piston rings to be used in a cylinder, one at a time, into that cylinder, and press them approximately 1″ below the deck with an inverted piston. Using feeler gauges, measure the ring end-gap, and compare to specifications. Pull the ring out of the cylinder and file the ends with a fine file to obtain proper clearance. CAUTION: *If inadequate ring end-gap is utilized, ring breakage will result.*
Install the piston rings: *[Illustration: PISTON RING, FEELER GAUGE, RING GROOVE]* Check the piston ring side clearance	Inspect the ring grooves in the piston for excessive wear or taper. If necessary, recut the groove(s) for use with an overwidth ring or a standard ring and spacer. If the groove is worn uniformly, overwidth rings, or standard rings and spaces may be installed without recutting. Roll the outside of the ring around the groove to check for burrs or deposits. If any are found, remove with a fine file. Hold the ring in the groove, and measure side clearance. If necessary, correct as indicated above. NOTE: *Always install any additional spacers above the piston ring.* The ring groove must be deep enough to allow the ring to seat below the lands (see illustration). In many cases, a "go-no-go" depth gauge will be provided with the piston rings. Shallow grooves may be corrected by recutting, while deep

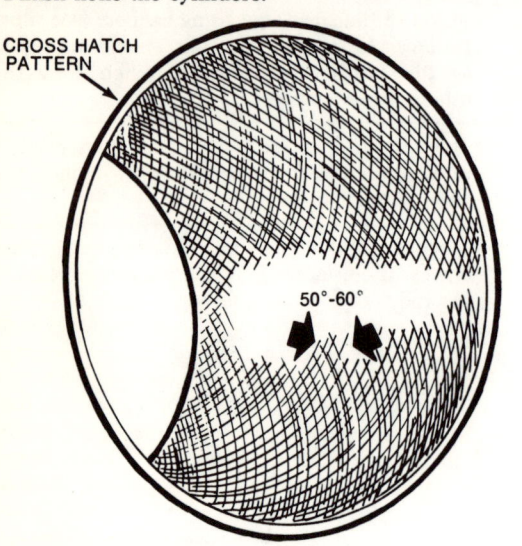

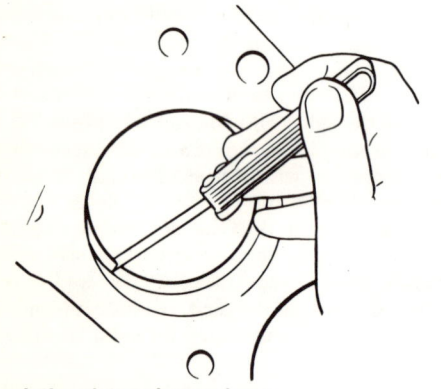

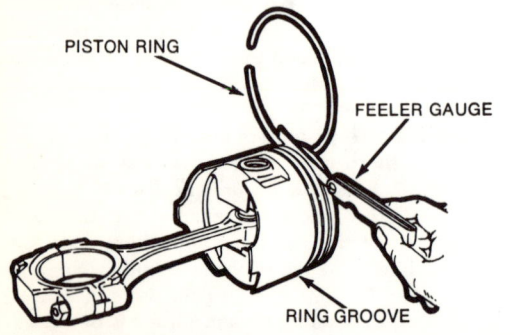

ENGINE AND ENGINE REBUILDING

Cylinder Block Reconditioning

Procedure	Method
	grooves require some type of filler or expander behind the piston. Consult the piston ring supplier concerning the suggested method. Install the rings on the piston, lowest ring first, using a ring expander. NOTE: *Position the rings as specified by the manufacturer.* Consult the engine service procedures earlier in this chapter for details concerning specific engines.
Install the rear main seal:	See the engine service procedures earlier in this chapter for details concerning specific engines.
Install the crankshaft: **Remove or install the upper bearing insert using a roll-out pin** **Home-made bearing roll-out pin** **Aligning the thrust bearing**	Thoroughly clean the main bearing saddles and caps. Place the upper halves of the bearing inserts on the saddles and press into position. NOTE: *Ensure that the oil holes align.* Press the corresponding bearing inserts into the main bearing caps. Lubricate the upper main bearings, and lay the crankshaft in position. Place a strip of Plastigage on each of the crankshaft journals, install the main caps, and torque to specifications. Remove the main caps, and compare the Plastigage to the scale on the Plastigage envelope. If clearances are within tolerances, remove the Plastigage, turn the crankshaft 90°, wipe off all oil and retest. If all clearances are correct, remove all Plastigage, thoroughly lubricate the main caps and bearing journals, and install the main caps. If clearances are not within tolerance, the upper bearing inserts may be removed, without removing the crankshaft, using a bearing roll out pin (see illustration). Roll in a bearing that will provide proper clearance, and retest. Torque all main caps, excluding the thrust bearing cap, to specifications. Tighten the thrust bearing cap finger tight. To properly align the thrust bearing, pry the crankshaft the extent of its axial travel several times, the last movement held toward the front of the engine, and torque the thrust bearing cap to specifications. Determine the crankshaft end-play (see below), and bring within tolerance with thrust washers.
Measure crankshaft end-play:	Mount a dial indicator stand on the front of the block, with the dial indicator stem resting on the

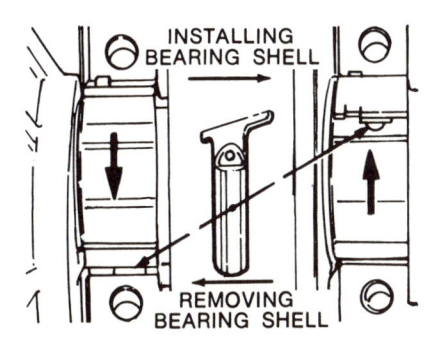

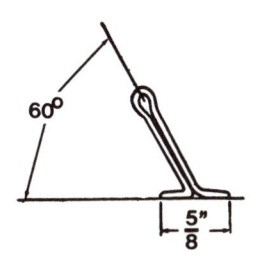

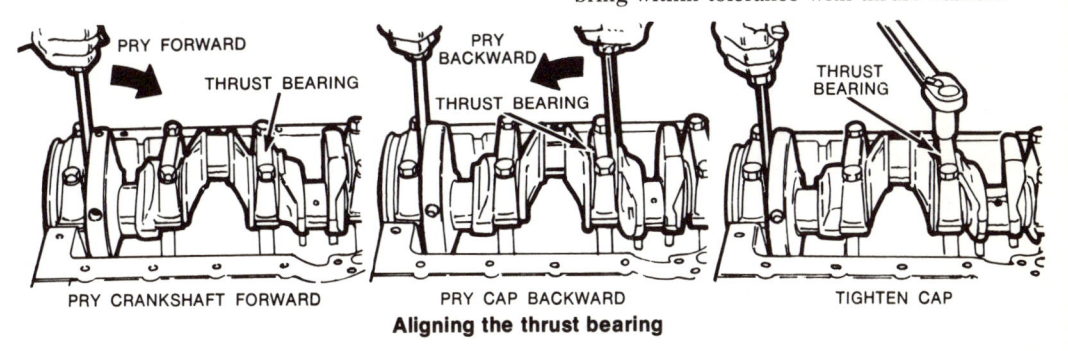

68 ENGINE AND ENGINE REBUILDING

Cylinder Block Reconditioning

Procedure	Method

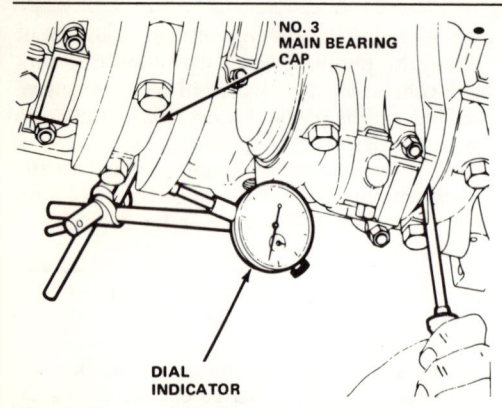

Check the crankshaft end-play with a dial indicator

nose of the crankshaft, parallel to the crankshaft axis. Pry the crankshaft the extent of its travel rearward, and zero the indicator. Pry the crankshaft forward and record crankshaft end-play.

NOTE: *Crankshaft end-play also may be measured at the thrust bearing, using feeler gauges* (see illustration).

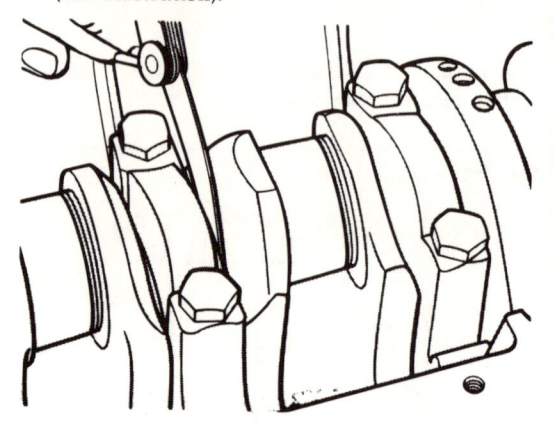

Check the crankshaft end-play with a feeler gauge

Install the pistons:

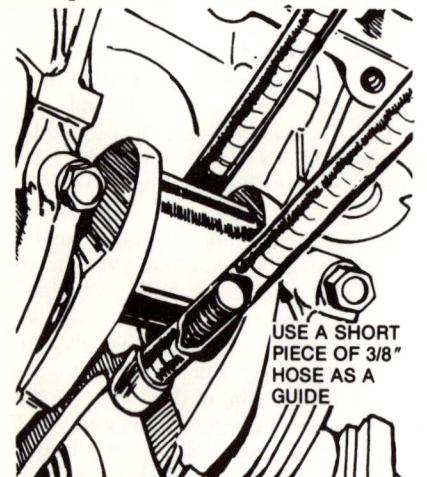

Use lengths of vacuum hose or rubber tubing to protect the crankshaft journals and cylinder walls during piston installation

Press the upper connecting rod bearing halves into the connecting rods, and the lower halves into the connecting rod caps. Position the piston ring gaps according to specifications (see car section), and lubricate the pistons. Install a ring compressor on a piston, and press two long (8″) pieces of plastic tubing over the rod bolts. Using the tubes as a guide, press the pistons into the bores and onto the crankshaft with a wooden hammer handle. After seating the rod on the crankshaft journal, remove the tubes and install the cap finger tight. Install the remaining pistons in the same manner. Invert the engine and check the bearing clearance at two points (90° apart) on each journal with Plastigage.

NOTE: *Do not turn the crankshaft with Plastigage installed.*

If clearance is within tolerances, remove *all* Plastigage, thoroughly lubricate the journals, and torque the rod caps to specifications. If clearance is not within specifications, install different thickness bearing inserts and recheck.

CAUTION: *Never shim or file the connecting rods or caps.*

Always install plastic tube sleeves over the rod bolts when the caps are not installed, to protect the crankshaft journals.

Install the piston using a ring compressor

ENGINE AND ENGINE REBUILDING

Cylinder Block Reconditioning

Procedure	Method
Check connecting rod side clearance: Check the connecting rod side clearance with a feeler gauge	Determine the clearance between the sides of the connecting rods and the crankshaft using feeler gauges. If clearance is below the minimum tolerance, the rod may be machined to provide adequate clearance. If clearance is excessive, substitute an unworn rod, and recheck. If clearance is still outside specifications, the crankshaft must be welded and reground, or replaced.
Inspect the timing chain (or belt):	Visually inspect the timing chain for broken or loose links, and replace the chain if any are found. If the chain will flex sideways, it must be replaced. Install the timing chain as specified. Be sure the timing belt is not stretched, frayed or broken. NOTE: *If the original timing chain is to be reused, install it in its original position.* See the engine service procedures earlier in this chapter for details concerning specific engines.

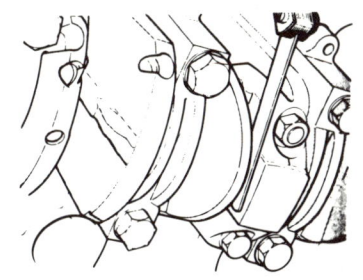

Completing the Rebuilding Process

Following the above procedures, complete the rebuilding process as follows:

Fill the oil pump with oil, to prevent cavitating (sucking air) on initial engine start up. Install the oil pump and the pickup tube on the engine. Coat the oil pan gasket as necessary, and install the gasket and the oil pan. Mount the flywheel and the crankshaft vibration damper or pulley on the crankshaft.

NOTE: *Always use new bolts when installing the flywheel.* Inspect the clutch shaft pilot bushing in the crankshaft. If the bushing is excessively worn, remove it with an expanding puller and a slide hammer, and tap a new bushing into place.

Position the engine, cylinder head side up. Install the cylinder head, and torque it as specified. Install the rocker arms and adjust the valves.

Install the intake and exhaust manifolds, the carburetor(s), the distributor and spark plugs. Adjust the point gap and the static ignition timing. Mount all accessories and install the engine in the car. Fill the radiator with coolant, and the crankcase with high quality engine oil.

Break-in Procedure

Start the engine, and allow it to run at low speed for a few minutes, while checking for leaks. Stop the engine, check the oil level, and fill as necessary. Restart the engine, and fill the cooling system to capacity. Check the point dwell angle and adjust the ignition timing and the valves. Run the engine at low to medium speed (800–2500 rpm) for approximately ½ hour, and retorque the cylinder head bolts. Road test the car, and check again for leaks.

Follow the manufacturer's recommended engine break-in procedure and maintenance schedule for new engines.

Emission Controls and Fuel System

4

EMISSION CONTROLS

Positive Crankcase Ventilation

Positive Crankcase Ventilation (PCV) is a system which returns combustible gases which have leaked past the piston rings into the crankcase, back through the intake manifold for reburning. This leakage is the normal result of the necessary working clearance of the piston rings. If these gases were to remain in the crankcase they would react with the oil to form sludge. Since there is also a certain amount of unburned fuel in the gases, dilution of the oil would occur. Both sludge and diluted oil will accelerate the wear of the engine.

Along with gases returning to the intake manifold, the PCV valve also returns a certain amount of additional air. The carburetor used with this system has been calibrated to compensate for the additional air intake.

The system consists of a hose connecting the air cleaner to the cam cover and another hose connecting the PCV valve mounted in a grommet in the cam cover and the intake manifold.

The PCV valve regulates the flow of combustion gases through the system. During engine idle and deceleration when intake manifold vacuum is high, the PCV valve restricts vapor flow to the intake manifold. When the engine is accelerated or is at constant speed, intake manifold vacuum is low and the PCV valve allows crankcase gases to flow into the intake manifold. Should the engine backfire, the plunger inside the valve is forced against its seat preventing the backfire from traveling through the PCV valve and into the engine crankcase.

The PCV valve is checked for proper operation simply by removing it from the grommet in the cam cover and shaking. If the plunger in the valve rattles, the valve is good and can be replaced. At 24 month or 30,000 mile intervals, install a new PCV valve and

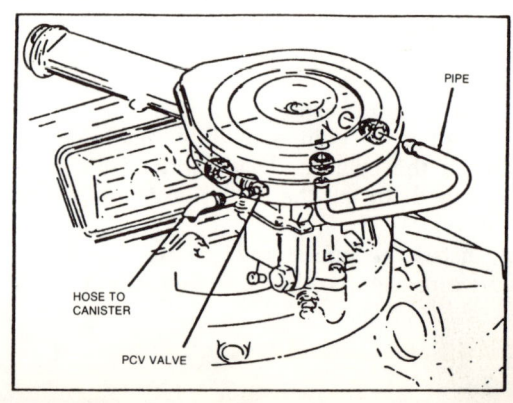

PCV system

EMISSION CONTROLS AND FUEL SYSTEM

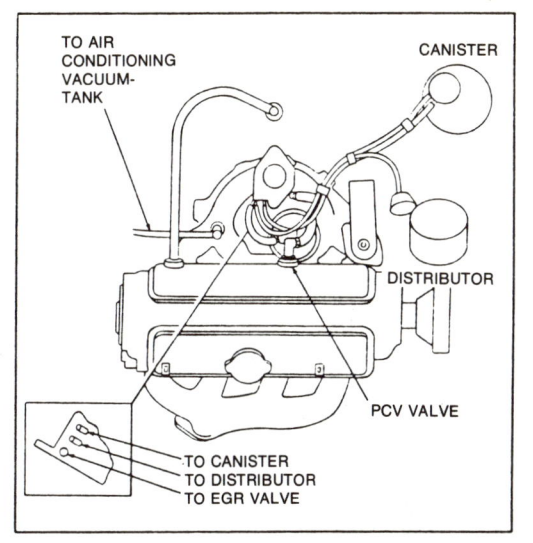

Emission hose routing without air injection (non-California)

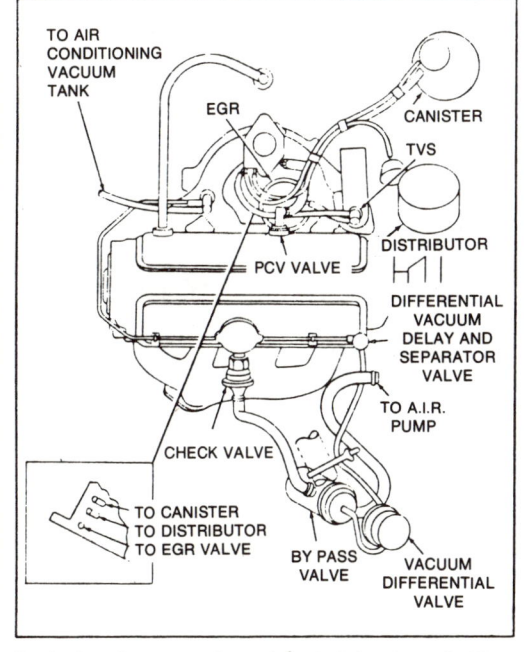

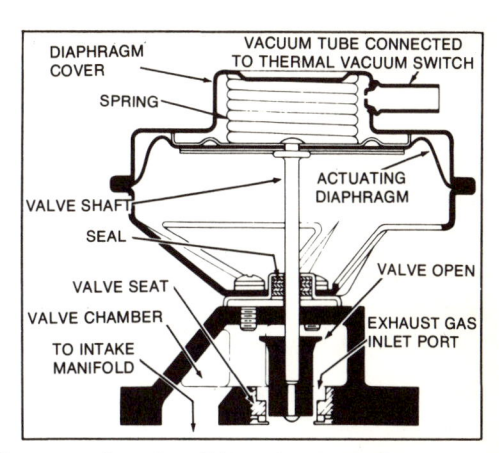

Cross-section of an EGR valve (typical)

Emission hose routing with air injection (California)

use compressed air to blow out the PCV valve hose to eliminate any restrictions.

PCV valve removal and installation procedures are covered in Chapter One.

Exhaust Gas Recirculation

Exhaust Gas Recirculation (EGR) is used to reduce oxides of nitrogen (NO_x) exhaust emissions. NO_x formation occurs at very high combustion temperatures so that the EGR system reduces combustion temperature slightly by introducing small amounts of inert exhaust gas into the intake manifold. The result is reduced formation of NO_x.

The EGR valve is mounted on the intake manifold and contains a vacuum diaphragm. The unit is operated by intake manifold vacuum and controls the flow of exhaust gases.

A vacuum signal supply port is located in the throttle body of the carburetor above the throttle plate. Vacuum is supplied to the EGR valve (causing recirculation), at part-throttle conditions. EGR does not occur at idle or at wide open throttle.

Some models also use a thermal vacuum switch (TVS), mounted in the outlet water housing to block vacuum to the EGR valve until engine coolant temperature is approximately 100° F.

An engine that idles roughly may be caused by a bad EGR valve. Push on the diaphragm plate to check for freedom of movement. If it sticks, replace the valve. Hook up a vacuum gauge between the signal tube and the vacuum hose. With the engine running and warmed up, increase the engine speed to obtain 5 hg.in. of vacuum. Remove the vacuum hose and check for the diaphragm plate to move downward. This should be accompanied by increased engine speed. Replace the vacuum hose and check to see that the plate moves upward. The engine speed should drop. If the diaphragm is not moving check for vacuum at the EGR hose. If there is none, check for leaking, plugged, or misplaced hoses. If the diaphragm moves but there is no change in rpm, check for blocked EGR manifold passages.

72 EMISSION CONTROLS AND FUEL SYSTEM

EGR VALVE REMOVAL AND INSTALLATION

1. Disconnect the vacuum line at the EGR valve.
2. Remove the bolt securing the EGR valve and remove the valve from the intake manifold.
3. Use a new gasket and install the EGR valve on the intake manifold. Torque the mounting bolt to 13–18 ft lbs.
4. Connect the vacuum line to the valve.

THERMAL VACUUM SWITCH CHECK

NOTE: *This test must be performed with the engine at normal operating temperatures, permitting the vacuum signal to reach the EGR valve.*

1. Remove EGR valve vacuum hose at EGR valve and attach the hose to a vacuum gauge.
2. Start the engine and open the throttle partially. Do not race the engine. As the throttle is opened, the vacuum gauge should respond proportionately.
3. If the vacuum gauge responds correctly, remove it and replace the hose to the EGR valve.
4. If the gauge does not react correctly, remove the carburetor to switch hose at the switch and attach the vacuum gauge to it. Repeat Step 2. If the gauge responds to the opening of the throttle, the switch is defective and must be replaced.
5. If the gauge does not respond to the opening throttle, suspect a plugged hose or a defective carburetor.

Location of EGR thermal vacuum switch

THERMAL VACUUM SWITCH REMOVAL AND INSTALLATION

1. Disconnect the vacuum lines.
2. Remove the switch from the thermostat housing.
3. Use sealer on the threads of the switch, install the switch and torque to 15 ft lbs.
4. Turn the switch head if necessary to align for hose routing and connect vacuum hoses.

Air Injection Reactor

The Air Injection Reactor (AIR) system reduces carbon monoxide and unburned hydrocarbon emissions by injecting air into the exhaust system at the rear of the exhaust valves. The AIR system is used on California cars only. The system consists of an air pump, air injection tubes (one for each cylinder), a vacuum differential valve, an air by-pass valve, a differential vacuum delay and separator valve, a check valve, and the required hoses to connect the components.

The air pump (with an integral filter), compresses and injects the air through the air manifolds into the exhaust system to the rear of the exhaust valves. The additional air brings about further combustion of hydrocarbons and carbon monoxide in the exhaust manifold. The vacuum differential valve stops air injection to prevent backfiring during engine deceleration by activating the air by-pass valve. The vacuum differential valve is triggered by sharp increases in manifold vacuum. On engine deceleration total air pump output is vented to the atmosphere through a muffler in the air by-pass valve. Also in the air by-pass valve is a pressure relief valve which vents excess air from the air pump at high engine speeds. The by-pass valve also vents air through its muffler at times of low intake manifold vacuum (engine acceleration). This low manifold vacuum venting is controlled by the differential vacuum delay and separator valve which blocks this venting during very short periods of 20 seconds or less to prevent possible overheating of the catalytic converter. The check valve prevents exhaust gases from entering the air pump.

When properly installed and maintained, the AIR system will effectively reduce contaminating exhausts. However, if any AIR component or any engine component that operates in conjunction with the AIR system

EMISSION CONTROLS AND FUEL SYSTEM

malfunctions, the pollutant level will be increased. Whenever the AIR system seems to be malfunctioning, the engine tune-up should be checked, particularly the PCV system, carburetor, and other systems which directly affect the fuel-air ratio.

AIR PUMP REMOVAL AND INSTALLATION

CAUTION: *Do not pry on the pump housing or clamp the pump in a vise; the housing is soft and may become distorted.*

1. Disconnect the air output hose at the pump.
2. Hold the pump pulley from rotating and loosen the pulley bolts. Remove the drive belt and pump pulley.

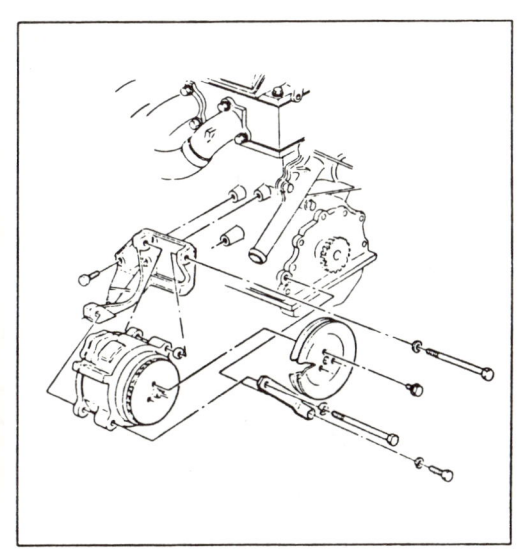

Air pump mounting details

3. Remove the air pump mounting bolts and remove the air pump.
4. Install the air pump by reversing the removal procedure.

Pulse Air System—PAIR

The PAIR system is used only on California cars. It consists of a pulse air valve which has four check valves. The firing of the engine creates a pulsating flow of exhaust gases which are either positive or negative, depending whether the exhaust valve is seated or not.

If the pressure is positive the check valve is forced closed and no exhaust gas will be able to flow past the valve and into the fresh air supply.

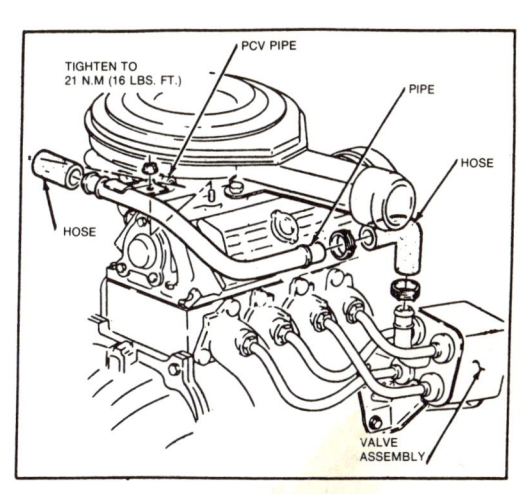

Pulse Air System—PAIR

If there is negative pressure, a vacuum, in the exhaust system, the check valve will open and allow fresh air to be drawn in and mixed with the exhaust gases. During high engine rpm the check valve will remain closed.

If one or more of the check valves has failed the engine may surge or perform poorly. A short hissing noise may also indicate a defective pulse air valve. Inspect the valve.

When exhaust gases are allowed to pass through the pulse air valve, excessive heat will be transferred to the valve body. This will be indicated by burned off paint or deteriorated rubber hoses. Replace the air valve as necessary.

To inspect the pulse air valve create a vacuum at the hose end of the valve to 5kPa (15 in.Hg.). The vacuum is permitted to drop to 17 kPa (5 in.Hg.) in two seconds. If the vacuum drops in less than two seconds, replace the valve.

PULSE AIR VALVE REMOVAL AND INSTALLATION.

1. Remove the air cleaner and disconnect the rubber hose from the pulse air valve.
2. Disconnect the support bracket and remove the attaching bolts.
3. Remove the pulse air valve.
4. Install the new pulse air valve and tighten the attaching bolts to 14–18 N·m (10–13 ft lbs.)
5. Connect the support bracket.
6. Connect the rubber hose to the pulse air valve and install the air cleaner.

NOTE: *In some cases the support bracket is not present in the vehicle. If so, simply omit this step.*

74 EMISSION CONTROLS AND FUEL SYSTEM

Evaporative Emission Control

The Evaporative Control System (ECS) limits gasoline vapor escape into the atmosphere. A domed fuel tank and pressure-vacuum filler cap is used with a plastic, charcoal-filled storage canister.

Fuel vapors travel from the fuel tank vent pipe (located above fuel level in the dome of the fuel tank), by way of steel tubing and fuel-resistant rubber hose to the plastic vapor storage canister in the engine compartment. Fuel vapors are routed into the PCV system for burning when ported carburetor vacuum operates a valve in the canister. As fuel is pumped from the tank, a relief valve in the tank cap opens to allow air to enter the fuel tank.

CHARCOAL CANISTER REMOVAL AND INSTALLATION

1. Carefully note the installed position of the hose connected to the canister, then disconnect the hoses.
2. Loosen the mounting clamps and remove the canister. To replace the canister filter, remove the filter from the bottom of the canister with your fingers.

Check to ensure that the hose connection openings are clear and check the purge valve by applying vacuum to it. If OK, it will hold vacuum. Check the condition of the hoses and replace as necessary. When replacing ECS hoses, use only fuel-resistant hose marked "EVAP."

If the purge valve is defective, disconnect the lines at the valve and snap off the valve cap. Turn the cap slowly as the diaphragm is under spring tension. Remove the diaphragm, spring retainer, and spring. Check all orifices and replace parts as necessary. Install the spring, spring retainer, diaphragm, and cap. Connect the lines to the valve.

3. Install a new filter in the bottom of the charcoal canister.
4. Install the canister and tighten its mounting clamp bolts.
5. Connect the hoses to the top of the canister in their original positions.

Controlled Combustion System

The Controlled Combustion System (CCS) increases combustion efficiency by means of leaner carburetor mixtures and revised distributor calibration. Also, a thermostatically-controlled damper in the air cleaner snorkel maintains warm air intake to the carburetor to optimize fuel vaporization.

An air intake duct routes air from the radiator support to the air cleaner snorkel, then to the air cleaner. Air temperature is automatically controlled by a thermostatic damper inside the air cleaner snorkel. The damper selects warm air from the exhaust manifold heat stove when air temperature is below 50° F. When air temperature is above 110° F, the damper selects outside air from the air intake duct.

When replacing the air cleaner, remove the air cleaner from the air intake snorkel and the carburetor and throw it away. Check the carburetor air horn gasket and replace it if damaged or cracked, and install a new air cleaner.

Catalytic Converter

All models are equipped with an underfloor catalytic converter. The converter contains pellets coated with the catalyst material containing platinum and palladium. The converter reduces hydrocarbon and carbon monoxide emissions by transforming them into carbon dioxide and water through a chemical reaction which takes place at great heat.

Unleaded fuel only must be used with converter equipped cars because lead in leaded fuel is not consumed in the combustion process and will enter the converter and coat the pellets, eventually rendering the catalytic converter useless for emission control. To ensure the use of unleaded fuel only, all models have a small diameter fuel inlet filler which

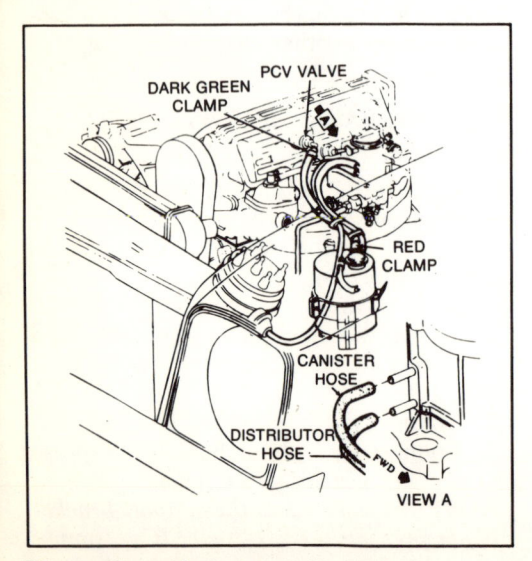

Evaporative emission control system

CHILTON'S
FUEL ECONOMY & TUNE-UP TIPS

Tune-Up • Spark Plug Diagnosis • Emission Controls
Fuel System • Cooling System • Tires and Wheels
General Maintenance

35 WAYS TO IMPROVE FUEL ECONOMY

CHILTON'S FUEL ECONOMY & TUNE-UP TIPS

Fuel economy is important to everyone, no matter what kind of vehicle you drive. The maintenance-minded motorist can save both money and fuel using these tips and the periodic maintenance and tune-up procedures in this Repair and Tune-Up Guide.

There are more than 130,000,000 cars and trucks registered for private use in the United States. Each travels an average of 10-12,000 miles per year, and, in total they consume close to 70 billion gallons of fuel each year. This represents nearly ⅔ of the oil imported by the United States each year. The Federal government's goal is to reduce consumption 10% by 1985. A variety of methods are either already in use or under serious consideration, and they all affect your driving and the cars you will drive. In addition to "down-sizing", the auto industry is using or investigating the use of electronic fuel delivery, electronic engine controls and alternative engines for use in smaller and lighter vehicles, among other alternatives to meet the federally mandated Corporate Average Fuel Economy (CAFE) of 27.5 mpg by 1985. The government, for its part, is considering rationing, mandatory driving curtailments and tax increases on motor vehicle fuel in an effort to reduce consumption. The government's goal of a 10% reduction could be realized — and further government regulation avoided — if every private vehicle could use just 1 less gallon of fuel per week.

How Much Can You Save?

Tests have proven that almost anyone can make at least a 10% reduction in fuel consumption through regular maintenance and tune-ups. When a major manufacturer of spark plugs sur-

TUNE-UP

1. Check the cylinder compression to be sure the engine will really benefit from a tune-up and that it is capable of producing good fuel economy. A tune-up will be wasted on an engine in poor mechanical condition.

2. Replace spark plugs regularly. New spark plugs alone can increase fuel economy 3%.

3. Be sure the spark plugs are the correct type (heat range) for your vehicle. See the Tune-Up Specifications.

Heat range refers to the spark plug's ability to conduct heat away from the firing end. It must conduct the heat away in an even pattern to avoid becoming a source of pre-ignition, yet it must also operate hot enough to burn off conductive deposits that could cause misfiring.

The heat range is usually indicated by a number on the spark plug, part of the manufacturer's designation for each individual spark plug. The numbers in bold-face indicate the heat range in each manufacturer's identification system.

Manufacturer	Typical Designation
AC	R **45** TS
Bosch (old)	WA **145** T30
Bosch (new)	HR **8** Y
Champion	RBL **15** Y
Fram/Autolite	**4**15
Mopar	P-**62** PR
Motorcraft	BRF-**42**
NGK	BP **5** ES-15
Nippondenso	W **16** EP
Prestolite	14GR **5** 2A

Periodically, check the spark plugs to be sure they are firing efficiently. They are excellent indicators of the internal condition of your engine.

On AC, Bosch (new), Champion, Fram/Autolite, Mopar, Motorcraft and Prestolite, a higher number indicates a hotter plug. On Bosch (old), NGK and Nippondenso, a higher number indicates a colder plug.

4. Make sure the spark plugs are properly gapped. See the Tune-Up Specifications in this book.

5. Be sure the spark plugs are firing efficiently. The illustrations on the next 2 pages show you how to "read" the firing end of the spark plug.

6. Check the ignition timing and set it to specifications. Tests show that almost all cars

veyed over 6,000 cars nationwide, they found that a tune-up, on cars that needed one, increased fuel economy over 11%. Replacing worn plugs alone, accounted for a 3% increase. The same test also revealed that 8 out of every 10 vehicles will have some maintenance deficiency that will directly affect fuel economy, emissions or performance. Most of this mileage-robbing neglect could be prevented with regular maintenance.

Modern engines require that all of the functioning systems operate properly for maximum efficiency. A malfunction anywhere wastes fuel. You can keep your vehicle running as efficiently and economically as possible, by being aware of your vehicles operating and performance characteristics. If your vehicle suddenly develops performance or fuel economy problems it could be due to one or more of the following:

PROBLEM	POSSIBLE CAUSE
Engine Idles Rough	Ignition timing, idle mixture, vacuum leak or something amiss in the emission control system.
Hesitates on Acceleration	Dirty carburetor or fuel filter, improper accelerator pump setting, ignition timing or fouled spark plugs.
Starts Hard or Fails to Start	Worn spark plugs, improperly set automatic choke, ice (or water) in fuel system.
Stalls Frequently	Automatic choke improperly adjusted and possible dirty air filter or fuel filter.
Performs Sluggishly	Worn spark plugs, dirty fuel or air filter, ignition timing or automatic choke out of adjustment.

Check spark plug wires on conventional point type ignition for cracks by bending them in a loop around your finger.

Be sure that spark plug wires leading to adjacent cylinders do not run too close together. (Photo courtesy Champion Spark Plug Co.)

have incorrect ignition timing by more than 2°.

7. If your vehicle does not have electronic ignition, check the points, rotor and cap as specified.

8. Check the spark plug wires (used with conventional point-type ignitions) for cracks and burned or broken insulation by bending them in a loop around your finger. Cracked wires decrease fuel efficiency by failing to deliver full voltage to the spark plugs. One misfiring spark plug can cost you as much as 2 mpg.

9. Check the routing of the plug wires. Misfiring can be the result of spark plug leads to adjacent cylinders running parallel to each other and too close together. One wire tends to pick up voltage from the other causing it to fire "out of time".

10. Check all electrical and ignition circuits for voltage drop and resistance.

11. Check the distributor mechanical and/or vacuum advance mechanisms for proper functioning. The vacuum advance can be checked by twisting the distributor plate in the opposite direction of rotation. It should spring back when released.

12. Check and adjust the valve clearance on engines with mechanical lifters. The clearance should be slightly loose rather than too tight.

SPARK PLUG DIAGNOSIS

Normal

APPEARANCE: This plug is typical of one operating normally. The insulator nose varies from a light tan to grayish color with slight electrode wear. The presence of slight deposits is normal on used plugs and will have no adverse effect on engine performance. The spark plug heat range is correct for the engine and the engine is running normally.

CAUSE: Properly running engine.

RECOMMENDATION: Before reinstalling this plug, the electrodes should be cleaned and filed square. Set the gap to specifications. If the plug has been in service for more than 10-12,000 miles, the entire set should probably be replaced with a fresh set of the same heat range.

Oil Deposits

APPEARANCE: The firing end of the plug is covered with a wet, oily coating.

CAUSE: The problem is poor oil control. On high mileage engines, oil is leaking past the rings or valve guides into the combustion chamber. A common cause is also a plugged PCV valve, and a ruptured fuel pump diaphragm can also cause this condition. Oil fouled plugs such as these are often found in new or recently overhauled engines, before normal oil control is achieved, and can be cleaned and reinstalled.

RECOMMENDATION: A hotter spark plug may temporarily relieve the problem, but the engine is probably in need of work.

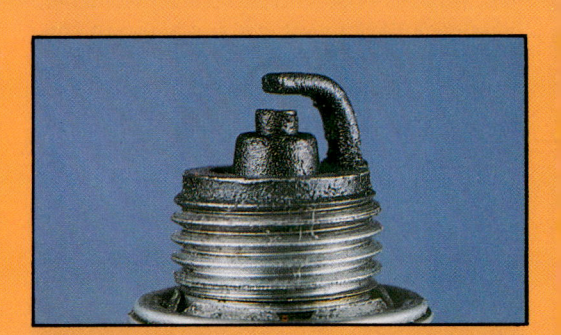

Incorrect Heat Range

APPEARANCE: The effects of high temperature on a spark plug are indicated by clean white, often blistered insulator. This can also be accompanied by excessive wear of the electrode, and the absence of deposits.

CAUSE: Check for the correct spark plug heat range. A plug which is too hot for the engine can result in overheating. A car operated mostly at high speeds can require a colder plug. Also check ignition timing, cooling system level, fuel mixture and leaking intake manifold.

RECOMMENDATION: If all ignition and engine adjustments are known to be correct, and no other malfunction exists, install spark plugs one heat range colder.

Photos Courtesy Champion Spark Plug Co.

Carbon Deposits

APPEARANCE: Carbon fouling is easily identified by the presence of dry, soft, black, sooty deposits.

CAUSE: Changing the heat range can often lead to carbon fouling, as can prolonged slow, stop-and-start driving. If the heat range is correct, carbon fouling can be attributed to a rich fuel mixture, sticking choke, clogged air cleaner, worn breaker points, retarded timing or low compression. If only one or two plugs are carbon fouled, check for corroded or cracked wires on the affected plugs. Also look for cracks in the distributor cap between the towers of affected cylinders.

RECOMMENDATION: After the problem is corrected, these plugs can be cleaned and reinstalled if not worn severely.

MMT Fouled

APPEARANCE: Spark plugs fouled by MMT (Methycyclopentadienyl Maganese Tricarbonyl) have reddish, rusty appearance on the insulator and side electrode.
CAUSE: MMT is an anti-knock additive in gasoline used to replace lead. During the combustion process, the MMT leaves a reddish deposit on the insulator and side electrode.
RECOMMENDATION: No engine malfunction is indicated and the deposits will not affect plug performance any more than lead deposits (see Ash Deposits). MMT fouled plugs can be cleaned, regapped and reinstalled.

High Speed Glazing

APPEARANCE: Glazing appears as shiny coating on the plug, either yellow or tan in color.
CAUSE: During hard, fast acceleration, plug temperatures rise suddenly. Deposits from normal combustion have no chance to fluff-off; instead, they melt on the insulator forming an electrically conductive coating which causes misfiring.
RECOMMENDATION: Glazed plugs are not easily cleaned. They should be replaced with a fresh set of plugs of the correct heat range. If the condition recurs, using plugs with a heat range one step colder may cure the problem.

Ash (Lead) Deposits

APPEARANCE: Ash deposits are characterized by light brown or white colored deposits crusted on the side or center electrodes. In some cases it may give the plug a rusty appearance.
CAUSE: Ash deposits are normally derived from oil or fuel additives burned during normal combustion. Normally they are harmless, though excessive amounts can cause misfiring. If deposits are excessive in short mileage, the valve guides may be worn.
RECOMMENDATION: Ash-fouled plugs can be cleaned, gapped and reinstalled.

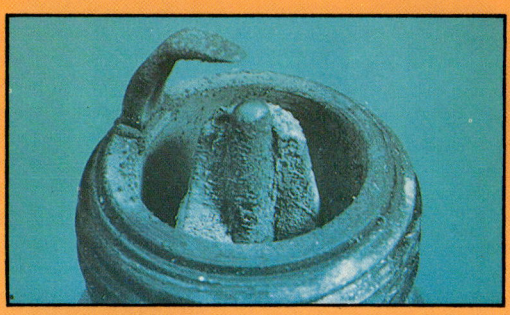

Detonation

APPEARANCE: Detonation is usually characterized by a broken plug insulator.
CAUSE: A portion of the fuel charge will begin to burn spontaneously, from the increased heat following ignition. The explosion that results applies extreme pressure to engine components, frequently damaging spark plugs and pistons.

Detonation can result by over-advanced ignition timing, inferior gasoline (low octane) lean air/fuel mixture, poor carburetion, engine lugging or an increase in compression ratio due to combustion chamber deposits or engine modification.
RECOMMENDATION: Replace the plugs after correcting the problem.

Photos Courtesy Fram Corporation

EMISSION CONTROLS

13. Be aware of the general condition of the emission control system. It contributes to reduced pollution and should be serviced regularly to maintain efficient engine operation.

14. Check all vacuum lines for dried, cracked or brittle conditions. Something as simple as a leaking vacuum hose can cause poor performance and loss of economy.

15. Avoid tampering with the emission control system. Attempting to improve fuel econ-

FUEL SYSTEM

Check the air filter with a light behind it. If you can see light through the filter it can be reused.

Extremely clogged filters should be discarded and replaced with a new one.

18. Replace the air filter regularly. A dirty air filter richens the air/fuel mixture and can increase fuel consumption as much as 10%. Tests show that 1/3 of all vehicles have air filters in need of replacement.

19. Replace the fuel filter at least as often as recommended.

20. Set the idle speed and carburetor mixture to specifications.

21. Check the automatic choke. A sticking or malfunctioning choke wastes gas.

22. During the summer months, adjust the automatic choke for a leaner mixture which will produce faster engine warm-ups.

COOLING SYSTEM

29. Be sure all accessory drive belts are in good condition. Check for cracks or wear.

30. Adjust all accessory drive belts to proper tension.

31. Check all hoses for swollen areas, worn spots, or loose clamps.

32. Check coolant level in the radiator or expansion tank.

33. Be sure the thermostat is operating properly. A stuck thermostat delays engine warm-up and a cold engine uses nearly twice as much fuel as a warm engine.

34. Drain and replace the engine coolant at least as often as recommended. Rust and scale

TIRES & WHEELS

38. Check the tire pressure often with a pencil type gauge. Tests by a major tire manufacturer show that 90% of all vehicles have at least 1 tire improperly inflated. Better mileage can be achieved by over-inflating tires, but never exceed the maximum inflation pressure on the side of the tire.

39. If possible, install radial tires. Radial tires deliver as much as 1/2 mpg more than bias belted tires.

40. Avoid installing super-wide tires. They only create extra rolling resistance and decrease fuel mileage. Stick to the manufacturer's recommendations.

41. Have the wheels properly balanced.

emission controls is
economy than im-
changes on modern
ersible.
the EGR valve and

lines as recommended.

17. Be sure that all vacuum lines and hoses are reconnected properly after working under the hood. An unconnected or misrouted vacuum line can wreak havoc with engine performance.

23. Check for fuel leaks at the carburetor, fuel pump, fuel lines and fuel tank. Be sure all lines and connections are tight.

24. Periodically check the tightness of the carburetor and intake manifold attaching nuts and bolts. These are a common place for vacuum leaks to occur.

25. Clean the carburetor periodically and lubricate the linkage.

26. The condition of the tailpipe can be an excellent indicator of proper engine combustion. After a long drive at highway speeds, the inside of the tailpipe should be a light grey in color. Black or soot on the insides indicates an overly rich mixture.

27. Check the fuel pump pressure. The fuel pump may be supplying more fuel than the engine needs.

28. Use the proper grade of gasoline for your engine. Don't try to compensate for knocking or "pinging" by advancing the ignition timing. This practice will only increase plug temperature and the chances of detonation or pre-ignition with relatively little performance gain.

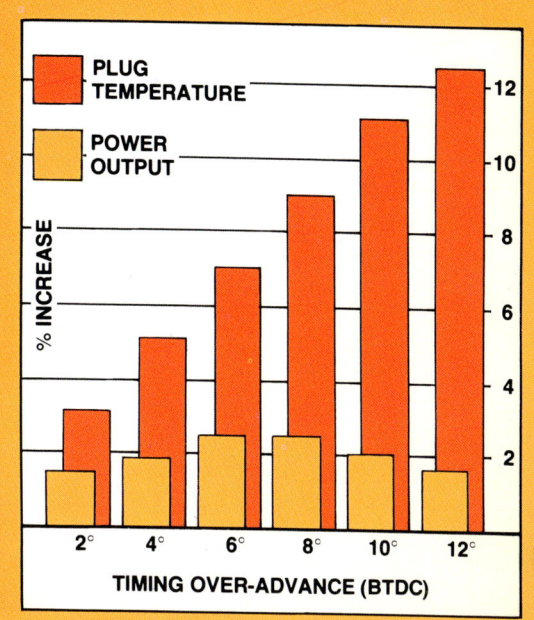

Increasing ignition timing past the specified setting results in a drastic increase in spark plug temperature with increased chance of detonation or preignition. Performance increase is considerably less. (Photo courtesy Champion Spark Plug Co.)

that form in the engine should be flushed out to allow the engine to operate at peak efficiency.

35. Clean the radiator of debris that can decrease cooling efficiency.

36. Install a flex-type or electric cooling fan, if you don't have a clutch type fan. Flex fans use curved plastic blades to push more air at low speeds when more cooling is needed; at high speeds the blades flatten out for less resistance. Electric fans only run when the engine temperature reaches a predetermined level.

37. Check the radiator cap for a worn or cracked gasket. If the cap does not seal properly, the cooling system will not function properly.

42. Be sure the front end is correctly aligned. A misaligned front end actually has wheels going in different directions. The increased drag can reduce fuel economy by .3 mpg.

43. Correctly adjust the wheel bearings. Wheel bearings that are adjusted too tight increase rolling resistance.

Check tire pressures regularly with a reliable pocket type gauge. Be sure to check the pressure on a cold tire.

GENERAL MAINTENANCE

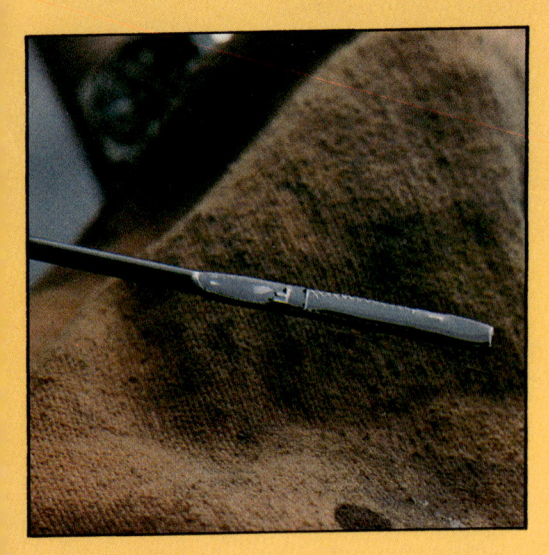

Check the fluid levels (particularly engine oil) on a regular basis. Be sure to check the oil for grit, water or other contamination.

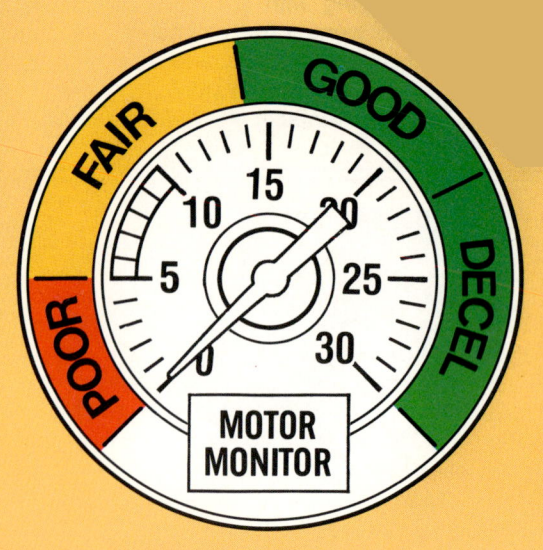

A vacuum gauge is another excellent indicator of internal engine condition and can also be installed in the dash as a mileage indicator.

44. Periodically check the fluid levels in the engine, power steering pump, master cylinder, automatic transmission and drive axle.

45. Change the oil at the recommended interval and change the filter at every oil change. Dirty oil is thick and causes extra friction between moving parts, cutting efficiency and increasing wear. A worn engine requires more frequent tune-ups and gets progressively worse fuel economy. In general, use the lightest viscosity oil for the driving conditions you will encounter.

46. Use the recommended viscosity fluids in the transmission and axle.

47. Be sure the battery is fully charged for fast starts. A slow starting engine wastes fuel.

48. Be sure battery terminals are clean and tight.

49. Check the battery electrolyte level and add distilled water if necessary.

50. Check the exhaust system for crushed pipes, blockages and leaks.

51. Adjust the brakes. Dragging brakes or brakes that are not releasing create increased drag on the engine.

52. Install a vacuum gauge or miles-per-gallon gauge. These gauges visually indicate engine vacuum in the intake manifold. High vacuum = good mileage and low vacuum = poorer mileage. The gauge can also be an excellent indicator of internal engine conditions.

53. Be sure the clutch is properly adjusted. A slipping clutch wastes fuel.

54. Check and periodically lubricate the heat control valve in the exhaust manifold. A sticking or inoperative valve prevents engine warm-up and wastes gas.

55. Keep accurate records to check fuel economy over a period of time. A sudden drop in fuel economy may signal a need for tune-up or other maintenance.

© 1980 Chilton Book Company, Radnor, PA 19089

EMISSION CONTROLS AND FUEL SYSTEM

will accept only the smaller unleaded fuel nozzle.

FUEL SYSTEM

All 1976–78 Chevettes use a Rochester 1ME carburetor. The unit incorporates an automatic choke with an electronically heated choke coil. The choke coil is heated in a housing which is mounted on a bracket connected to the fuel bowl.

The internal fuel filter is made of pleated paper and is located in the fuel bowl behind the fuel inlet nut. The throttle body of the 1ME is made of aluminum for better heat dispersement.

The carburetor identification number is stamped on the float bowl, right next to the fuel inlet nut. When replacing the fuel bowl, be sure to transfer the identification number to the new float bowl.

The 1979–80 Chevettes are equipped with a 2-bbl Holley carburetor. This provides a slight increase in horsepower and at the same time, improves the fuel economy.

FUEL PUMP REMOVAL AND INSTALLATION

NOTE: *Air conditioned cars require removal of the rear compressor bracket to gain working room.*

1. Working from under the car, remove the ignition coil.
2. Disconnect the fuel inlet and outlet lines at the pump and plug the inlet line.
3. Remove the two pump mounting bolts and lockwashers and remove the fuel pump and gasket.
4. Install the fuel pump with a new gasket coated with sealer. Tighten the two mounting bolts.
5. Connect the fuel inlet and outlet lines at the pump. Install the ignition coil.
6. Start the engine and check for leaks.

Carburetor

REMOVAL AND INSTALLATION

1. Remove the air cleaner.
2. Disconnect the fuel line. Disconnect all vacuum lines, but note where they attach.
3. Disconnect the electrical connector at the choke.
4. Disconnect the accelerator linkage.
5. Disconnect the solenoid electrical connector.

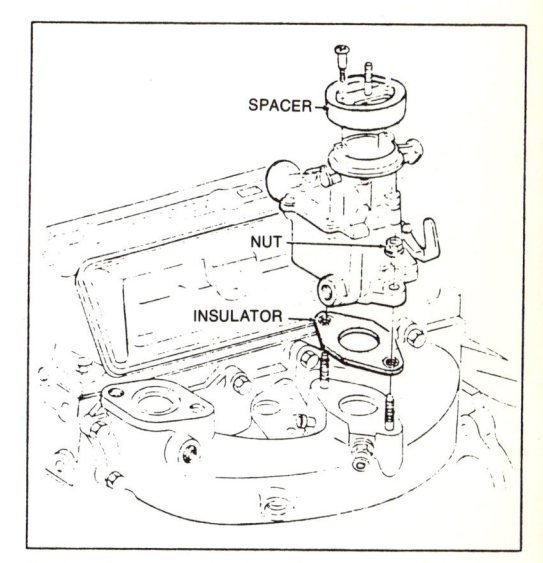

Carburetor mounting details

6. On cars with an automatic transmission, disconnect the detent cable.
7. Remove the carburetor retaining nuts and remove the carburetor/solenoid assembly.
8. Installation is the reverse of removal. Start the engine and check for leaks.

FLOAT LEVEL ADJUSTMENT

1. Remove the top of the carburetor.
2. Hold the float retaining pin in place and push down on the float arm at the outer end against the top of the float needle valve.
3. Measure the distance from the bump

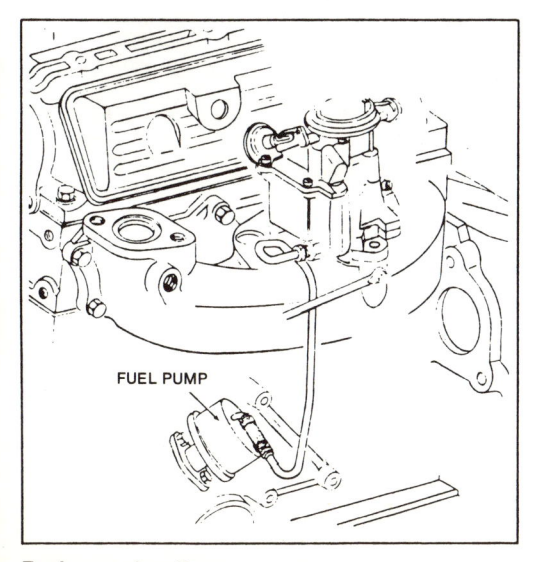

Fuel pump location

EMISSION CONTROLS AND FUEL SYSTEM

on the top of the float at the end to the bowl gasket surface, without the gasket.

4. To adjust, bend the float arm at the point where it joins the float.

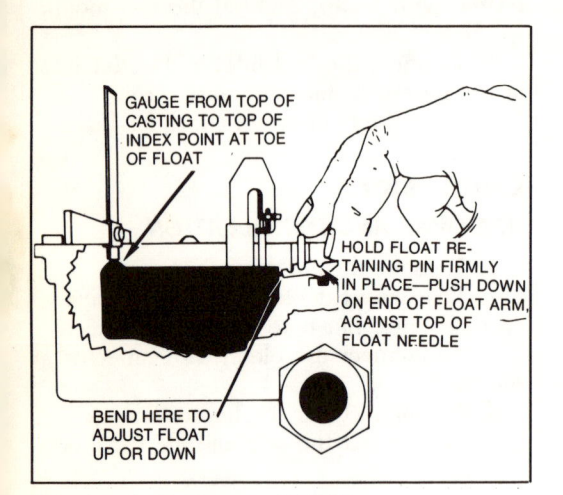

Float level adjustment—1976-78

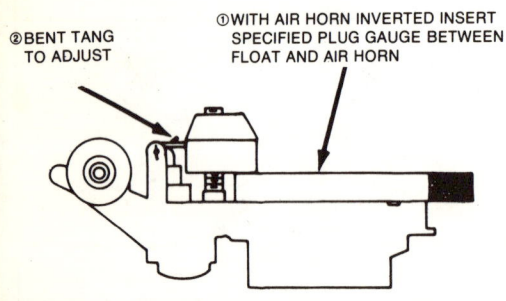

Float level adjustment 1979-80

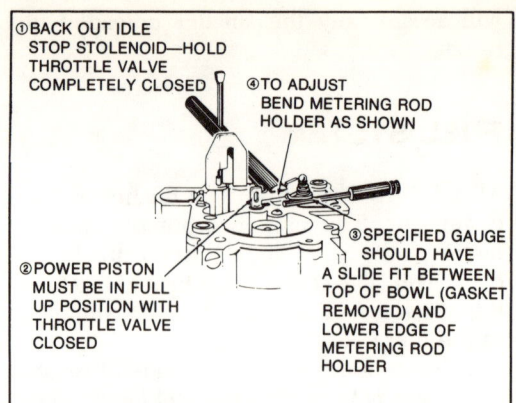

METERING ROD ADJUSTMENT
Through 1978

1. Remove the top of the carburetor.
2. Back out the idle stop solenoid and rotate the fast idle cam so that the fast idle screw does not contact the cam.
3. With the throttle valve completely closed, make sure that the power piston is all the way up.
4. Insert the specified size gauge between the bowl gasket surface with no gasket and the lower surface of the metering rod holder, next to the metering rod.
5. To adjust, carefully bend the metering rod holder.

FAST IDLE SPEED ADJUSTMENT

1. The engine should be at normal temperature with the air cleaner in place. Disconnect and plug the EGR valve vacuum line.
2. Make sure that the curb idle speed is as specified.
3. Place the fast idle screw on the highest cam step with the engine running.

Metering rod adjustment

Fast idle adjusting screw—1976-78

4. Adjust the fast idle speed screw to the correct fast idle speed.

FAST IDLE CAM ADJUSTMENT

1. Hold the fast idle speed screw on the second cam step against the shoulder of the high step.
2. Hold the choke valve closed with a finger.
3. Insert the specified gauge between the

EMISSION CONTROLS AND FUEL SYSTEM

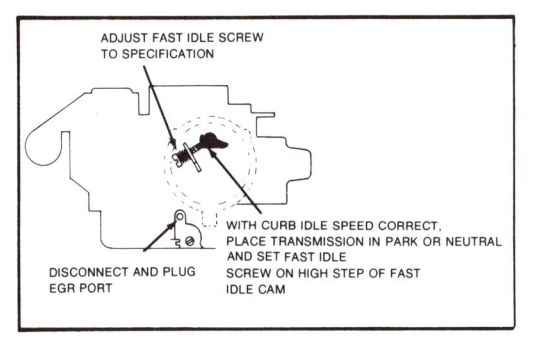

Fast idle adjusting screw 1979–80

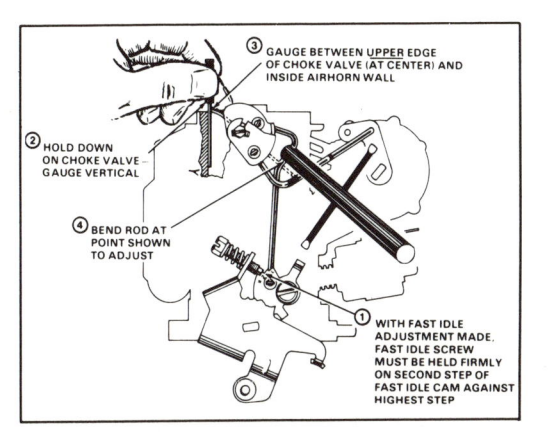

Fast idle cam adjustment—1976–78

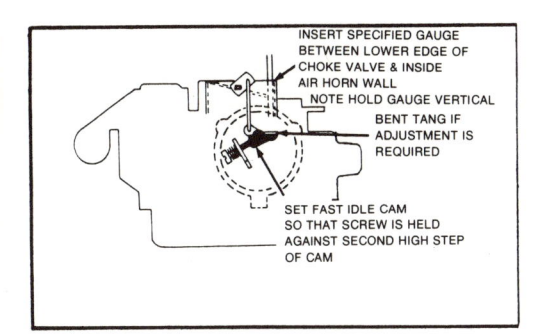

Fast idle cam adjustment 1979–80

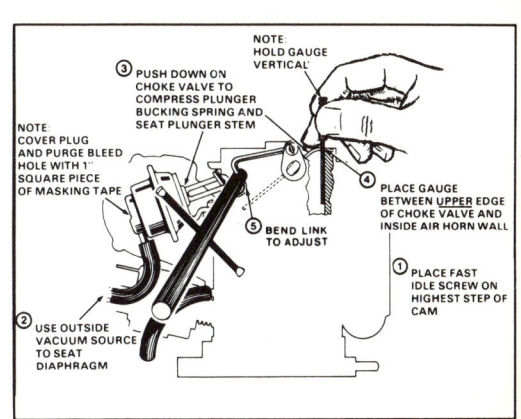

Vacuum break adjustment—1976–78

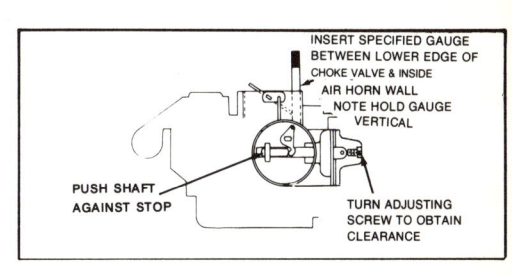

Vaccum break adjustment 1979–80

center upper edge of the choke valve and the airhorn wall.

4. Bend the linkage rod at the upper angle to adjust.

VACUUM BREAK ADJUSTMENT

1. Place the fast idle speed screw on the highest cam step.
2. Tape over the bleed hole in the diaphragm unit. Apply suction by mouth to seat the diaphragm.
3. Push down on the choke valve with a finger.
4. Insert the gauge between the upper edge of the choke valve and the airhorn wall.
5. Bend the link to adjust.

CHOKE UNLOADER ADJUSTMENT

1. Hold the throttle valve wide open.
2. Hold down the choke valve with a finger and insert the specified gauge between the upper edge of the choke valve and the airhorn wall.
3. Bend the linkage tang to adjust.

CHOKE COIL LEVER ADJUSTMENT

1. Place the fast idle speed screw on the highest cam step.
2. Hold the choke valve closed.
3. Insert a 0.120 in. gauge through the hole in the arm on the choke housing and into the hole in the casting.
4. Bend the link to adjust.

ELECTRIC CHOKE ADJUSTMENT
1976–78

1. Place the fast idle cam follower on the high step.
2. Loosen the three retaining screws and rotate the cover counterclockwise until the choke valve just closes.
3. Align the index mark on the cover with the specified housing mark.
4. Tighten the three screws.

EMISSION CONTROLS AND FUEL SYSTEM

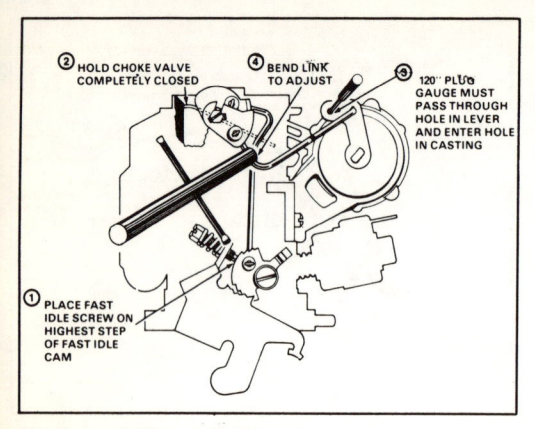

Choke coil lever adjustment

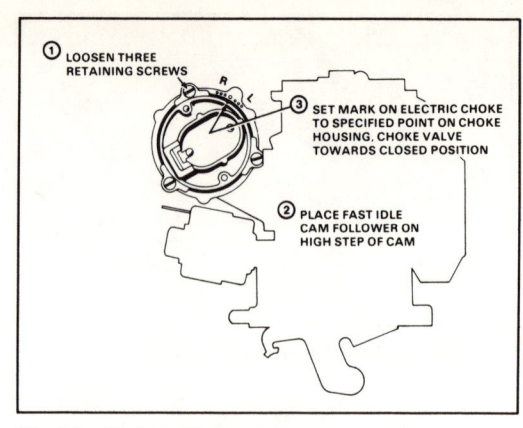

Electric choke adjustment

OVERHAUL

Whenever wear or dirt causes a carburetor to perform poorly, there are two possible solutions to the problem. The simplest is to trade in the old unit for a rebuilt one. The other, cheaper alternative is to purchase a carburetor overhaul kit and rebuild the original unit. Some of the better overhaul kits contain complete step by step instructions along with exploded views and gauges. Other kits, probably intended for the professional, have only a few general overhaul hints. The second type can be moderately confusing to the novice, especially since a kit may have extra parts so that one kit can cover several variations of the same carburetor. In any event, it is inadvisable to dismantle any carburetor without at least replacing all the gaskets. The

Carburetor Specifications

Year	Carburetor Identification Number [1]	Float Level (in.)	Metering Rod (in.)	Fast Idle Speed (rpm)	Fast Idle Cam (in.)	Vacuum Break (in.)	Choke Unloader (in.)	Choke Setting (notches)
1976–77	17056030 17056036 17056031 17056037	5/32	0.072	2000 [2]	0.065	0.070	0.165	3 Rich
	17056032 17056034 17056033 17056035	5/32	0.073	2000 [3]	0.045	0.070	0.200	3 Rich
	17056330 17056331	5/32	0.072	2000	0.065	0.070	0.165	3 Rich
	17056332 17056333 17056334	5/32	0.073	2000	0.045	0.070	0.200	3 Rich
	17056335	5/32	0.073	2000	0.045	0.120	0.200	3 Rich

EMISSION CONTROLS AND FUEL SYSTEM

Carburetor Specifications (cont.)

Year	Carburetor Identification Number①	Float Level (in.)	Metering Rod (in.)	Fast Idle Speed (rpm)	Fast Idle Cam (in.)	Vacuum Break (in.)	Choke Unloader (in.)	Choke Setting (notches)
1978	17058031	5/32	0.080	2400	.105	.150	.500	2 Rich
	17058032 17058034 17058036 17058038	5/32	0.080	2400	.080	.130	.500	3 Rich
	17058033 17058037	5/32	0.080	2400	.080	.130	.500	2 Rich
	17058042 17058044 17058332 17058334	5/32	0.080	2400	.080	.130④	.500	2 Rich
	17058035	5/32	0.080	2300	.080	.130	.500	3 Rich
	17058045 17058335	5/32	0.080	2300⑤	.080	.130④	.500	2 Rich
1979	466361 466363 466369 466371	.50	NA	2500	.110	.245	.350	2 Rich
	466362 466364 466370 466372	.50	NA	2500	.110	.250	.350	2 Rich
	466365 466366 466367 466368 466373 466374 466375 466376	.50	NA	2500	.130	.300	.350	1 Rich

① Stamped on float bowl, next to fuel inlet nut
② 2200 rpm for the first two numbers
③ 2200 rpm for the last two numbers
④ .160 above 30,000 miles
⑤ Non-adjustable by design
NA—Not available

80 EMISSION CONTROLS AND FUEL SYSTEM

carburetor adjustments should all be checked after overhaul.

FUEL TANK

REMOVAL AND INSTALLATION

1. Disconnect the battery.
2. Drain the fuel tank.
3. Raise the rear of the car and support it safely on jackstands.
4. Disconnect the meter wire at the rear harness connector and the ground strap at the fuel tank reinforcement.
5. Disconnect the fuel filler neck hose and the vent hose.
6. Disconnect the fuel feed line and the vapor line at the hose connections.
7. Remove the fuel tank strap rear support bolts and lower and remove the fuel tank.

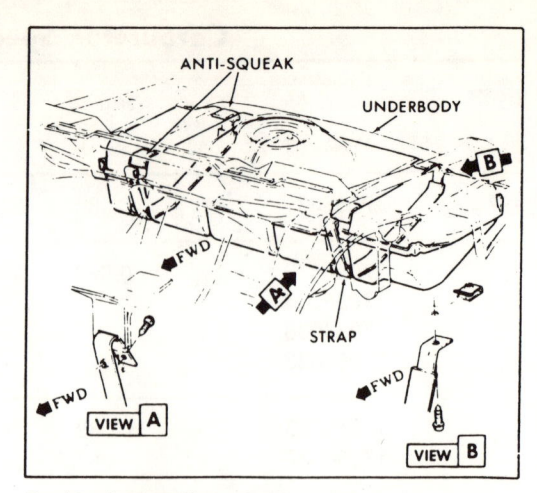

Fuel tank mounting

8. To install the tank, reverse the above steps.

Chassis Electrical

HEATER

Blower
REMOVAL AND INSTALLATION

1. Disconnect the negative battery cable.
2. Disconnect the electrical lead from the blower motor.
3. Scribe a mark to reference the blower motor flange-to-case position.
4. Remove the blower motor-to-case attaching screws and remove the blower motor and wheel as an assembly. Pry the flange gently if the sealer acts as an adhesive.
5. Remove the blower wheel retaining nut and separate the motor and wheel.
6. Reverse Steps 1–5 to install. Be sure to align the scribe marks made during removal.

NOTE: *Assemble the blower wheel to the motor with the open end of the wheel away from the motor. If necessary, replace the sealer at the motor flange.*

The heater blower is located on the passenger side of the firewall

Heater Core
REMOVAL AND INSTALLATION

1. Disconnect the negative battery cable.
2. Drain the radiator.
3. Disconnect the heater hoses at the heater core tube connections. Use care when detaching the hoses as the core tube attachments can easily be damaged if too much force is used on them. If the hoses will not come off, cut the hose just forward of the core tube connection. Remove the remaining piece by splitting it lengthwise. When the hoses are removed, install plugs in the core tubes to prevent coolant spilling out when the core is removed.

NOTE: *The larger diameter hose goes to*

82 CHASSIS ELECTRICAL

the water pump; the smaller diameter hose goes to the thermostat housing.

4. Remove the screws around the perimeter of the heater core cover on the engine side of the dash panel.
5. Pull the heater core cover from its mounting in the dash panel.
6. Remove the core from the distributor assembly.
7. Reverse the removal procedure to install. Be sure that the core-to-case sealer is intact before replacing the core; use new sealer if necessary. When installation is complete, check for coolant leaks.

RADIO

REMOVAL AND INSTALLATION

1. Disconnect the negative battery cable.
2. Remove the nut from the mounting stud on the bottom of the radio.
3. Remove all control knobs and/or spacers from the right and left radio control shafts.

NOTE: *The volume control knob and tuning control knob will fit on either shaft but are not interchangeable. The tone control knob and balance control knob are interchangeable.*

4. Remove the four screws from the center trim plate and pull the trim plate and the radio forward slightly.
5. Disconnect the antenna lead from the rear of the radio.
6. Disconnect the speaker and electrical connectors from the radio harness.

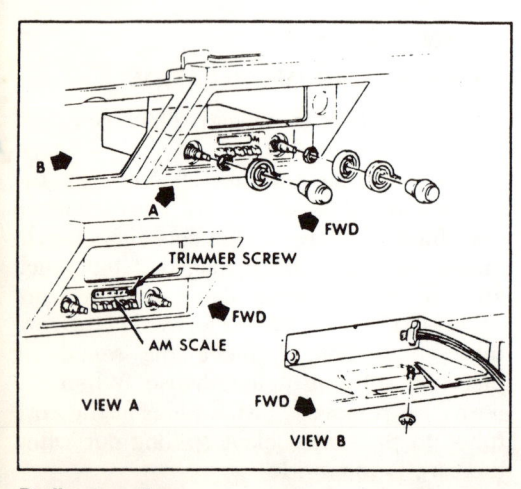

7. Disconnect the electrical connectors from the rear window defogger and cigarette lighter.
8. Use a deep well socket to remove the retaining nuts from both control shafts and remove the radio.
9. To install, reverse the removal procedure.

WINDSHIELD WIPERS

Motor

REMOVAL AND INSTALLATION

1. Working inside the car, reach up under the instrument panel above the steering column and loosen, but do not remove, the transmission drive link-to-motor crank arm attaching nuts.
2. Disconnect the transmission drive link from the motor crank arm.
3. Raise the hood and disconnect the motor wiring.
4. Remove the three motor attaching bolts.
5. Remove the motor while guiding the crank arm through the hole.

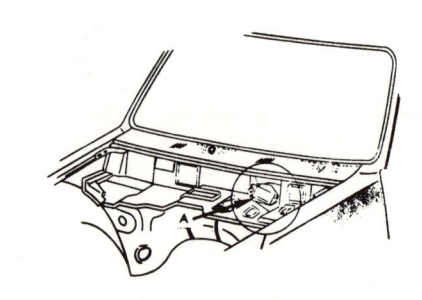

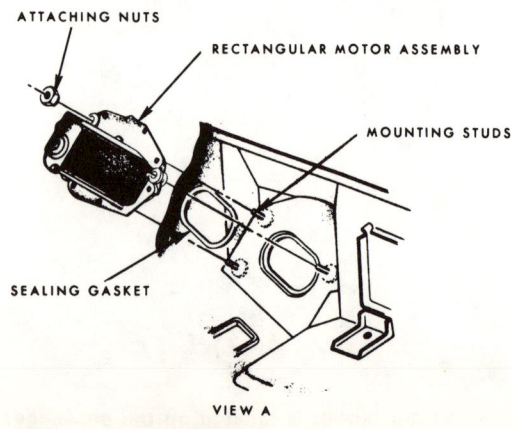

Radio mounting

Wiper motor mounting

CHASSIS ELECTRICAL 83

6. To install, align the sealing gasket to the base of the motor and reverse the rest of the removal procedure. Tighten the motor attaching bolts to 30–45 in. lbs. Tighten the transmission drive link-to-motor crank arm attaching nuts to 25–35 in. lbs.

NOTE: *If the wiper motor-to-dash panel sealing gasket is damaged during removal, it should be replaced with a new gasket to prevent possible water leaks.*

Wiper Blade
REMOVAL AND INSTALLATION

1. To replace the wiper blade, lift up on the spring release tab on the wiper arm connector.
2. Work the blade assembly off.
3. Snap the new blade assembly into place.

NOTE: *To only replace the rubber insert, press down and away from the wiper blade to free it. Insert the rubber wiper. Bend the insert upward slightly to engage the retaining clips.*

INSTRUMENT PANEL

The standard instrument cluster contains a speedometer and fuel gauge with warning lights for oil pressure, coolant temperature, alternator, brakes, and seat belts. The optional cluster adds a tachometer, but retains all warning lights.

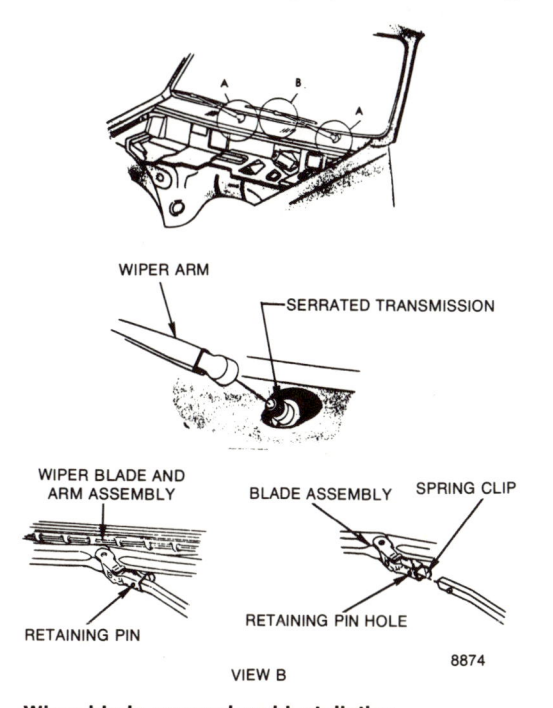

REMOVAL AND INSTALLATION

The instrument cluster must be removed to replace light bulbs, gauges, and printed circuit.
1. Disconnect the negative battery cable.
2. Remove the clock stem knob.
3. Remove the four screws and remove the instrument cluster bezel and lens.
4. Remove the two nuts securing the instrument cluster to the instrument panel and pull the cluster slightly forward.
5. Disconnect the electrical connector and speedometer cable from the cluster and remove it.
6. Installation is the reverse of removal.

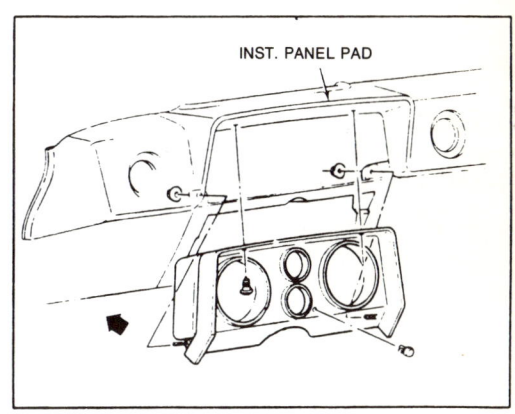

Instrument cluster mounting

Wiper blade removal and installation

Headlight Switch
REMOVAL AND INSTALLATION

1. Disconnect the negative battery cable.
2. Pull the headlight switch control knob to the "On" position.
3. Reach up under the instrument panel and depress the switch shaft retainer button while pulling on the switch control shaft knob.
4. Remove the three screws and remove the headlight switch trim plate.
5. Use a large-bladed screwdriver to remove the light switch ferrule nut from the front of the instrument panel.
6. Disconnect the multi-contact connector

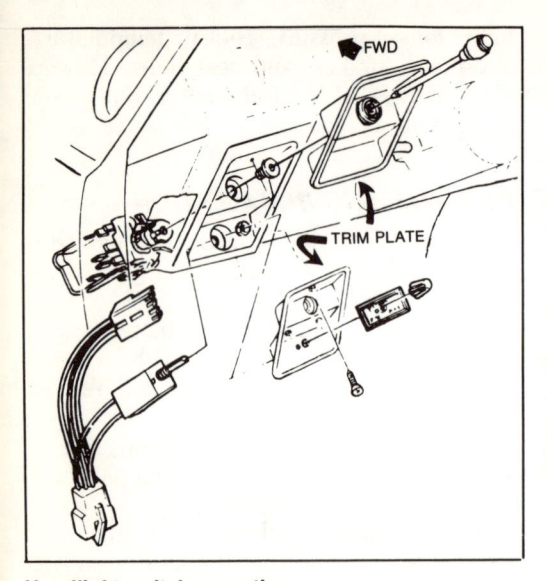

84 CHASSIS ELECTRICAL

Headlight switch mounting

These are the headlight aiming screws, don't touch them when removing the headlight

from the bottom of the headlight switch. (A small screwdriver will aid removal).

7. Installation is the reverse of removal.

HEADLIGHTS

REMOVAL AND INSTALLATION

1. Remove the four phillips screws that retain the headlight bezel.
2. Remove the three screws and remove the headlight retaining ring.
3. Pull out the headlight and detach the electrical connector.

Unsnap the connector from the headlight

4. Install the new headlight in the reverse order of removal.

Front Parking Lights, Turn Signals and Side Marker Lights

REMOVAL AND INSTALLATION

The bulb socket for these lights is reached from under the front bumper or under the front wheel well.

1. Turn the bulb socket counterclockwise 90° and lift it out.

Arrows point out the headlight bezel retaining screw

CHASSIS ELECTRICAL

Light Bulb Specifications

Bulb	Candle Power	Trade No.
Headlamp Unit		
High Beam	60W	6012
Low Beam	50W	
Front Park and Directional Signal	32–3	1157
Front Fender Side Marker Lamp	2	194
Rear Side Marker Lamp	3	168
Tail and Stop Lamp	32–3	1157
Directional Signal (Rear)	32	1156
(Front)	32–3	1157
Back-Up Lamp	32	1156
Courtesy Lamp	6	631
Dome Lamp	12	561
Instrument Panel Cluster Illumination	2	194
Indicator Lamps		
High Beam Headlamp	2	194
Oil Pressure	2	194
Temperature	2	194
Directional Signal	2	194
Parking Brake Warning	2	194
Seatbelt Warning	2	194
Generator	2	194
Transmission Control Illumination	2	194
Underhood Lamp	15	93
Heater or A/C Control Panel Lamp	2	194
Radio Dial		
AM Radio	5	37
AM/FM Radio	2	1893
License Plate Lamp	3	168
Dome Lamp	12	561

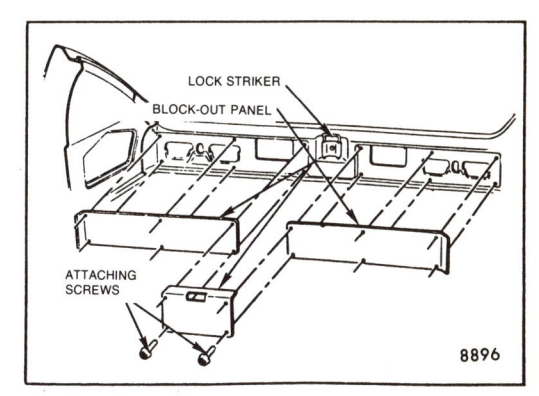

Block-out panel

2. Pull the bulb out of the socket and replace it with a new bulb. Test the operation of the bulb.

3. Replace the bulb socket in the housing and turn it clockwise 90° to lock it in place.

Rear Parking Lights and Turn Signals

REMOVAL AND INSTALLATION

1. Remove the tail lamp lens attaching screws and remove the lens.
2. On the inside of the car, remove the block-out panel.
3. Remove the bulb from the socket and replace as necessary.
4. To install, reverse the procedure.

Rear Side Marker Lamp

1. Remove the lens attaching screws and lens.
2. Remove the bulb from the socket and replace it with a new bulb.
3. Install the lens with the attaching screws.

FUSES AND FLASHERS

The fuse panel is located under the instrument panel on the left-hand side. The headlight circuit is protected by a circuit breaker in the light switch. An electrical overload will cause the lights to go on and off, or in some cases to stay off. If this condition develops, check the wiring circuits immediately.

An Air Conditioning high blower speed fuse, 30 amp, is located in an in-line fuse

CHASSIS ELECTRICAL

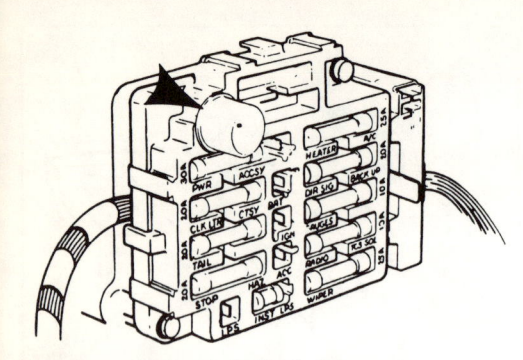

Fuse box—flasher is indicated by arrow

holder running from the junction block to the Air Conditioning relay.

A Fusible link is incorporated into the wiring system. This is a wire of such a gauge that it will fuse (or melt) before damage occurs to an entire wiring harness in the event of an electrical overload.

WIRING DIAGRAMS

Wiring diagrams have been left out of this book. As cars have become more complex, and available with longer and longer option lists, wiring diagrams have grown in size and complexity. It has become virtually impossible to provide a readable reproduction in a reasonable number of pages. Information on ordering wiring diagrams from the vehicle manufacturer can be found in the owners manual.

Radio and Idle Stop Solenoid	10 Amp.
Directional Signal and Backup Lamps	20 Amp.
Tail, License, Sidemarker and Parking Lamps	20 Amp.
Clock, Lighter, Key Warning Buzzer, Courtesy, Dome and Glove Box Lamps	20 Amp.
Windshield Wiper	25 Amp.
Gauges and Warning Lamps	10 Amp.
Instrument Lamps	4 Amp.
Stop and Hazard Warning Lamps	20 Amp.
Heater and Air Conditioning	25 Amp.

Clutch and Transmission 6

CLUTCH

Chevette manual transmission models use a cable-operated, diaphragm spring-type clutch. The clutch cable is attached to the clutch pedal at its upper end and is threaded at its lower end where it attaches to the clutch fork. The clutch release fork pivots on a ball stud located opposite the clutch cable attaching point. The pressure plate, clutch disc, and throwout bearing are of conventional design.

When the clutch pedal is depressed, the clutch release fork pivots on the ball stud and pushes the throwout bearing forward. The throwout bearing presses against the inner ends of the pressure plate diaphragm spring fingers to release pressure on the clutch disc, disengaging the clutch. The return spring preloads the clutch release mechanism to remove any looseness. Clutch pedal free-play will increase with release mechanism wear and will decrease with clutch disc wear.

CLUTCH DISC REMOVAL AND INSTALLATION

1. Raise the car.
2. Remove the transmission.
3. Remove the throwout bearing from the clutch fork by sliding the fork off the ball stud against spring tension. If the ball stud is to be replaced, remove the locknut and stud from the bellhousing.
4. If the balance marks on the pressure plate and the flywheel are not easily seen, remark them with paint or centerpunch.
5. Alternately loosen the pressure plate-to-flywheel attaching bolts one turn at a time until spring tension is released.
6. Support the pressure plate and cover assembly, then remove the bolts and the clutch assembly.
    CAUTION: *Do not disassemble the clutch cover and pressure plate for repair. If defective, replace the assembly.*
7. Align the balance marks on the clutch assembly and the flywheel. Place the clutch disc on the pressure plate with the long end of the splined hub facing forward and the damper springs inside the pressure plate. Insert a used or dummy shaft through the cover and clutch disc.
8. Position the assembly against the flywheel and insert the dummy shaft into the pilot bearing in the crankshaft.
9. Align the balance marks and install the pressure plate-to-flywheel bolts finger-tight.
    CAUTION: *Tighten all bolts evenly and gradually until tight to avoid possible clutch distortion. Torque the bolts to 18 ft lbs and remove the dummy shaft.*
10. Pack the groove on the inside of the

88 CLUTCH AND TRANSMISSION

throwout bearing with graphite grease. Coat the fork groove and ball stud depression with the lubricant.

11. Install the throwout bearing and release fork assembly in the bellhousing with the fork spring hooked under the ball stud and the fork spring fingers inside the bearing groove.

12. Position the transmission and clutch housing and install the clutch housing attaching bolts and lockwashers. Torque the bolts to 25 ft lbs (33 Nm).

13. Complete the transmission installation.

CAUTION: *Check position of the engine in the front mounts and realign as necessary.*

NOTE: *A special gauge (part no. J-28449 or its equivalent) is necessary to adjust the ball stud position.*

14. Perform "Initial Ball Stud Adjustment" and "Clutch Cable Attachment and Adjustment." Adjust clutch pedal free-play if necessary.

15. Lower the car and check operation of the clutch and transmission.

INITIAL BALL STUD ADJUSTMENT

1. Install throwout bearing assembly, release fork, and ball stud to the transmission.
2. Install and secure the transmission to the engine.
3. Cycle the clutch once.
4. Place the special gauge (Part No. J-28449) so that the flat end is against the front face of the clutch housing and the hooked end is located at the bottom depression in the clutch fork.
5. Turn the ball stud inward by hand until the throwout bearing makes contact with the clutch spring.
6. Install the locknut and tighten it to 25 ft lbs (33 Nm), being careful not to change the ball stud adjustment.
7. Remove the gauge by pulling outward at the housing end.

CLUTCH CABLE ATTACHMENT AND ADJUSTMENT
1976–77

These adjustments are made before the return spring is installed and with the clutch cable attached to the clutch pedal at its upper end.

1. Place the clutch cable through the hole in the clutch fork.
2. Pull the clutch cable until the clutch pedal is firmly against the pedal bumper and hold it in position.
3. Push the release fork forward until the throwout bearing contacts the clutch spring fingers and hold it in position.
4. Thread the nut or the cable until it bottoms out against the spherical surface of the release fork.
5. Depress the clutch pedal to the floor a

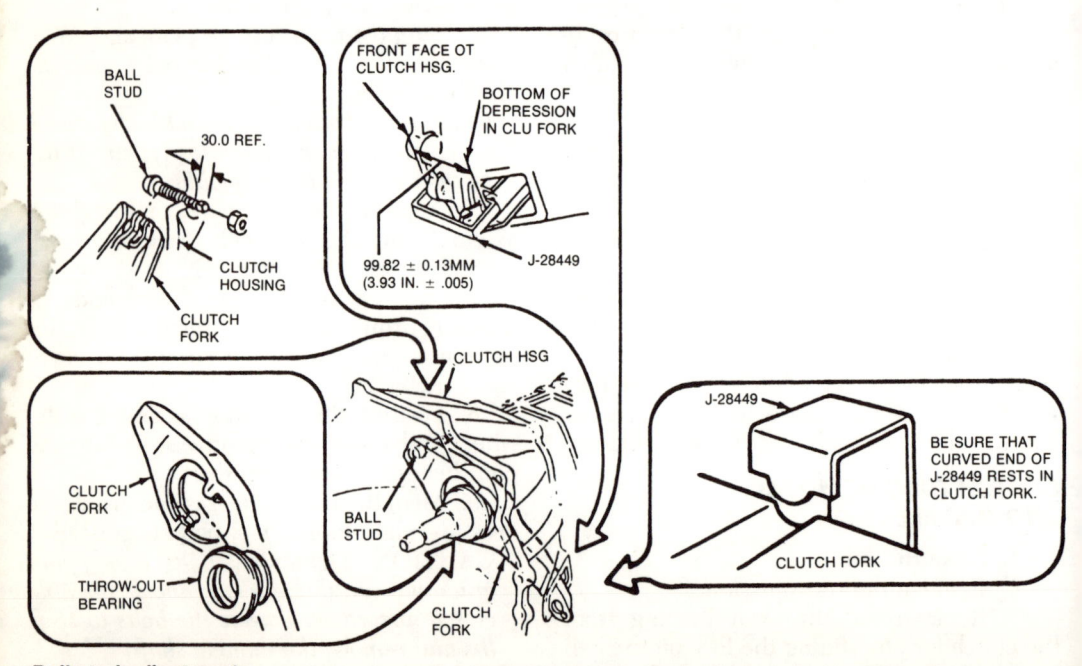

Ball stud adjustment

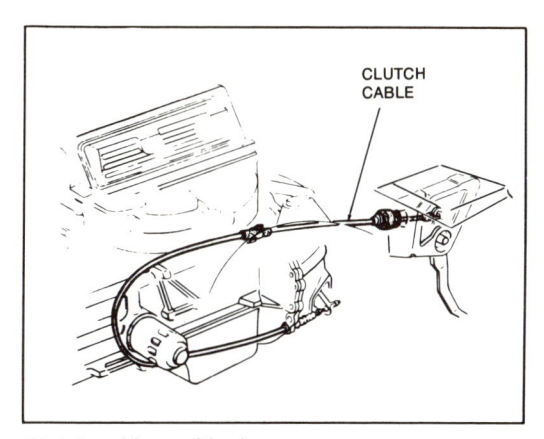

CLUTCH AND TRANSMISSION

Clutch cable positioning

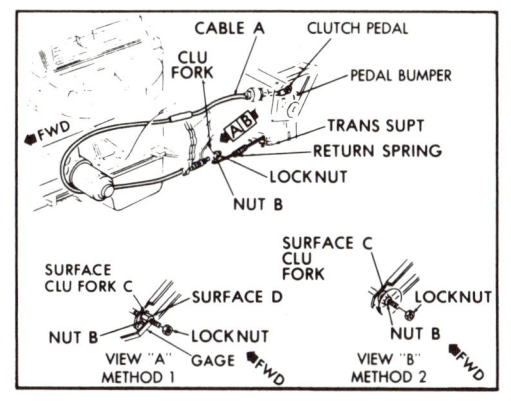

Clutch cable adjustment 1976–77

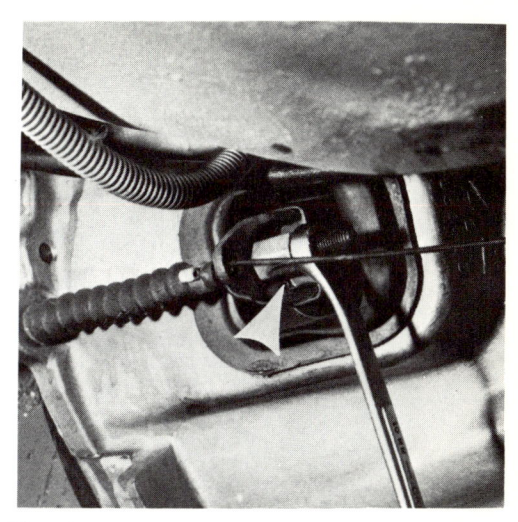

The clutch fork locknut is a 10 mm nut

1978–80

The following adjustments are to be made with the cable and loose parts assembled to the front of the dash and the cable attached to the clutch pedal.

1. Place the cable through the hole in the clutch fork and properly seat it.
2. Install the return spring.
3. From the engine compartment, pull the cable away from the dash until the clutch pedal is firmly seated against the pedal bumper.
4. Holding the pedal in position, install the circlip in the first fully visible groove in the cable from the sleeve. Release the cable.

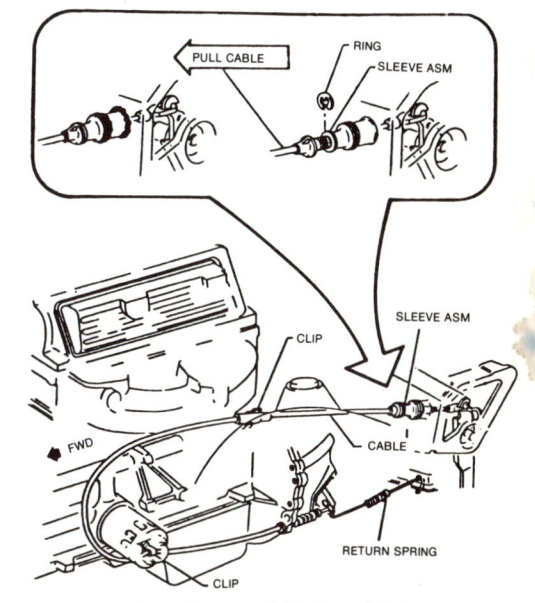

Clutch cable adjustment 1978 and later

minimum of four times to establish cable position at clearance points.

6. To obtain the correct clutch pedal lash, use either Step 7 or Step 8.

7. See View "A" of the accompanying illustration.
   a. Place a 0.171 in. (4.35 mm) thick gauge or shim stock against surface "D" of nut "B."
   b. Thread the locknut on the cable "A" until the locknut contacts the gauge.
   c. Remove the gauge and back off nut "B" until it contacts the locknut.
   d. Tighten the locknut to 4 ft lbs.

8. See View "B" of the accompanying illustration.
   a. Turn nut "B" 4.35 turns counterclockwise.
   b. Thread the locknut on the cable "A" until the locknut contacts nut "B."
   c. Tighten the locknut to 4 ft lbs.

9. Attach the return spring.
10. This procedure should yield 0.812 ±0.25 in. (20.6 ±6 mm) lash at the clutch pedal.

CLUTCH AND TRANSMISSION

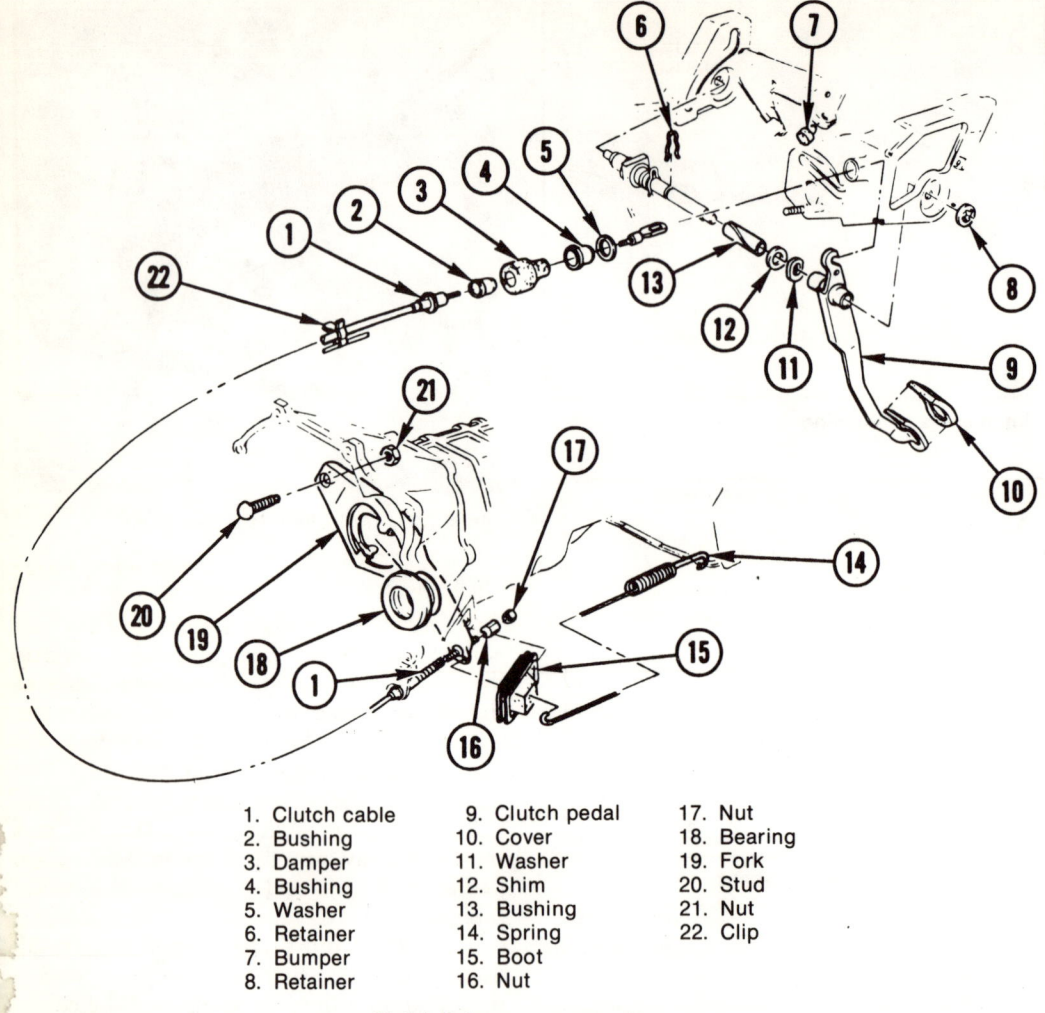

1. Clutch cable
2. Bushing
3. Damper
4. Bushing
5. Washer
6. Retainer
7. Bumper
8. Retainer
9. Clutch pedal
10. Cover
11. Washer
12. Shim
13. Bushing
14. Spring
15. Boot
16. Nut
17. Nut
18. Bearing
19. Fork
20. Stud
21. Nut
22. Clip

Clutch linkage components

5. Depress the clutch cable at least four times to make sure that all the elements are properly seated.

6. This procedure should produce a lash of 0.83 ± .25 in. (21 ± 6mm) at the clutch pedal.

NOTE: *If the above procedure produces excessive pedal lash, remove the circlip from the cable and move it into the dash by one ring. If the lash is insufficient remove the circlip and move it away from the dash one ring.*

CLUTCH PEDAL FREE-PLAY ADJUSTMENT

1976–77

Adjustment for normal wear is made by turning the release fork ball stud counterclockwise to give 0.812 ± 0.25 in. (20.6 ± 6mm) lash at the clutch pedal.

1. Loosen the locknut on the ball stud end located to the right of the transmission on the clutch housing.

2. Adjust the ball stud to obtain the correct free-play (lash) as mentioned previously.

3. Tighten the locknut to 25 ft lbs, being careful not to change the adjustment.

4. Check for proper clutch operation.

1978–80

1. If there is insufficient play in the pedal, remove the circlip from the cable and allow the cable to move into the dash by one notch. Reinstall the circlip.

2. If there is excessive pedal lash, remove the circlip and pull the cable out of the dash by one notch and reinstall the circlip ring.

CLUTCH CABLE REPLACEMENT

1. Disconnect the return spring and clutch cable at the clutch release fork.

CLUTCH AND TRANSMISSION

2. Disconnect the cable from the upper end of the clutch pedal.

3. Pull the cable through the body reinforcement and disconnect it from the fender retainer.

4. Push the new cable through the body reinforcement and attach the cable end to the clutch pedal.

5. Route the cable down to the clutch release fork. Install the cable end in the release fork and install the nuts.

6. Perform "Initial Ball Stud Adjustment" and "Clutch Cable Attachment and Adjustment." Also, adjust clutch pedal free-play if necessary.

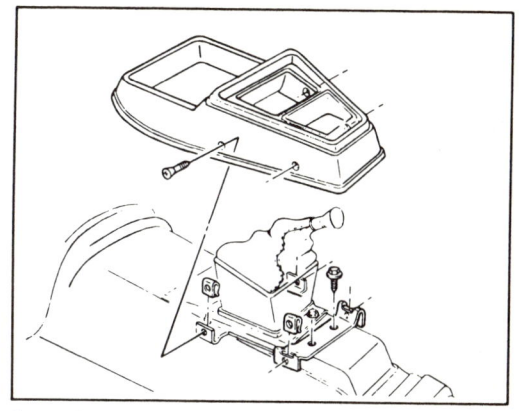

Console removal

MANUAL TRANSMISSION

Chevette models use a four-speed fully synchronized transmission. This transmission is identified as the "70 mm" four-speed transmission. Helical gears are used throughout the transmission. The mainshaft gears are free to rotate independently on the mainshaft and are in constant mesh with the countershaft gears. The countershaft gears are integral with the shaft and rotate at all times of clutch engagement being in constant mesh with the main drive gear. The reverse idler gear is carried on a bushing and is not synchronized. The synchronizer assemblies consist of a hub, sleeve, two key energizer springs, and three synchronizer keys. The synchronizer hubs are splined to the mainshaft and are retained by snap-rings. Gear shifting is accomplished by an internal shifter shaft. No adjustment of the mechanism is possible.

TRANSMISSION REMOVAL AND INSTALLATION

1. Remove the shift lever as outlined in this chapter.

2. Raise the car on a hoist and drain the lubricant from the transmission.

3. Remove the driveshaft as described in the next chapter.

4. Disconnect the speedometer cable and back-up light switch.

5. Disconnect the return spring and clutch cable at the clutch release fork.

6. Remove the crossmember-to-transmission mount bolts.

7. Remove the exhaust manifold nuts and converter-to-tailpipe bolts and nuts. Remove the converter-to-transmission bracket bolts and remove the converter.

8. Remove the crossmember-to-frame bolts and remove the crossmember.

9. Remove the dust cover.

10. Remove the clutch housing-to-engine retaining bolts, slide the transmission and clutch housing to the rear, and remove the transmission.

To install:

11. Place the transmission in gear, position the transmission and clutch housing, and slide forward. Turn the output shaft to align the input shaft splines with the clutch hub.

12. Install the clutch housing retaining bolts and lockwashers. Torque the bolts to 25 ft lbs.

13. Install the dust cover.

14. Position the crossmember to the frame and loosely install the retaining bolts. Install the crossmember-to-transmission mounting bolts. Torque the center nuts to 33 ft lbs; the end nuts to 21 ft lbs. Torque the crossmember-to-frame bolts to 40 ft lbs.

15. Install the exhaust pipe to the manifold and the converter bracket on the transmission. Torque the converter bracket rear support nuts to 150 in. lbs.

16. Connect the clutch cable. Perform "Initial Ball Stud Adjustment" and "Clutch Cable Attachment and Adjustment." Also, adjust clutch pedal free-play, if necessary.

17. Connect the speedometer cable and back-up light switch.

18. Install the driveshaft.

19. Fill the transmission to the correct level with SAE 80W or SAE 80W-90 GL-5 gear lubricant. Lower the car.

20. Install the shift lever and check operation of the transmission.

92 CLUTCH AND TRANSMISSION

1. Drive gear
2. Bearing retainer
3. Pilot bearings
4. Case
5. Bellhousing
6. 3-4 Synchronizer assembly
7. 3-4 Shifter fork
8. Third speed gear
9. Detent bushing
10. Second speed gear
11. 1-2 Shifter fork
12. 1-2 Synchronizer assembly
13. First speed gear
14. Shifter shaft
15. Extension
16. Speedometer drive gear and clip
17. Mainshaft
18. Rear oil seal
19. Retainer oil seal
20. Snap ring—bearing to gear
21. Drive gear bearing
22. Snap ring—bearing to case
23. Countergear roller bearings
24. Countergear assembly
25. Counter reverse gear
26. Reverse idler gear
27. Reverse gear
28. Snap ring—bearing to extension
29. Rear bearing

Cross-section of the manual transmission

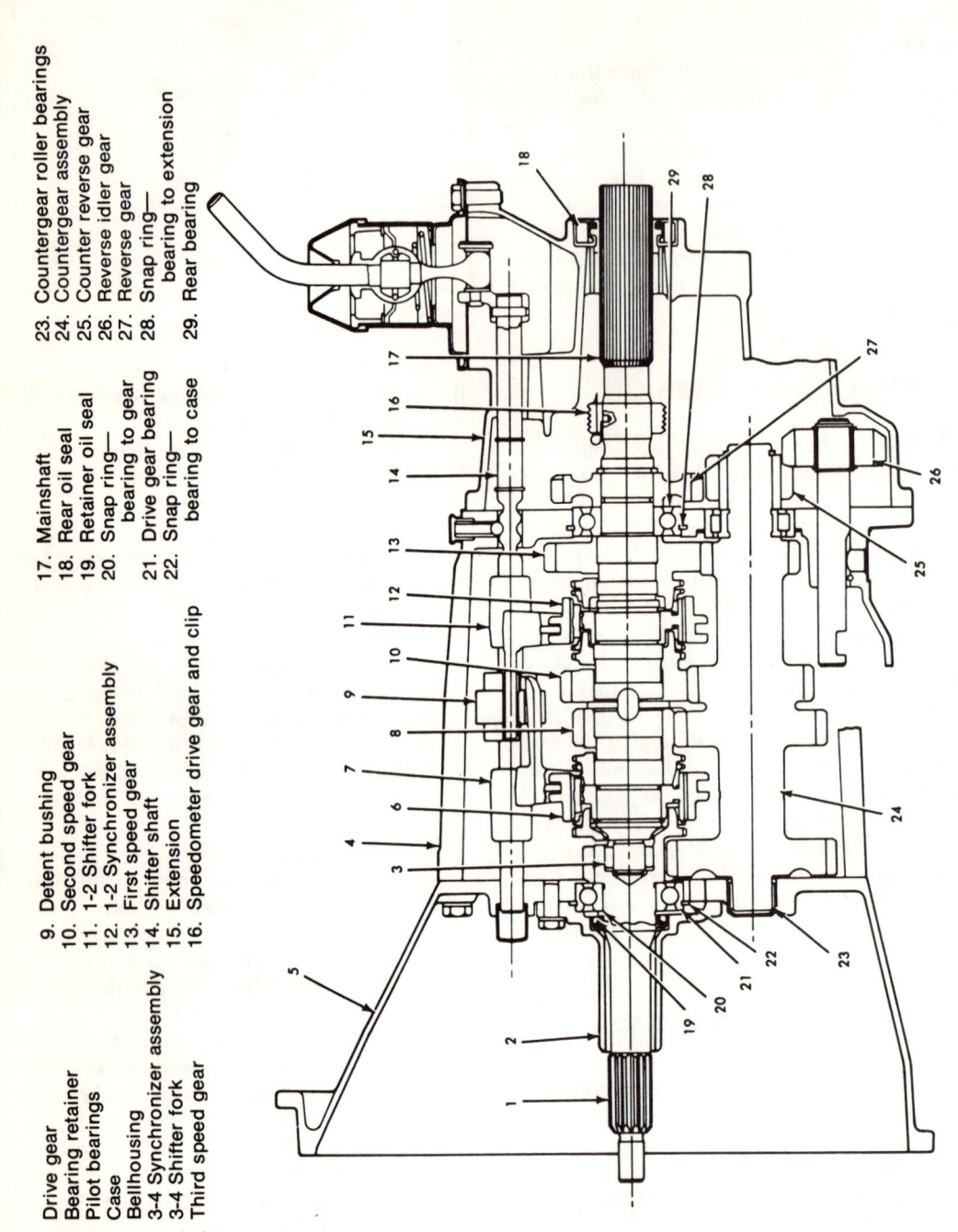

CLUTCH AND TRANSMISSION

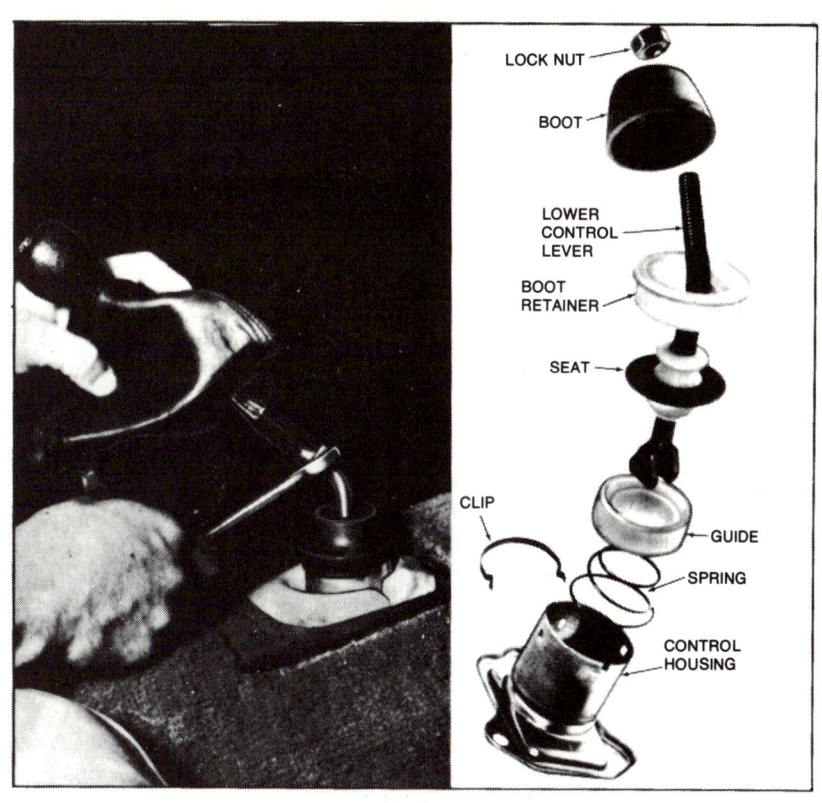

Shift lever removal

SHIFT LEVER REPLACEMENT

1. Remove the floor console and/or boot retainer.
2. Raise the shift lever boot to gain access to the locknut on the lever. Loosen the locknut and unscrew the upper portion of the shift lever with the knob attached.
3. Remove the foam insulator to gain access to the control assembly bolts.
4. Remove the three bolts on the extension and remove the control assembly.
5. Use caution when removing the clip on the control housing as the internal components are under spring pressure.
6. Remove the locknut, boot retainer, and seat from the threaded end of the shift lever.
7. Remove the spring and guide from the forked end of the shift lever.
8. To assemble the shift lever, install the spring and guide on the forked end of the lever.
9. Install the seat, boot retainer, and the locknut over the threaded end of the lever.
10. Assemble the components in the control housing and install the clip on the control housing.
11. Install the control assembly on the extension making sure that the fork at the lower end of the lever engages the shifter shaft lever arm pin. Torque the shift lever retaining bolts to 35 in. lbs.
12. Install the foam insulator, boot, retainer, and/or floor console.
13. Slide the boot below the threaded portion of the shift lever and install the upper shift lever. Tighten the locknut.

AUTOMATIC TRANSMISSION

1976–77 Chevettes equipped with automatic transmission use the Turbo Hydra-Matic 200 transmission. Later models are equipped with a model 180 automatic transmission. Both units are fully automatic and provide three forward speeds and reverse.

NEUTRAL SAFETY SWITCH REPLACEMENT

1. Remove the floor console cover.
2. Disconnect the electrical connectors on the back-up, seat belt warning, and neutral starter contacts on the switch.
3. Place the shift lever in Neutral.
4. Remove the two switch attaching screws and remove the switch.

CLUTCH AND TRANSMISSION

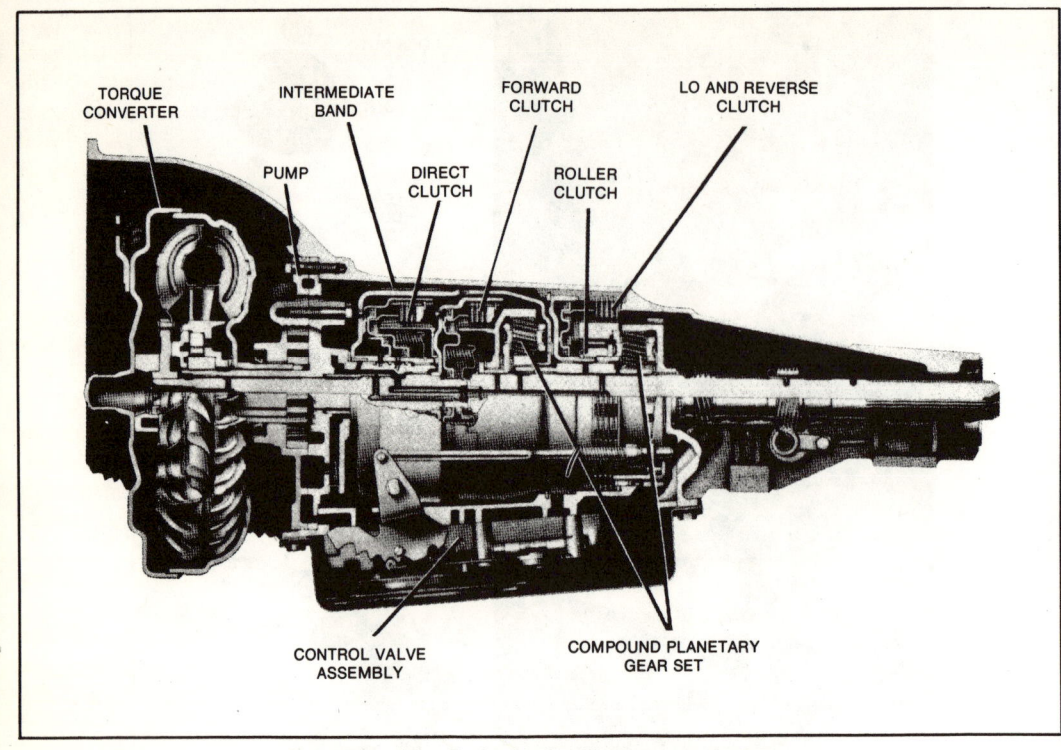

Cutaway of the Turbo Hydra-Matic transmission

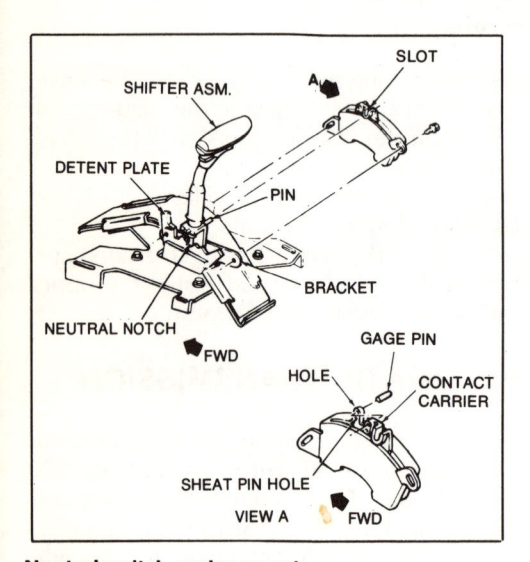

Neutral switch replacement

5. Make sure that the shift lever is in the Neutral position before installing the switch assembly.
6. Place the neutral start switch assembly in position on the shift lever making sure that the pin on the lever is in the slot of the switch.

NOTE: *When installing the same switch, align the contact support slot with the service adjustment hole in the switch and insert a 3/32 in. drill bit to hold the switch in Neutral. Remove the dill bit after the switch is fastened to the shift lever mounting bracket.*

7. Install the two switch attaching screws.
8. Move the shift lever out of Neutral to shear the plastic pin.
9. Connect the electrical connectors to the switch contacts. Apply the parking brake and start the engine. Check to make sure that the engine starts only in Park or Neutral. Make sure that the back-up lights work only in Reverse. Check that the seat belt warning system operates.
10. Stop the engine and install the floor console cover.

SHIFT LINKAGE ADJUSTMENT

1. Place the shift lever in the Neutral position of the detent plate.
2. Disconnect the rod from the lower end of the shift lever. Place the transmission lever in the Neutral position. Do this by moving the lever clockwise to the maximum detent (Park), then moving the lever counterclockwise two (2) detent positions (Neutral).

CLUTCH AND TRANSMISSION 95

sults in a loss of fluid pressure and in turn, only a partial engagement of the affected clutches. A partial engagement of the clutches with sufficient pressure to cause apparently normal operation of the vehicle will result in the failure of clutches or various other internal parts after only a few miles of operation.

DOWNSHIFT CABLE ADJUSTMENT

The transmission has a cable between the carburetor linkage and the transmission which provides transmission downshifting.

1. Remove the air cleaner.
2. Disengage the snap lock by pushing up on the bottom. Release the lock and cable.
3. Disconnect the snap lock assembly from the bracket by compressing the locking tabs.
4. Disconnect the cable from the carburetor.
5. Remove the clamp around the oil filler tube. Remove the screw and the washer that secure the cable to the transmission and disconnect the cable.
6. Install a new seal on the cable and lubricate it with transmission fluid.
7. Connect the transmission end of the cable and attach it to the transmission with the screw and washer.
8. Feed the cable in front of the oil filler tube and attach it to the tube with the clamp.
9. Feed the cable through the mounting

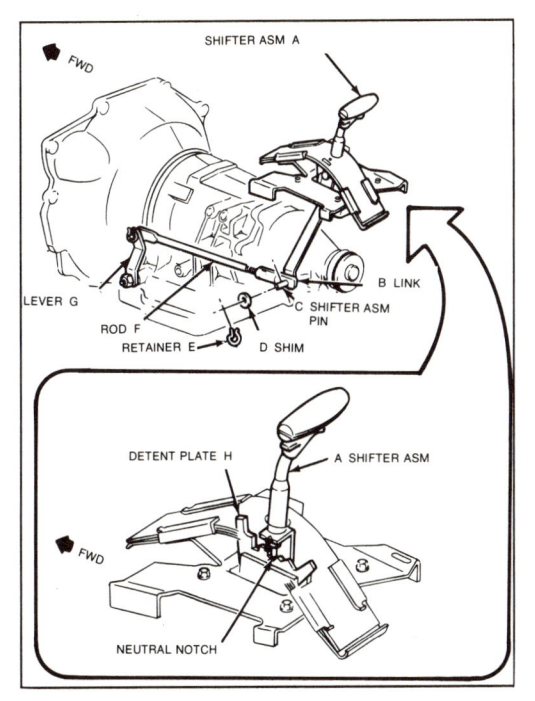

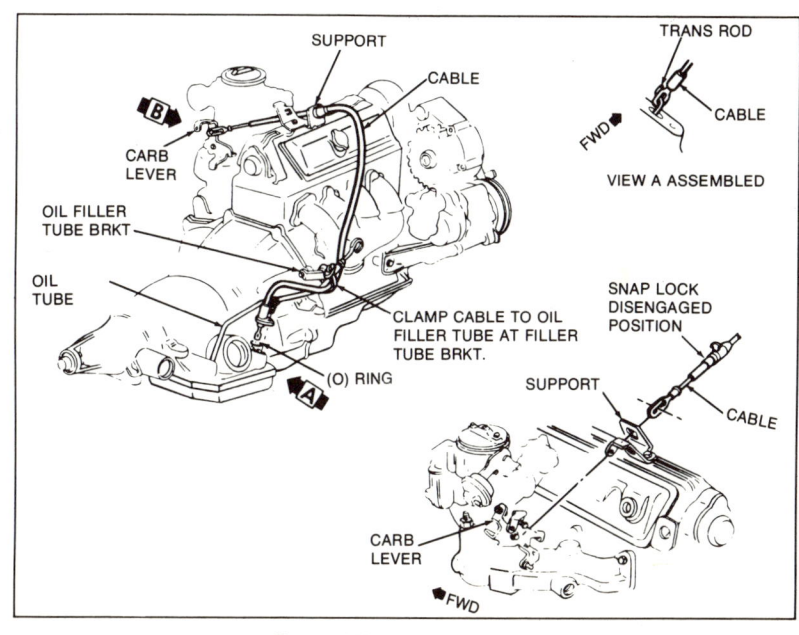

Shift linkage adjustment

3. Adjust the rod until the hole in the rod aligns with the pin on the lower end of the shift lever. Install the rod on the pin and secure it by adding the washer and spring clip.

NOTE: *Any inaccuracies in the adjustment may result in a premature failure of the transmission due to operation without the controls in full detent. Such operation re-*

Downshift cable adjustment

CLUTCH AND TRANSMISSION

bracket and snap lock assembly and attach it to the carburetor lever.

10. With the cable attached to both the transmission and the carburetor lever, move the carburetor lever to the wide open throttle position. Push the snap lock flush and return carburetor lever to normal position.

11. Install the air cleaner.

PAN REMOVAL AND INSTALLATION, FLUID AND FILTER CHANGE

Transmission fluid should be drained while at normal operating temperature.

CAUTION: *Transmission fluid temperature can exceed 350° F.*

1. Raise the car and support the transmission with a suitable jack at the transmission vibration damper.
2. Place a receptacle of at least three quarts capacity under the transmission oil pan. Remove the oil pan attaching bolts from the front and side of the pan.
3. Loosen the rear pan attaching bolts approximately four turns.
4. Drain the fluid by carefully prying the oil pan loose with a screwdriver.
5. After the fluid has drained, remove the remaining oil pan attaching bolts. Remove the oil pan and gasket. Throw the old gasket away.
6. Drain the remaining fluid from the pan. Thoroughly clean the pan with solvent and dry with compressed air.
7. Remove the two screen-to-valve body bolts and remove the screen and gasket. Discard the gasket.
8. Thoroughly clean the screen in solvent and dry with compressed air.
9. Install the new gasket on the screen and install the bolts. On 1976–77 models, torque the bolts to 6–10 ft lbs. On 1978–80 models, torque the bolts to 13–15 ft lbs.
10. Install a new gasket on the oil pan and install the oil pan. Tighten the bolts to 10–13 ft lbs. on 1976–77 models and to 7–10 ft lbs. on 1978–80 models.
11. Lower the car and add about 6 pints of Dexron® II automatic transmission fluid through the filler tube. If the transmission has been overhauled add about 4.9 quarts of fluid.
12. With the transmission in Park, apply the parking brake, start the engine and let it idle (not fast idle). Do not race the engine.
13. Move the gear selector lever slowly through all positions, return the lever to Park, and check the transmission fluid level.
14. Add fluid as necessary to raise the level between the dimples on the dipstick. Be careful not to overfill the transmission; approximately one pint of fluid will raise the level to the correct amount.

Drive Train
7

DRIVELINE

Driveshaft and U-joints

A one-piece driveshaft is mounted to the companion flange with a conventional universal joint at the rear. The driveshaft is connected to the transmission output shaft with a splined slip yoke. The slip yoke contains a thrust spring which seats against the end of the transmission output shaft. The thrust spring MUST be installed for proper operation

The unversal joints are of the long-life design and do not require periodic inspection or lubrication. When the joints are disassembled, repack the bearings and lubricate the reservoirs at the end of the trunnions with chassis grease and replace the dust seals.

DRIVESHAFT REMOVAL AND INSTALLATION

1. Raise the car. Scribe matchmarks on the driveshaft and the companion flange and disconnect the rear universal joint by removing the trunnion bearing straps.
2. Move the driveshaft to the rear under the axle to remove the slip yoke from the transmission. Watch for oil leakage from the transmission output shaft housing.
3. Install the driveshaft in the reverse

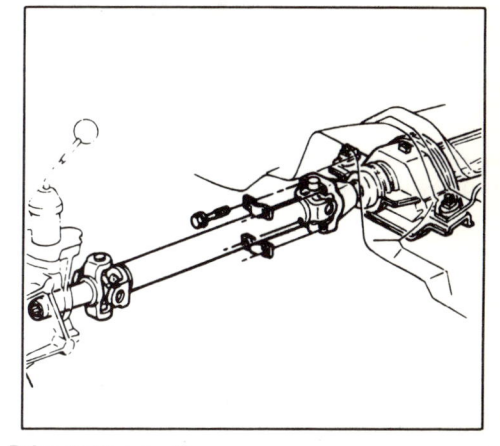

Driveshaft mounting

order of removal. Tighten the trunnion strap bolts to 16 ft lbs.

UNIVERSAL JOINT REMOVAL AND INSTALLATION

1. Remove the driveshaft.
2. For reassembly purposes, scribe a line on the transmission end of the driveshaft and on the slip yoke. Remove the snap-rings from the trunnion yoke.
3. Support the trunnion yoke on a piece of 1¼ in. ID pipe on an arbor press or bench vise. Use a suitable socket or rod to press on the trunnion until the bearing cup is almost

DRIVE TRAIN

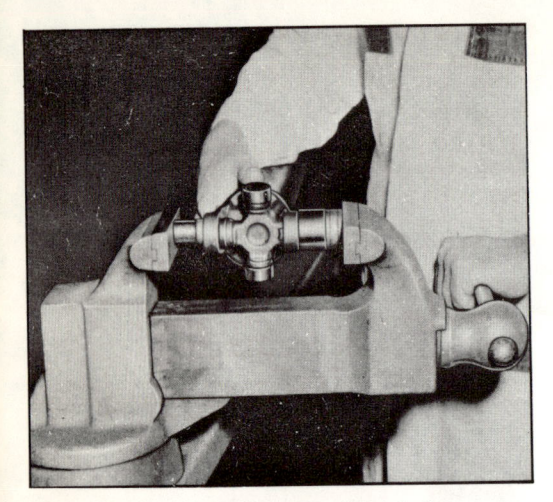

Removing the U-joint from the driveshaft

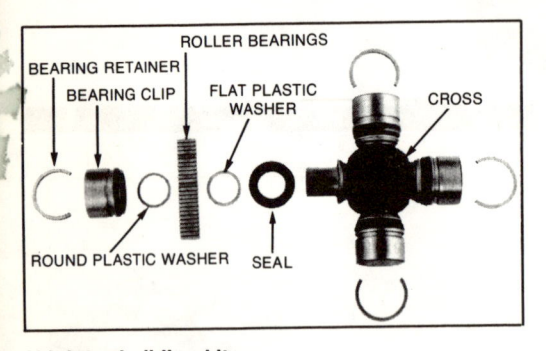

U-joint rebuilding kit

out. Grasp the cup in the vise and work the cup out of the yoke. Press the trunnion in the opposite direction to remove the other cup.

4. Clean and inspect the dust seals, bearing rollers, and trunnions. Lubricate the bearings. Make sure that the lubricant reservoir at the end of each trunnion is completely filled with lubricant. A squeeze bottle is recommended to fill the reservoirs from the bottom to prevent air pockets.

5. When installing a U-joint rebuilding kit, place the dust seals on the trunnions with the cavities of the seals toward the end of the trunnions. Use caution when pressing the seals onto the trunnions to prevent seal distortion and to assure proper seal seating.

NOTE: *Install the transmission yoke on the front of the driveshaft as marked in Step 2. If this is not done, driveline vibration may result.*

6. To assemble, position the trunnion into the yoke. Partially install one bearing cup into the yoke and start the trunnion into the bearing cup. Partially install the other cup, align the trunnion into the cup, and press the cups into the yoke.

7. Install the snap-rings.
8. Install the driveshaft.

REAR AXLE

Axle Shaft, Bearing, and Seal
REMOVAL AND INSTALLATION

1. Raise the car. Remove the wheel and tire assembly and the brake drum.
2. Clean the area around the differential carrier cover.
3. Remove the differential carrier cover to drain the rear axle lubricant.
4. Use a metric allen wrench to unscrew the differential pinion shaft lockscrew and remove the differential pinion shaft. It may be necessary to shorten the allen wrench to do this.
5. Push the flanged end of the axle shaft toward the center of the car and remove the "C" lock from the bottom end of the shaft.
6. Remove the axle shaft from the housing making sure not to damage the oil seal.
7. If replacing the seal only, remove the oil seal by using the button end of the axle shaft. Insert the button end of the shaft behind the steel case of the oil seal and carefully pry the seal out of the bore.
8. To remove bearings, insert a bearing and seal remover into the bore so that the tool head grasps behind the bearing. Slide the washer against the seal or bearing and turn the nut against the washer. Attach a slide hammer and remove the bearing.
9. Lubricate a new bearing with hypoid lubricant and install it into the housing with a bearing installer tool. Make sure that the tool contacts the end of the axle tube to make sure that the bearing is at the proper depth.
10. Lubricate the cavity between the seal lips with a high melting point wheel bearing grease. Place a new oil seal on the seal installation tool and position the seal in the axle housing bore. Tap the seal into the bore flush with the end of the housing.
11. To install the axle shaft, slide the axle shaft into place making sure that the splines on the end of the shaft do not damage the oil seal and that they engage the splines of the differential side gear. Install the "C" lock on

DRIVE TRAIN 99

Rear axle assembly

Cross-section of the differential

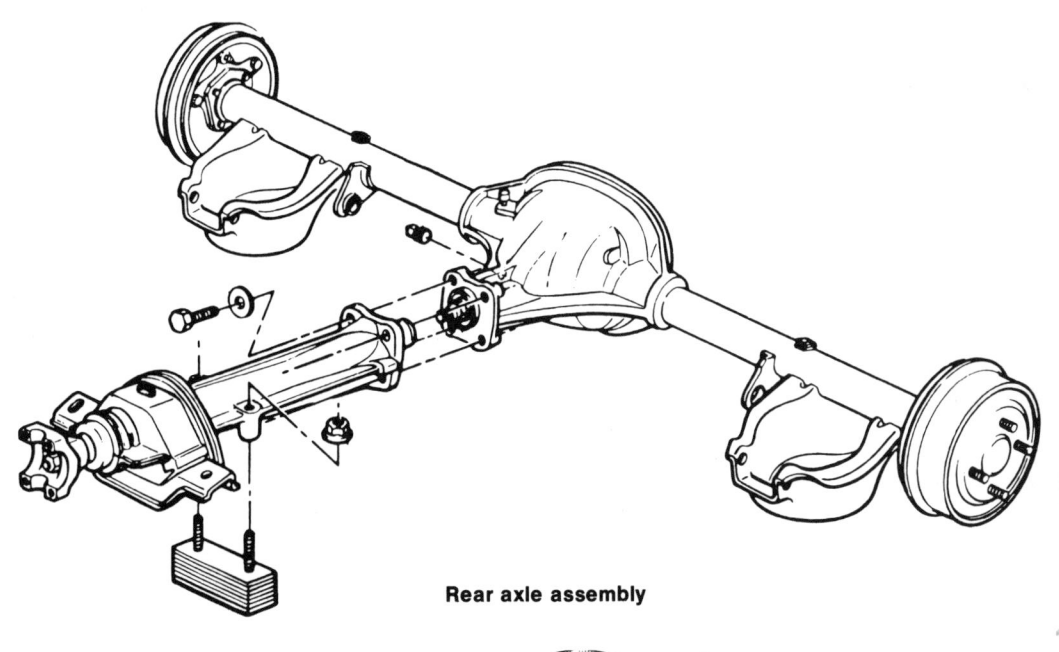

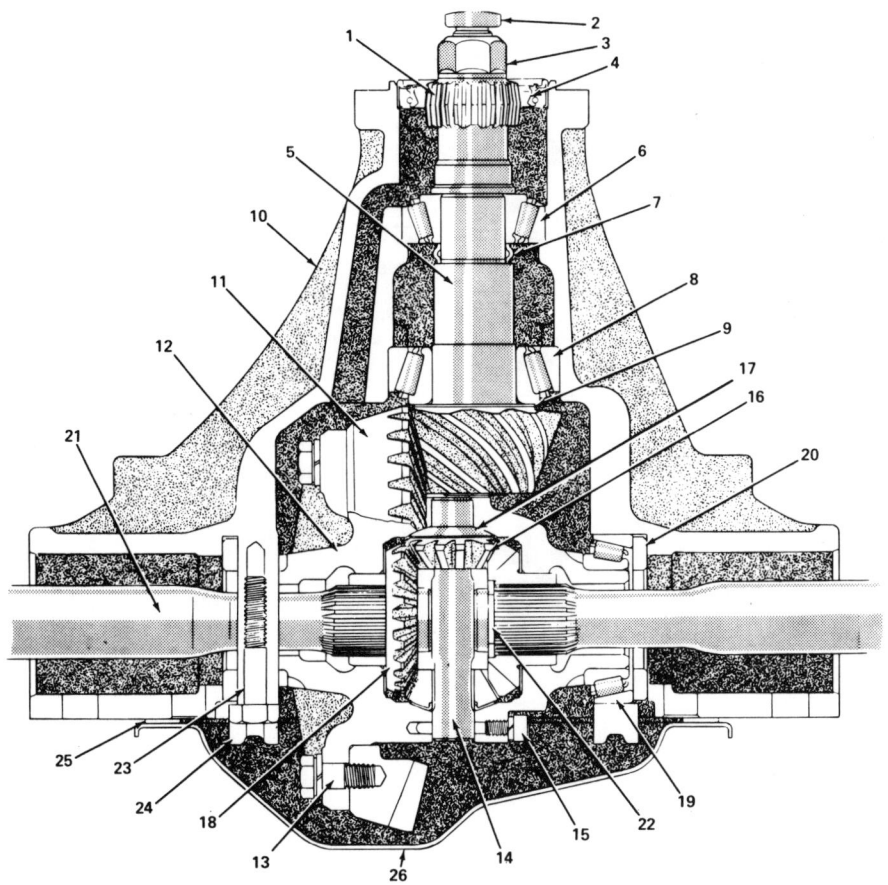

1. Drive coupling
2. Thrust washer
3. Lock nut
4. Oil seal
5. Drive pinion
6. Pinion front bearing
7. Preload spacer
8. Pinion rear bearing
9. Pinion depth shim
10. Differential carrier
11. Ring gear
12. Differential case
13. Ring gear bolt
14. Pinion shaft
15. Lock screw
16. Pinion gear
17. Thrust washer
18. Side gear
19. Differential bearing
20. Shim/spacer
21. Axle shaft
22. Axle shaft 'C' lock
23. Bearing cap bolt
24. Bearing cap
25. Differential cover gasket
26. Differential cover

100 DRIVE TRAIN

Remove the lock screw with a metric allen wrench. It may be necessary to shorten the wrench.

the button end of the axle shaft and push the shaft outward so that the shaft lock seats in the counterbore of the differential side gear.

12. Position the differential pinion shaft through the case and pinions, aligning the hole in the shaft with the lockscrew hole. Install the lockscrew.

13. Clean the gasket mounting surfaces on the differential carrier and the carrier cover. Install the carrier cover using a new gasket and tighten the cover bolts in a crosswise pattern to 22 ft lbs.

14. Fill the rear axle with lubricant to the bottom of the filler hole.

15. Install the brake drum and the wheel and tire assembly.

16. Lower the car.

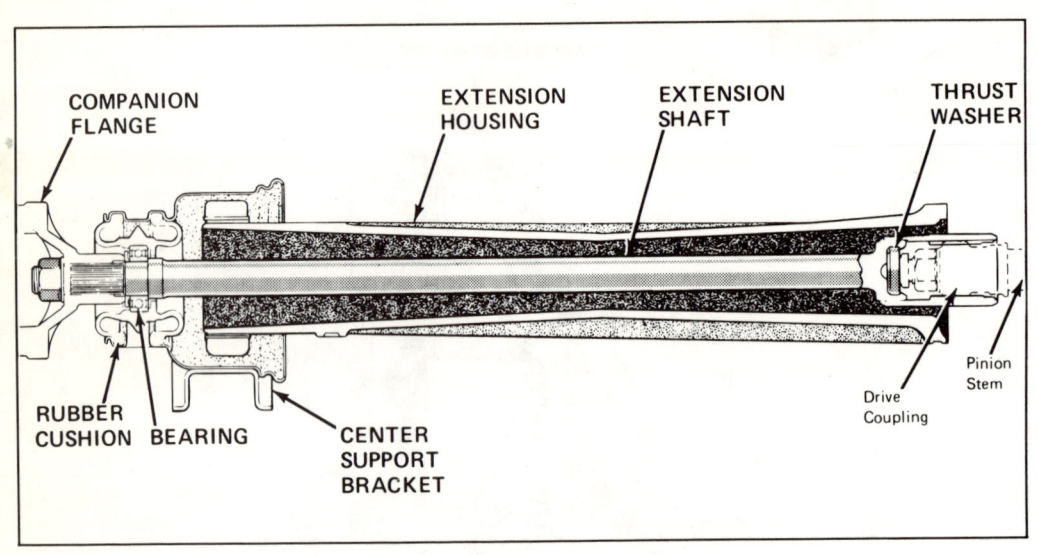

Cross-section of rear axle extension

Suspension and Steering

8

FRONT SUSPENSION

The Chevette front suspension is of conventional long and short control arm design with coil springs. The control arms attach with bolts and bushings at the inner pivot points and to the steering knuckle/front wheel spindle assembly at the outer pivot points. Lower ball joints are the wear indicator type. A front stabilizer bar is used.

Shock Absorber

REMOVAL AND INSTALLATION

1. Hold the shock absorber upper stem and remove the nut, upper retainer, and rubber grommet.
2. Raise the car.
3. Remove the bolt from the lower end of the shock absorber and remove the shock absorber.

To install:

4. With the lower retainer and rubber grommet in position, extend the shock absorber stem and install the stem through the wheelhouse opening.
5. Install and torque the lower bolt to 35–50 ft lbs.
6. Lower the car.
7. Install the upper rubber grommet, retainer, and nut to the shock absorber stem.

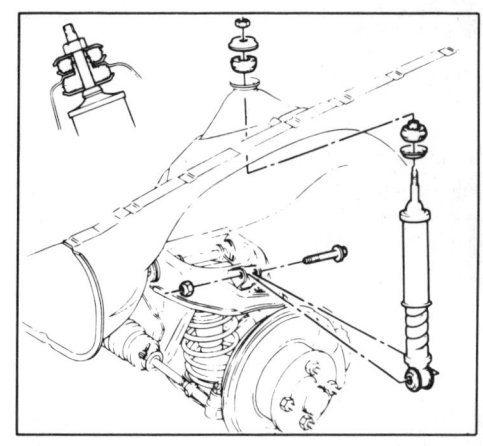

Front shock absorber mounting

8. Hold the shock absorber upper stem and torque the nut to 60–120 in. lbs.

NOTE: *The required torque is produced by running the nut to the unthreaded part of the stud.*

Lower Ball Joint

REMOVAL AND INSTALLATION

1. Raise the car.
2. Remove the tire and wheel.
3. Support the lower control arm with a hydraulic floor jack.

SUSPENSION AND STEERING

4. Loosen, but do not remove the lower ball stud nut.

5. Install a ball joint removal tool with the cup end over the upper ball stud nut.

6. Turn the threaded end of the ball joint removal tool until the ball stud is free of the steering knuckle.

7. Remove the ball joint removal tool and remove the nut from the ball stud.

8. Remove the ball joint.

NOTE: *Inspect the tapered hole in the steering knuckle. Clean the area. If any out-of-roundness, deformation, or damage is found, the steering knuckle MUST be replaced.*

9. To install the lower ball joint, mate the ball stud through the lower control arm and into the steering knuckle.

NOTE: *The ball joint studs use a special nut which must be discarded whenever loosened and removed. On assembly, use a standard nut to draw the ball joint into position on the knuckle, then remove the standard nut and install a new special nut for final installation.*

10. Install and torque the ball stud nut to 41–54 ft lbs.

11. Install the tire and wheel.

12. Lower the car.

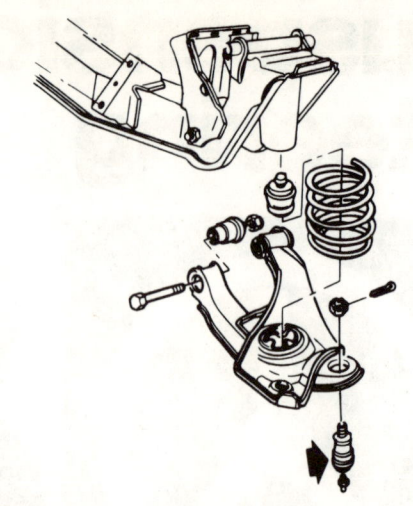

Exploded view of control arm assembly. The arrow points out the ball joints

The upper nut is 14 mm. Hold the shock absorber stem (arrow) while loosening the nut

The lower bolt and nut will require two 17 mm wrenches

Lower Control Arm and Coil Spring

REMOVAL AND INSTALLATION

1. Raise the car.
2. Remove the wheel and tire.
3. Disconnect the stabilizer bar from the lower control arm and disconnect the tie-rod from the steering knuckle.
4. Support the lower control arm with a jack.
5. Remove the nut from the lower ball joint, then use a ball joint removal tool to press out the lower ball joint.
6. Swing the knuckle and hub aside and attach them securely with wire.
7. Loosen the lower control arm pivot bolts.
8. As a safety precaution, install a chain through the coil spring.
9. Slowly lower the jack.
10. When the spring is extended as far as possible, use a pry bar to carefully lift the spring over the lower control arm seat. Remove the spring.
11. Remove the pivot bolts and remove the lower control arm.

SUSPENSION AND STEERING 103

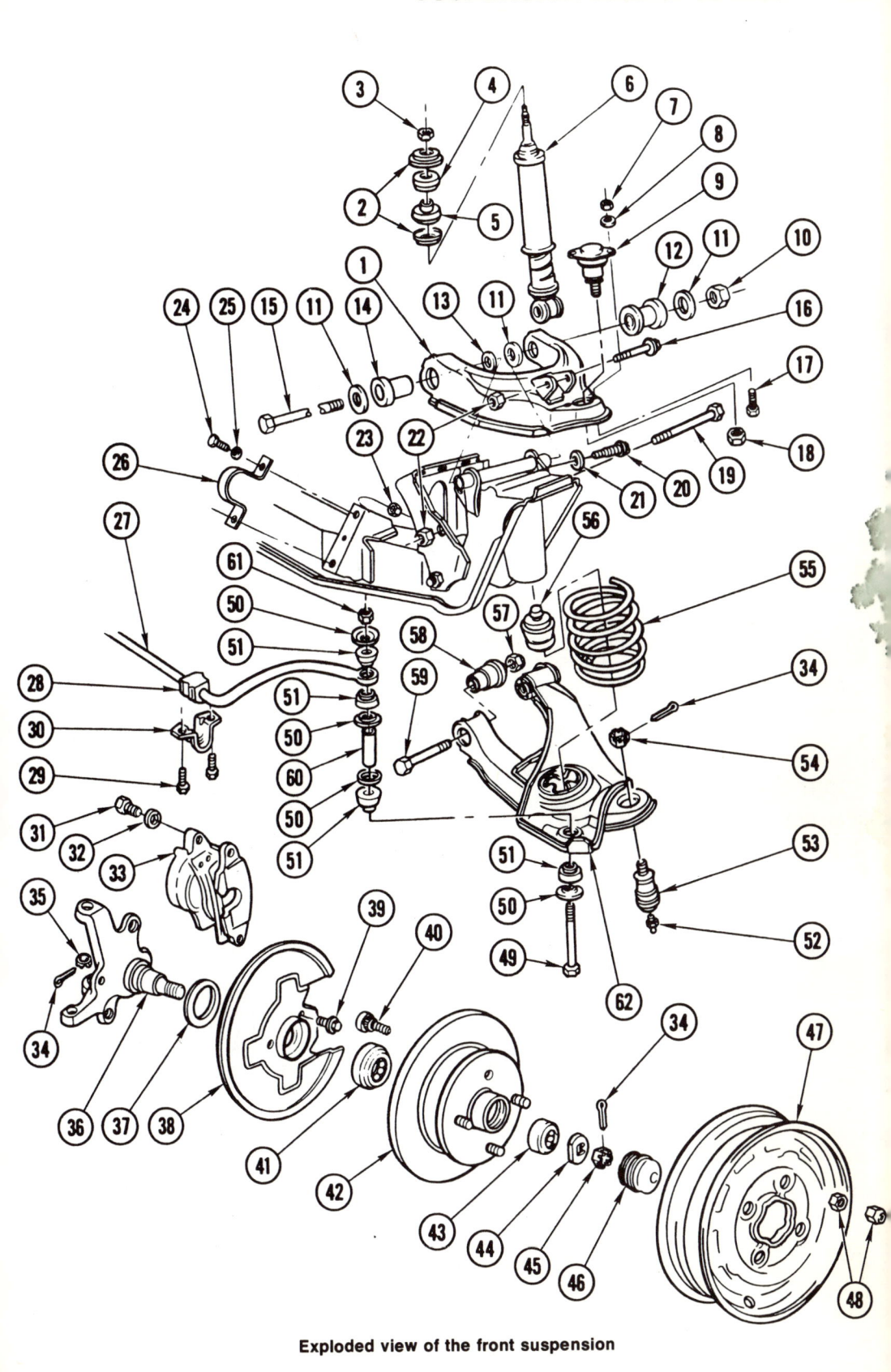

Exploded view of the front suspension

SUSPENSION AND STEERING

To install:

12. Install the lower control arm and pivot bolts to the underbody brackets. Torque the lower control arm pivot bolts to 40 ft lbs.
13. Position the spring correctly and install it in the upper pocket. Use tape to hold the insulatator onto the spring.
14. Install the lower end of the spring onto the lower control arm. An assistant may be necessary to compress the spring far enough to slide it over the raised area of the lower control arm seat.
15. Use a jack to raise the lower control arm and compress the coil spring.

NOTE: *The ball joint studs use a special nut which must be discarded whenever loosened and removed. On assembly, use a standard nut to draw the ball joint into position on the knuckle, then remove the standard nut and install a new special nut for final installation.*

16. Install the ball joint through the lower control arm and into the steering knuckle. Install the nut on the ball stud nut and torque to 41–54 ft lbs.
17. Connect the stabilizer bar to the lower control arm and torque its attaching bolt to 15 ft lbs. Connect the tie-rod to the steering knuckle. Install the wheel and tire.
18. Lower the car.

Upper Ball Joint
REMOVAL AND INSTALLATION

1. Raise the car and support it safely on jackstands.
2. Remove the tire and wheel.
3. Support the lower control arm with a floor jack.
4. Loosen, but do not remove the upper ball stud nut.
5. Install a ball joint removal tool with the cup end over the lower ball stud nut.
6. Turn the threaded end of the ball joint removal tool until the upper ball stud is free of the steering knuckle.
7. Remove the ball joint removal tool and remove the nut from the ball stud.
8. Remove the two nuts and bolts attaching the ball joint to the upper control arm and remove the ball joint.

NOTE: *Inspect the tapered hole in the steering knuckle. Clean the area. If any out-of-roundness, deformation, or damage is found, the steering knuckle MUST be replaced.*

9. To install the upper ball joint, install the nuts and bolts attaching the ball joint to the upper control arm. Torque the nuts to 20 ft lbs. Then mate the upper control arm ball stud to the steering knuckle.

NOTE: *The ball joint studs use a special nut which must be discarded whenever loosened and removed. On assembly, use a standard nut to draw the ball joint into position on the knuckle, then remove the standard nut and install a new special nut for final installation.*

10. Install and torque the ball stud nut to 29–36 ft lbs.
11. Install the tire and wheel.
12. Lower the car.

Upper Control Arm
REMOVAL AND INSTALLATION

1. Raise the car.
2. Remove the tire and wheel.

1. Steering arm	22. Nut	43. Bearing
2. Retainer	23. Nut	44. Washer
3. Nut	24. Bolt	45. Nut
4. Grommet	25. Washer	46. Nut
5. Grommet	26. Bracket	47. Wheel
6. Absorber	27. Stabilizer shaft	48. Nut
7. Nut	28. Bushing	49. Bolt
8. Washer	29. Screw	50. Retainer
9. Ball joint	30. Bracket	51. Grommet
10. Nut	31. Washer	52. Fitting
11. Washer	32. Bolt	53. Ball joint
12. Bushing	33. Caliper	54. Nut
13. Washer	34. Cotter pin	55. Spring
14. Bushing	35. Nut	56. Bumper
15. Bolt	36. Knuckle	57. Nut
16. Bolt	37. Washer	58. Bushing
17. Bolt	38. Shield	59. Bolt
18. Nut	39. Screw and washer	60. Spacer
19. Bolt	40. Bolt	61. Nut
20. Bolt	41. Bearing	62. Arm
21. Washer	42. Hub and bearing	

SUSPENSION AND STEERING

3. Support the lower control arm with a floor jack.
4. Remove the upper ball joint from the steering knuckle as previously described.
5. Remove the upper control arm pivot bolts and remove the upper control arm.
6. To install the upper control arm, install the upper control arm with its pivot bolts.

NOTE: *The inner pivot bolt must be installed with the bolt head toward the front.*

7. Install the pivot bolt nut.
8. Position the upper control arm in a horizontal plane and torque the nut to 43–50 ft lbs.

NOTE: *The ball joint studs use a special nut which must be discarded whenever loosened and removed. On assembly, use a standard nut to draw the ball joint into position on the knuckle, then remove the standard nut and install a new special nut for final installation.*

9. Install the ball joint to the upper control arm and to the steering knuckle as previously described. Toruqe the ball joint-to-upper control arm attaching bolts to 20 ft lbs. Torque the ball stud nut to 29–36 ft lbs.
10. Install the tire and wheel.
11. Lower the car.

Stabilizer Bar
REMOVAL AND INSTALLATION

1. Raise the car.
2. Remove the stabilizer bar nuts and bolts from the lower control arms.
3. Remove the stabilizer bar brackets and remove the stabilizer bar.

To install:

4. Hold the stabilizer bar in place and install the body bushings and brackets. Torque the bracket bolts to 14 ft lbs.
5. Install the retainers, grommets, and spacer to the lower control arms and install the attaching nuts.
6. Lower the car.
7. Torque the attaching nuts to 15 ft lbs.

NOTE: *The correct torque is produced by running the nuts to the unthreaded portions of the link bolts.*

Front End Alignment
CAMBER ADJUSTMENT

Camber angle can be increased by approximately 1° by removing the upper ball joint, rotating it one-half turn, and reinstalling it with the flat of the upper flange on the inboard side of the control arm.

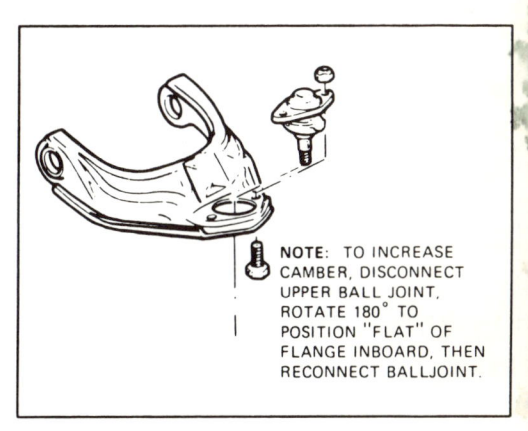

Camber adjustment

CASTER ADJUSTMENT

Caster angle can be changed with a realignment of the washers located between the legs of the upper control arm. To adjust the caster angle, an adjustment kit consisting of one 3 mm and one 9 mm washer must be used. Install as shown in the illustration.

NOTE: *You must always use two washers that total 12 mm, with one washer at each end of the floating tube.*

TOE-IN ADJUSTMENT

Toe-in is controlled by the position of the tie-rods. To adjust the toe, loosen the nuts at the steering knuckle end of the tie-rod, and the rubber cover at the other end, then rotate the rod as needed to adjust toe-in. Tighten the cover and the locknuts.

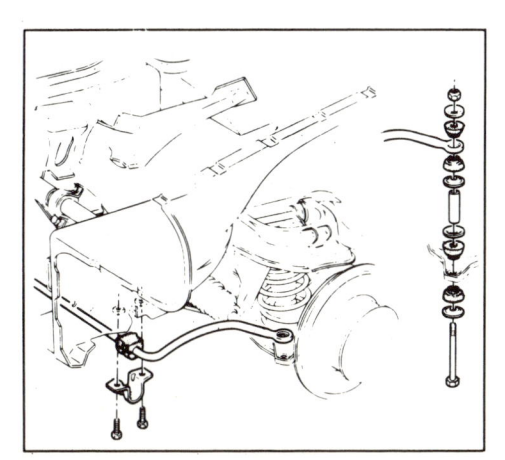

Front stabilizer bar mounting

106 SUSPENSION AND STEERING

Wheel Alignment Specifications

Year	Model	CASTER Range (deg)	CASTER Pref Setting (deg)	CAMBER Range (deg)	CAMBER Pref Setting (deg)	Toe-in (in.)	Steering Axis Inclination (deg)
1976–80	All	4P to 5P	4½P	¼N to ¾P	¼P	1/16	7½

N Negative
P Positive

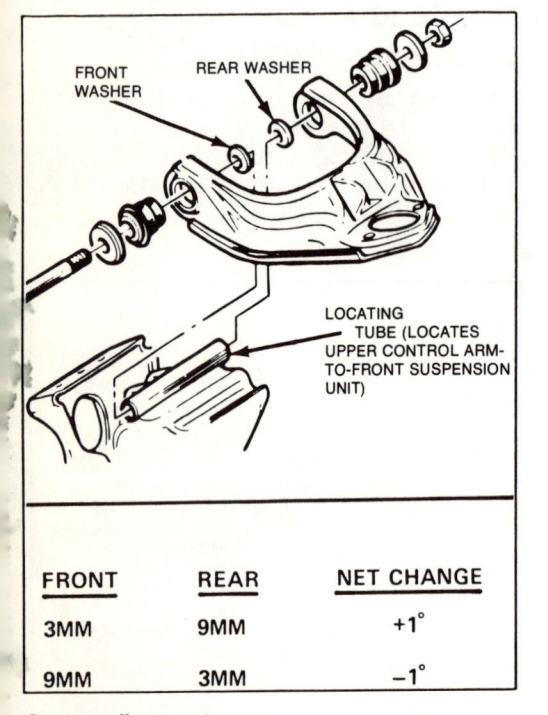

FRONT	REAR	NET CHANGE
3MM	9MM	+1°
9MM	3MM	−1°

Caster adjustment

Rear suspension

REAR SUSPENSION

Chevette models use a solid rear axle and coil springs. The axle is attached to the body by two tubular lower control arms, a straight track rod, two shock absorbers, and a bracket at the front end of the rear axle extension.

The lower control arms maintain fore and aft relationship of the axle to the chassis. The coil springs are located between brackets on the axle tube and spring seats in the frame. They are held in place by the weight of the car and, during rebound, by the shock absorbers which limit axle movement. The shock absorbers are angle-mounted on brackets behind the axle housing and the rear spring seats in the frame. A rear stabilizer bar is used.

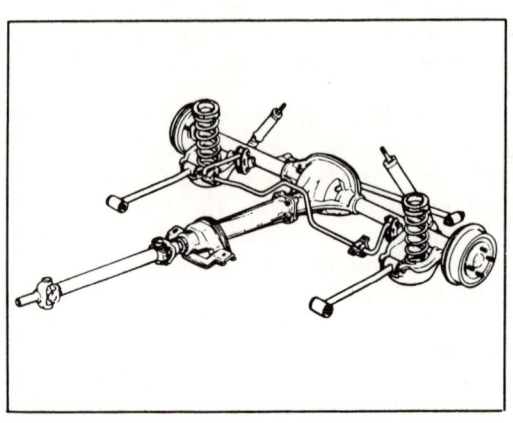

When using a hoist contacting the rear axle be sure that the stabilizer links and the track rod are not damaged.

Shock Absorber
REMOVAL AND INSTALLATION

1. Raise the car.
2. Support the rear axle.
3. Remove the shock absorber upper attaching nut and lower attaching bolt and nut, and remove the shock absorber.

To install:

4. Install the retainer and the rubber grommet onto the shock absorber.
5. Place the shock absorber into its installed position and install and tighten the upper retaining nut to 7 ft lbs.
6. Install the lower shock absorber nut and bolt and torque to 33 ft lbs.
7. Remove the rear axle supports and lower the car.

Springs
REMOVAL AND INSTALLATION

1. Raise the car.
2. Support the rear axle with a hydraulic jack.

SUSPENSION AND STEERING 107

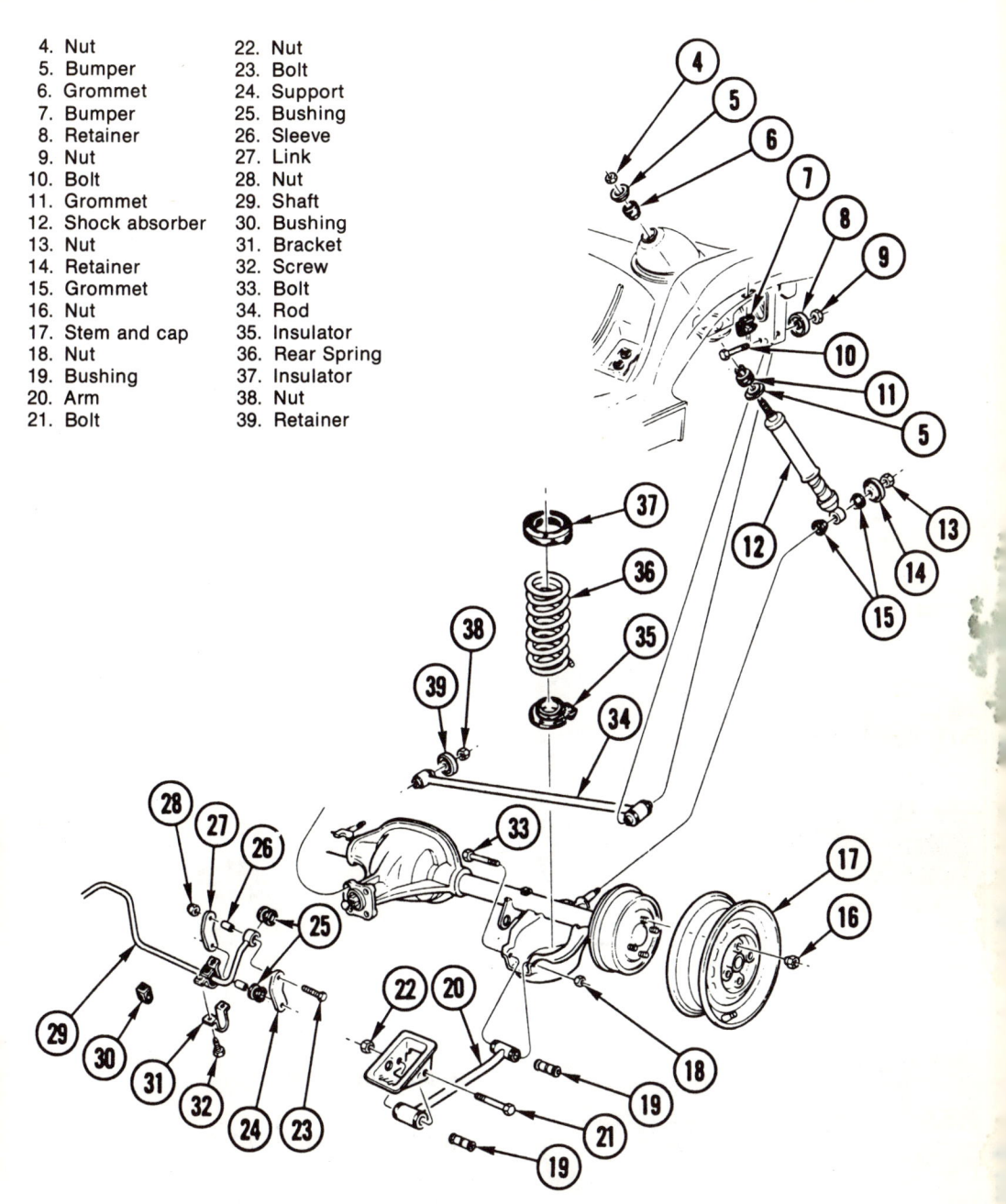

4. Nut
5. Bumper
6. Grommet
7. Bumper
8. Retainer
9. Nut
10. Bolt
11. Grommet
12. Shock absorber
13. Nut
14. Retainer
15. Grommet
16. Nut
17. Stem and cap
18. Nut
19. Bushing
20. Arm
21. Bolt
22. Nut
23. Bolt
24. Support
25. Bushing
26. Sleeve
27. Link
28. Nut
29. Shaft
30. Bushing
31. Bracket
32. Screw
33. Bolt
34. Rod
35. Insulator
36. Rear Spring
37. Insulator
38. Nut
39. Retainer

Exploded view of the rear suspension

3. Disconnect both shock absorbers from their lower brackets.

4. Disconnect the rear axle extension center support bracket from the underbody. Use caution when disconnecting the extension and safely support it when disconnected.

5. Lower the rear axle and remove the springs and spring insulators.

NOTE: *One or both springs can be removed now.*

CAUTION: *Do not stretch the rear brake hoses when lowering the rear axle.*

6. To install, place the insulators on top and on the bottom of the springs and position the springs between their upper and lower seats.

7. Raise the rear axle. Connect the rear axle extension center support bracket to the underbody. Torque the bolts to 37 ft lbs.

8. Connect the shock absorbers to their lower brackets. Torque the nuts to 33 ft lbs.

SUSPENSION AND STEERING

9. Remove the hydraulic jack from the axle.
10. Lower the car.

Stabilizer Bar

REMOVAL AND INSTALLATION

1. Raise the car.
2. Remove the bolts attaching the stabilizer bar to its brackets and links. Remove the stabilizer bar.
3. To install, place the stabilizer bar in position and install the attaching bolts and nuts in the brackets and links. Torque both the bracket and link bolts to 15 ft lbs.
4. Lower the car.

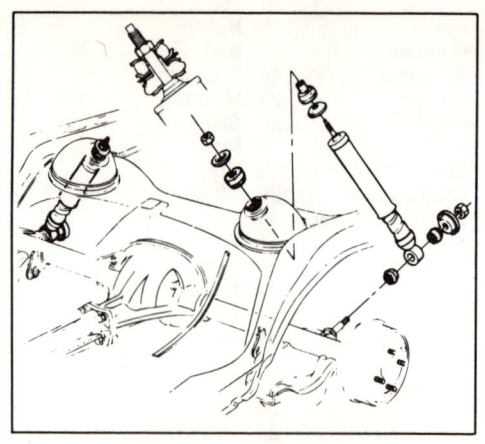

Rear shock absorber mounting detail

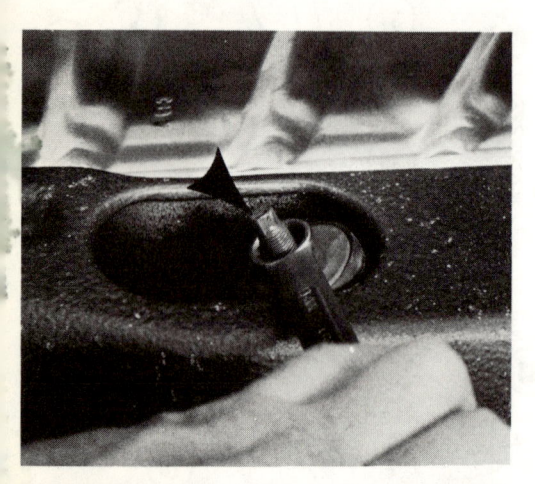

Rear shock absorber upper mount. Hold the shock absorber stem (arrow) while loosening the 14 mm locknut

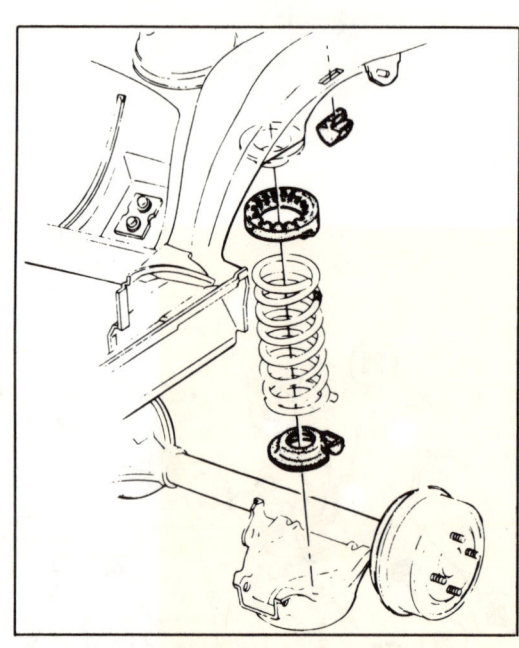

Rear spring installation

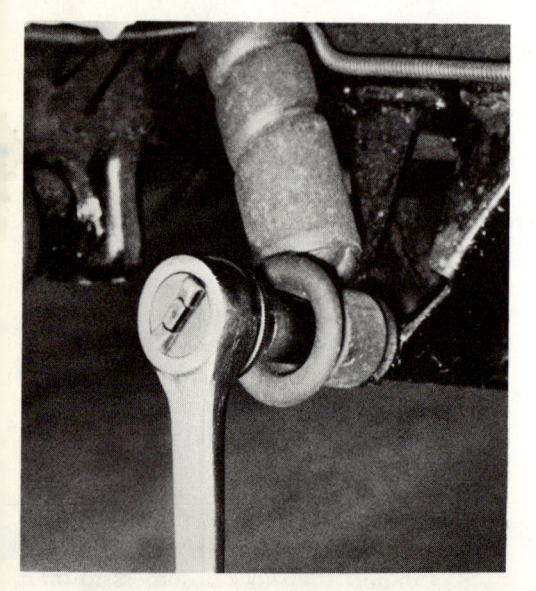

Lower Control Arm and Track Rod

REMOVAL AND INSTALLATION

CAUTION: *If both control arms are to be replaced, remove and replace one control arm at a time to prevent the axle from rolling or slipping sideways.*

1. Raise the car.
2. Support the rear axle.
3. Disconnect the stabilizer bar.
4. Remove the control arm front and rear attaching bolts and remove the control arm.
5. Remove the track rod attaching bolts and remove the track rod.
6. Press the rubber bushings out of the control arm and track rod with the proper

One nut retains the bottom shock absorber mount

SUSPENSION AND STEERING 109

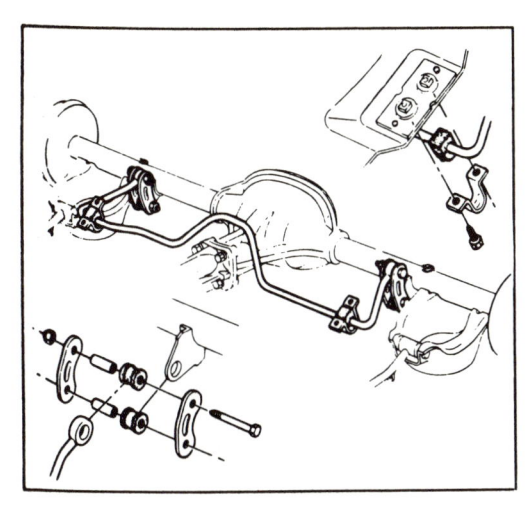

Rear stabilizer mounting

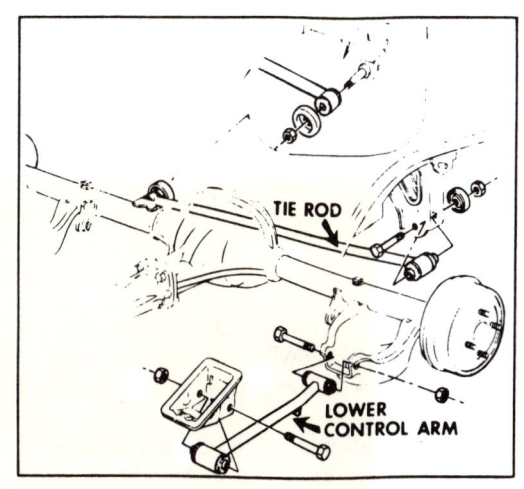

Lower control arm and track rod mounting

tools. Inspect the pivot ends of the control arm and track rod for distortion, burrs, etc., and press new bushings into place.

7. To install, place the lower control arm into position and install and torque the front and rear attaching bolts to 49 ft lbs.

8. Place the track rod in position and install the torque both the axle housing nut and body bracket bolt and nut to 49 ft lbs.

NOTE: *The car must be at curb height when tightening pivot bolts.*

9. Connect the stabilizer bar. Torque all stabilizer bar attaching bolts to 15 ft lbs.
10. Remove the support from the axle.
11. Lower the car.

STEERING

All Chevette models use manual rack and pinion steering which encloses the steering gear and linkage in one unit. Power steering is not available.

Rotary motion of the steering wheel is converted into linear motion to turn the wheels by the meshing of the helical pinion with the teeth of the rack. The pinion and a major portion of the rack are encased in a die cast aluminum housing. Inner tie-rod assemblies are threaded and staked to the rack. The inner tie-rods contain a belleville spring-loaded ball joint which permits both rocking and rotating tie-rod movement. The outer tie-rods thread onto the inners and are held in position by jam nuts. Two convoluted boots are secured by clamps to the housing and inner tie-rods to prevent the entrance of dirt. The rack and pinion assembly is secured to the front suspension crossmember with two clamps and bushings.

The energy-absorbing steering column has a "smart" switch which operates the turn signals (up and down movement), the headlight dimmer switch (front and back movement), the windshield wipers (rotation), and the windshield washers (by pushing the lever into the column).

Rack and Pinion Steering Assembly

REMOVAL AND INSTALLATION

1. Raise the car and support it safely on jackstands.
2. Remove the retaining bolts and the shield.
3. Remove both tie-rods cotter pins and nuts and remove the tie-rods.
4. Remove the flexible coupling pinch-bolt-to-shaft.
5. Remove the four bolts at the clamps and remove the rack and pinion steering assembly.

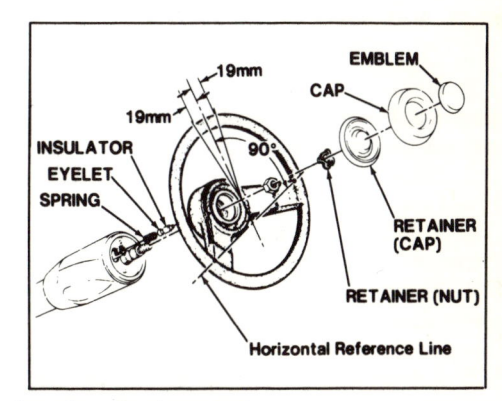

Steering wheel removal

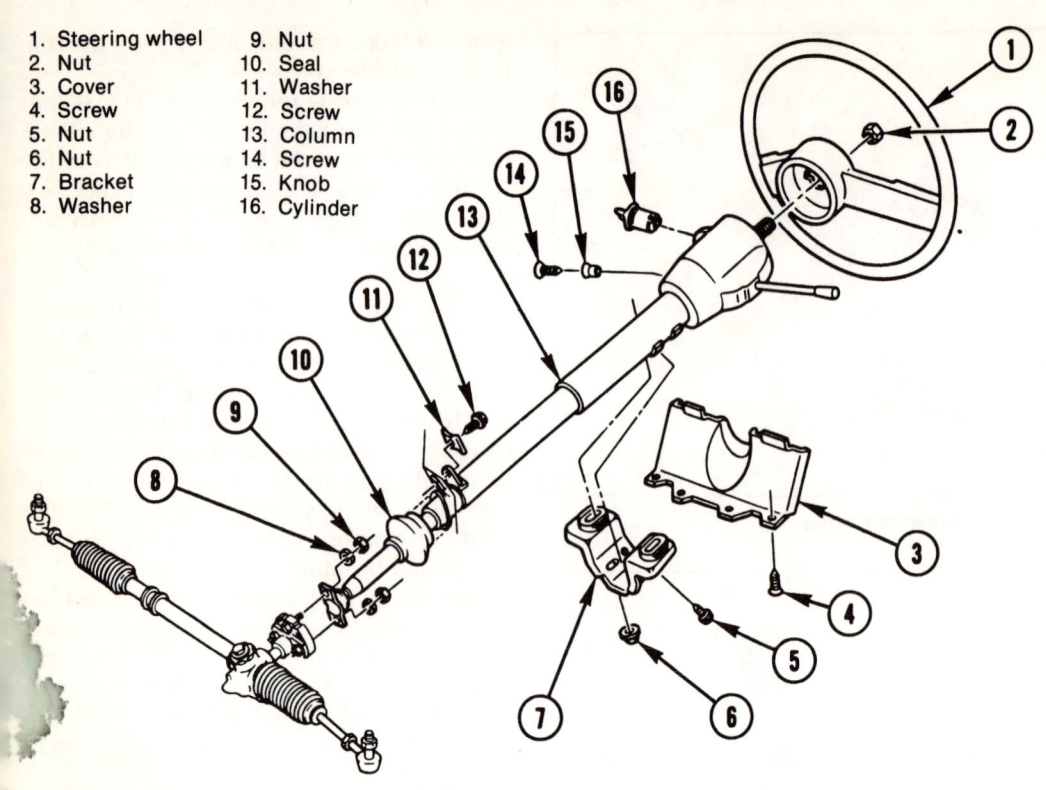

110 SUSPENSION AND STEERING

1. Steering wheel
2. Nut
3. Cover
4. Screw
5. Nut
6. Nut
7. Bracket
8. Washer
9. Nut
10. Seal
11. Washer
12. Screw
13. Column
14. Screw
15. Knob
16. Cylinder

Exploded view of the steering system

6. To install, position the assembly, install four new bolts into the clamps, and tighten the bolts to 14 ft lbs.
7. Install the flexible coupling pinch-bolt-to-shaft.
8. Install the tie-rods into the steering knuckles. Install the tie-rod nuts. If the cotter pin holes do not align, tighten the nut until the cotter pin can be inserted, and install the cotter pins.
9. Install the bolts and the shield.
10. Lower the car.

Steering Wheel

REMOVAL AND INSTALLATION

1. Disconnect the negative battery cable.
2. Remove the two steering wheel shroud screws at the underside of the steering wheel and remove the shroud.
3. Remove the wheel nut retainer and the wheel nut.
   CAUTION: *Do not overexpand the retainer.*
4. Using a steering wheel puller, thread the puller anchor screws into the threaded holes in the steering wheel. With the center bolt of the puller butting against the steering shaft, turn the center bolt clockwise to remove the steering wheel.
   NOTE: *The puller centering adapter need not be used.*
5. To install, place the turn signal lever in the neutral position and install the steering wheel. Torque the steering wheel nut to 30 ft lbs and install the nut retainer. Use caution not to overexpand the nut retainer.
6. Connect the negative battery cable.

Turn Signal Switch

REMOVAL AND INSTALLATION

1. Remove the steering wheel as previously described.
2. Position a screwdriver blade into one of the three cover slots. Pry up and out (at least two slots) to free the cover.
3. Place the U-shaped lockplate compressing tool on the end of the steering shaft and compress the lockplate. The full load of the spring should not be relieved because the ring will rotate and make removal difficult. Pry the round wire snap-ring out of the shaft groove and discard it. Remove the lockplate compressing tool and lift the lockplate off the end of the shaft.

SUSPENSION AND STEERING

This lockplate compressor is necessary for turn signal switch removal

CAUTION: *If the steering column is being disassembled out of the car, with the snap-ring removed, the shaft could slide out of the lower end of the mast jacket and be damaged.*

4. Slide the turn signal cancelling cam, upper bearing preload spring, and thrust washer off the end of the shaft.

5. Remove the multi-function lever by rotating it clockwise to its stop (off position), then pull the lever straight out to disengage it.

6. Push the hazard warning knob in and unscrew the knob.

7. Remove the two screws, pivot arm, and spacer.

8. Wrap the upper part of the connector with tape to prevent snagging the wires during switch removal.

9. Remove the three switch mounting screws and pull the switch straight up, guiding the wiring harness through the column housing.

CAUTION: *On installation it is extremely important that only the specified screws, bolts, and nuts be used. The use of overlength screws could prevent the steering column from compressing under impact.*

10. Position the switch into the housing.

11. Install the three switch mounting screws. Replace the spacer and pivot arm. Be sure that the spacer protrudes through the hole in the arm and that the arm finger encloses the turn signal switch frame. Tighten the truss head screw (secures the spacer to the signal switch) to 20 in. lbs and the flat head screw to 35 in. lbs.

12. Install the hazard warning knob.

13. Make sure that the turn signal switch is in the neutral position and that the hazard warning knob is out. Slide the thrust washer, upper bearing preload spring, and the cancelling cam into the upper end of the shaft.

14. Place the lockplate and a NEW snap-ring onto the end of the shaft. Using the lockplate compressing tool, compress the lockplate as far as possible. Slide the new snap-ring into the shaft groove and remove the lockplate compressing tool.

CAUTION: *On assembly, always use a new snap-ring.*

15. Install the multi-function lever, guiding the wire harness through the column housing. Align the lever pin with the switch slot. Push on the end of the lever until it is seated securely.

16. Install the steering wheel as previously described.

Wiper/Washer Switch
REMOVAL AND INSTALLATION

The wiper/washer switch is located on the left-side of the column under the turn signal switch.

1. Remove the steering wheel and turn signal switch as previously described. The ignition switch is mounted on top of the mast jacket near the front of the dash.

2. Remove the upper attaching screw on the ignition and dimmer switch; this releases the dimmer switch and actuator rod assembly.

NOTE: *Do not move the ignition switch. If this happens, refer to the switch adjustment procedure in "Ignition Switch and Dimmer Switch Removal and Installation."*

3. The wiper/washer switch and pivot assembly now can be removed from the column housing.

4. To install, place the wiper/washer switch and pivot assembly into the housing and guide the connector down through the bowl and shroud assembly.

5. Install the turn signal switch as previously described.

6. Fit the pinched end of the dimmer switch actuator rod into the dimmer switch. Feed the other end of the rod through the hole in the shroud into the hole in the wiper/washer switch and pivot assembly drive, but do not tighten the attaching screw. Depress the dimmer switch slightly to insert a $3/32$ in. drill bit to lock the switch to the body. Push the switch up to remove the lash between both the igniton and dimmer switches and the actuator rod. Install the

112 SUSPENSION AND STEERING

wiper/washer switch mounting screw and tighten it to 35 in. lbs. Remove the drill and check dimmer switch operation with the actuating lever.

Ignition Key Buzzer Switch
REMOVAL AND INSTALLATION

1. Remove the steering wheel and turn signal switch as previously described.
2. Make a right angle bend in a short piece of small wire about ¼ in. from one end. The wire should be inserted in the exposed loop of the wedge spring, then a straight pull on the wire will remove both the spring and the switch.

CAUTION: *Do not attempt to remove the switch separately as the clip may fall into the column. If this happens, the clip must be found before assembly.*
NOTE: *The lock cylinder must be in the "Run" position if it is in the housing. Also, if the lock cylinder is in place, the buzzer switch actuating button on the lock cylinder must be depressed before the buzzer switch can be installed.*

3. Install the buzzer switch with the contacts toward the upper end of the steering column and with the formed end of the spring clip around the lower end of the switch. Push the switch and spring assembly into the hole with the internal switch contacts toward the lock cylinder bore.
4. Install the turn signal switch and the steering wheel as previously described.

Lock Cylinder
REMOVAL AND INSTALLATION

The lock cylinder is located on the right-side of the steering column and should be removed only in the "Run" position. Removal in any other position will damage the key buzzer switch. The lock cylinder cannot be disassembled; if replacement is required, a new cylinder coded to the old key must be installed.

1. Remove the steering wheel and turn signal switch as previously described.
2. Do not remove the buzzer switch or damage to the lock cylinder will result.
3. Insert a small screwdriver or similar tool into the turn signal housing slot to the upper right of the steering shaft. Keep the tool to the right-side of the slot and depress the retainer at the bottom to release the lock cylinder. Remove the lock cylinder.
4. To install the lock cylinder, hold the cylinder sleeve in the left hand and rotate knob (key in) clockwise to stop. (This retracts the actuator.) Insert the cylinder into the housing bore with the key on the cylinder sleeve aligned with the keyway in the housing. Push the cylinder in until it bottoms. Rotate the knob counterclockwise while maintaining a light pressure inward until the drive section of the cylinder mates with the sector. Push the cylinder in fully until the retainer pops into the housing groove.
5. Install the turn signal switch and the steering wheel as previously described.

Ignition Switch and Dimmer Switch
REMOVAL AND INSTALLATION

The ignition switch is mounted on top of the mast jacket near the front of the dash. The switch is located inside the channel section of the brake pedal support and is completely inaccessible without first lowering the steering column.

1. Disconnect the negative battery cable.
2. Remove the steering wheel as previously described.

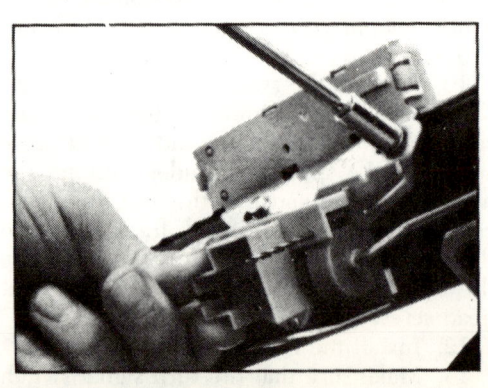

Lock cylinder removal

Installing the dimmer switch

SUSPENSION AND STEERING 113

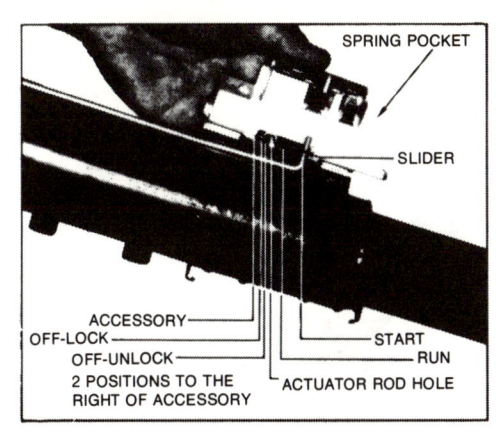

Positioning the ignition switch

7. Remove the two mounting screws and remove the ignition and dimmer switch.

8. Refer to the installation procedure previously described in "Lock Cylinder Removal and Installation."

9. Turn the cylinder clockwise to stop and then counterclockwise to stop ("Off-Unlock" position).

10. Place the ignition switch in the "Off-Unlock" position by positioning the switch as shown in the accompanying illustration. Move the slider two positions to the right from "Accessory" to the "Off-Unlock" position.

11. Fit the actuator rod into the slider hole and install the switch on the column. Be sure to use only the correct screws. Tighten only one bottom screw to 35 in. lbs. Be careful not to move the switch out of its detent.

12. Perform the dimmer switch adjustment procedure previously outlined in "Wiper/Washer Switch Removal and Installation."

13. Connect the ignition switch wiring harness.

14. Loosely install the column bracket-to-instrument panel nuts to within 1 mm±½ mm of being tight.

15. Install the floor pan bracket screw and tighten it to 25 ft lbs.

16. Tighten the column bracket-to-instrument panel nuts to 20 ft lbs.

17. Install the steering wheel as previously outlined.

18. Connect the battery negative cable.

3. Move the driver's seat as far back as possible.

4. Remove the floor pan bracket screw.

5. Remove the two column bracket-to-instrument panel nuts and lower the column far enough to disconnect the ignition switch wiring harness.

CAUTION: *Be sure that the steering column is properly supported before proceeding.*

6. The switch should be in the "Lock" position before removal. If the lock cylinder has already been removed, the actuating rod to the switch should be pulled up until there is a definite stop, then moved down one detent which is the "Lock" position.

Brakes

9

UNDERSTANDING THE BRAKES

Front disc brakes are standard equipment on all models. Power brakes are available as an option. The disc is 9.68 in. in diameter and ½ in. thick and is a one-piece casting with the hub. Single-piston sliding calipers are used.

The rear brakes are of conventional leading-trailing shoe design. Brake drum diameter is 7.87 in. Automatic adjusters are used in the rear brakes which provide adjustment when needed whenever the brakes are applied.

The master cylinder is a two-piece design: a cast housing containing the primary and secondary pistons and a stamped steel reservoir. The reservoir is attached to the cast housing with two retainers and sealed with two O-rings. The reservoir is not divided, however a dual braking system is used. The front (secondary) piston operates the rear brakes, while the rear (primary) piston operates the front brakes.

The front and rear brake lines are routed through a distributor and switch assembly located on the left-hand engine compartment side panel. The switch is a pressure differential type which lights the brake warning light on the instrument panel if either the front or rear hydraulic system fails. The switch is nonadjustable and nonserviceable; it must be replaced if defective.

Brake Adjustment

All Chevettes are equipped with front disc brakes which require no adjustment. Rear brake adjustment takes place every time the brakes are applied through the use of an automatic brake adjuster. Only an initial adjustment is necessary when the brakes have been installed. This is done by depressing the brake pedal a few times until the pedal becomes firm. Check the fluid level in the master cylinder frequently during the adjustment procedure.

HYDRAULIC SYSTEM

Master Cylinder

REMOVAL AND INSTALLATION

CAUTION: *Never allow brake fluid to spill on painted surfaces.*

1. Disconnect the master cylinder pushrod from the brake pedal.
2. Remove the pushrod boot.
3. Remove the air cleaner.

BRAKES 115

Master cylinder mounting

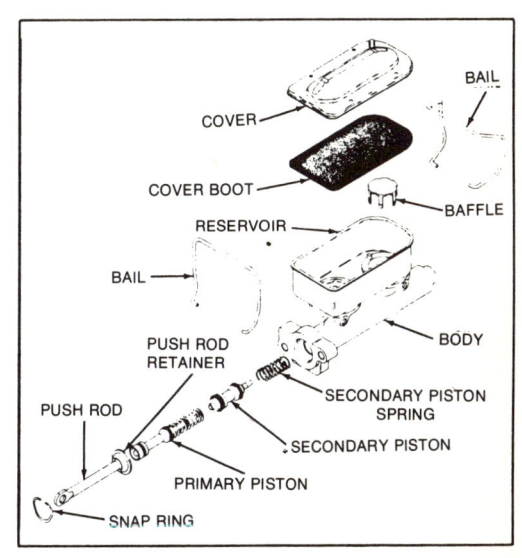

Exploded view of the master cylinder

4. Thoroughly clean all dirt from the master cylinder and the brake lines. Disconnect the brake lines from the master cylinder and plug them to prevent the entry of dirt.

5. Remove the master cylinder securing nuts and remove the master cylinder.

6. Install the master cylinder with its spacer. Tighten the securing nuts to 150 in. lbs.

7. Connect the brake lines to their proper ports. Tighten the nuts to 150 in. lbs.

8. Place the pushrod boot over the end of the pushrod. Secure the pushrod to the brake pedal with the pin and clip.

9. Fill the master cylinder and bleed the entire hydraulic system. After bleeding, fill the master cylinder to within ¼ in. from the top of the reservoir. Check for leaks.

10. Install the air cleaner.

11. Check brake operation before moving the car.

OVERHAUL

If the master cylinder leaks externally, or if the pedal sinks while being held down, the master cylinder is worn. There are three ways to correct this situation:

  a. Buy a new master cylinder;
  b. Trade in the worn unit for a rebuilt unit;

Location of the brake master cylinder

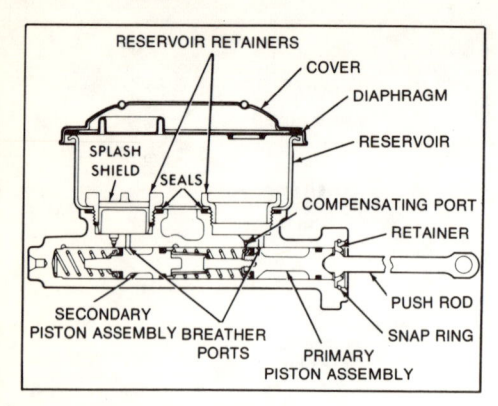

116 BRAKES

Cross-section of the master cylinder

c. Rebuild the old master cylinder with a rebuilding kit.

Your choice depends on the time and finances available.

To rebuild the master cylinder:

1. Remove the old master cylinder from the car as previously outlined.
2. Remove the cover and drain all fluid from the reservoir. Pump the fluid from the cylinder bore by depressing the pushrod.
3. Position the master cylinder in a vise. Use soft wood or rags to protect the cylinder from the vise jaws.
4. Remove the snap-ring.
5. Remove the pushrod and retainer as a unit.
6. Remove the primary piston.

NOTE: *A new primary piston is included in the rebuilding kit, so it's unnecessary to disassemble the old piston.*

7. Remove the secondary piston (it's at the front), and spring by applying air pressure through the front outlet.
8. Make sure that your hands are clean and then use new brake fluid to clean all metal parts thoroughly.
9. Check the cylinder bore for pitting or corrosion. Clean the outlet ports of any dirt and then rewash all parts.
10. Place the parts on a clean rag and allow them to air dry.

NOTE: *Be sure you have the correct rebuilding kit by checking the identification marks on the old secondary piston with those on the new one in the kit.*

11. Install the new secondary piston seals in the grooves of the piston. The seal that is nearest the front end of the piston will have its lip facing toward that end. Be sure that the seal protector is in place. The front seal has the smallest inside diameter.
12. Install the seal retainer and spring seat after the seal is in place.
13. Install the seal on the rear of the secondary piston. The seal should face toward the rear of the piston.
14. Use new brake fluid to coat the bore of the master cylinder and the primary and secondary seals of the front piston.
15. Install the secondary piston spring over the nose of the piston and onto the spring seat.
16. Install the primary piston and pushrod and retainer into the cylinder bore. Hold pressure on the pushrod and install the snap-ring.
17. Fill the master cylinder reservoir with fresh brake fluid and stroke the pushrod several times to bench bleed the cylinder. Snap the retaining bails over the cylinder cover.
18. Install the master cylinder as previously described.
19. Bleed the brakes.

Bleeding

The hydraulic system must be bled whenever the pedal feels spongy, indicating that compressible air has entered the system. The system must be bled whenever any component has been disconnected or there has been a leak.

Brake fluid sometimes becomes contaminated and loses its original qualities. Old brake fluid should be bled from the system and replaced if any part of the hydraulic system becomes corroded or if the fluid is dirty or discolored.

1. Clean off the top of the master cylinder and remove the cover. Check that the fluid

Bleeder valve location on rear brake

level in each reservoir is within ¼ in. of the top.

2. Attach a 7/32 in. inside diameter hose to the bleeder valve at the first wheel to be bled. Start at the wheel farthest from the master cylinder and work closer. Pour a few inches of brake fluid into a clear container and stick the end of the tube below the surface.

NOTE: *The tube and container of brake fluid are not absolutely necessary, but this is a very sloppy job without them.*

3. Open the bleed valve counterclockwise ⅓ turn. Have a helper slowly depress the pedal. Close the valve just before the pedal reaches the end of its travel. Have the helper let the pedal back up.

4. Check the fluid level. If the reservoir runs dry, the procedure will have to be restarted from the beginning.

5. Repeat Step 3 until no more bubbles come out the hose.

6. Repeat the bleeding operation, Steps 3 to 5, at the other three wheels.

7. Check the master cylinder level again.

8. If repeated bleeding has no effect, there is an air leak, probably internally in the master cylinder or in one of the wheel cylinders.

Brake Distribution and Warning Switch Assembly

BRAKE WARNING LIGHT CHECKING

1. Disconnect the electrical lead from the switch terminal and use a jumper wire to connect the lead to a good ground.

2. Turn the ignition to the "On" position. The instrument panel warning lamp should light. If it does not light, either the bulb is burned out or the circuit is defective. Replace the bulb or repair the circuit as necessary.

3. When the warning lamp lights, turn the ignition off, remove the jumper wire, and connect the electrical lead to the brake line switch.

BRAKE WARNING LIGHT SWITCH TESTING

1. Raise the car on a hoist and attach a bleeder hose to a rear brake bleed screw. Immerse the other end of the hose in a container partially filled with clean brake fluid. Check the master cylinder reservoir to make sure that it is full.

2. Turn the ignition switch to "On." Open

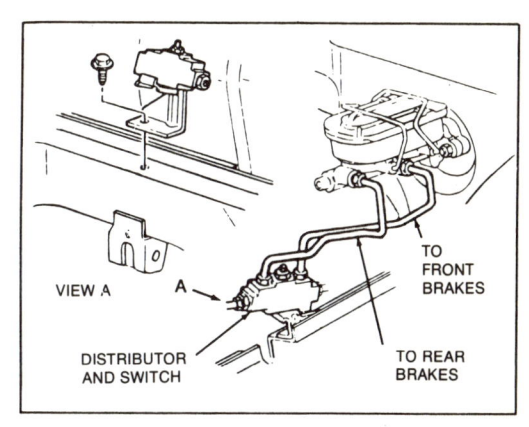

Brake distribution switch assembly mounting

the bleed screw while an assistant applies heavy pressure to the brake pedal. The warning lamp should light. Close the bleed screw before the assistant releases the brake pedal.

3. Repeat Step 2 on a front brake bleed screw. The warning lamp should light again. Turn the ignition off.

4. Lower the car. Check and fill the master cylinder reservoir to the correct level.

NOTE: *If the warning lamp does not light during Steps 2 and 3, but does light when a jumper wire is connected to ground, the warning light switch is defective and must be replaced.*

REMOVAL AND INSTALLATION

The distribution and warning switch assembly is nonadjustable and nonserviceable. It must be replaced if defective.

1. Disconnect the negative battery cable.

2. Clean the switch assembly thoroughly to remove dirt and foreign matter.

3. Disconnect the electrical lead from the switch.

4. Place dry rags below the switch to absorb any brake fluid which may be spilled.

5. Disconnect the hydraulic lines from the switch. If necessary, loosen the lines at the master cylinder to assist removal at the switch. Cover the open lines with clean, lint-free material to prevent the entry of dirt.

6. Remove the mounting screw and remove the switch.

7. Make sure that the new switch is clean and free of dust and lint. If there is any doubt, wash the switch in clean brake fluid and dry with compressed air.

8. Place the switch in its installed position and install its mounting screw. Tighten the mounting screw to 100 in. lbs.

9. Remove the protective covering from

118 BRAKES

the brake lines and connect the lines to the switch. If necessary, tighten the brake lines at the master cylinder. Tighten the brake line nuts at the switch and master cylinder to 150 in. lbs.

10. Connect the electrical lead to the switch.

11. Connect the negative battery cable.

12. Bleed the entire hydraulic system. Fill the master cylinder to within ¼ in. from the top of the reservoir after bleeding. Check for proper brake operation and leaks before moving the car.

FRONT DISC BRAKES

Instead of the traditional expanding brakes that press outward against a circular drum, disc brake systems consist of two cast iron discs with brake pads positioned on either side. Braking action is achieved by the pads squeezing either side of the rotating disc. Dirt and water do not greatly affect braking action since they are thrown off the rotor by centrifugal action or scraped off by the pads. The equal clamping action of the pads tends to ensure uniform, straight stopping. All disc brakes are self-adjusting.

Disc Brake Pads and Caliper

REPLACEMENT

1. Siphon off about one half of the brake fluid in the master cylinder. This is necessary because the new, thicker pads will push the caliper pistons in farther and cause the master cylinder to overflow.

2. Jack up the front of the car and support it safely on jackstands. Remove the wheels.

NOTE: *Always replace brake pads on both wheels. Never replace one pair. Replace pads when worn to within 1/32 in. of the metal pad backing.*

3. Mount a 7 in. C-clamp on the caliper with the solid end on the caliper housing and the screw end on the metal back of the outboard shoe (pad). Tighten the C-clamp to bottom the piston in the cylinder bore and remove the clamp.

4. Remove the two retaining bolts and remove the caliper from the rotor. Do not remove the socket head bolt. Hang the caliper from the front suspension with a chain or heavy wire. Coat hanger wire should be suf-

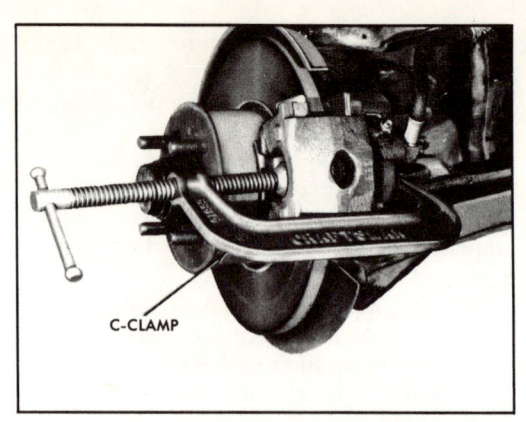

A 7 in. or larger C-clamp is necessary for pad replacement

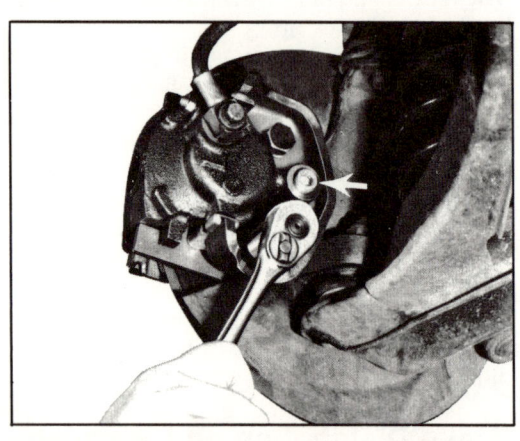

The caliper is retained by two hex head bolts. Don't remove the socket head bolt (arrow).

ficient. Don't let the caliper hang with the brake hose as its support.

5. Remove the old pads. If the shoe retaining spring doesn't come out with the inboard pad, remove it from the piston.

6. Blow any dirt out of the caliper and check that the piston boot isn't damaged or leaking fluid.

7. Install the new pads in the same locations as the old ones. Before installing the inboard pad, be sure that the retaining spring is properly positioned. Push the tab on the single leg end of the spring down into the pad hole, and then snap the other two legs over the edge of the pad notch.

8. Position the caliper over the rotor (disc). Install the two retaining bolts and tighten them to 70 ft lbs.

9. Using a large pair of Channel Lock® pliers, clinch the outboard pad to the caliper. Position the lower jaw of the pliers on the bottom edge of the outboard pad. Place the upper jaw of the pliers on the outboard pad

BRAKES 119

Clinching the brake pad tabs

tab. Squeeze the pliers firmly to bend the tab. Clinch the other end of the outboard pad the same way.

10. Install the wheels and lower the car.
11. Refill the master cylinder with fresh fluid.
12. Pump the brake pedal several times to push the pads in on the rotor. Check the fluid level in the master cylinder after this has been done. Do not move the car until a firm pedal is obtained.
13. Carefully road test the car.

CALIPER OVERHAUL

1. Remove the caliper as previously described. Disconnect the brake line and remove the brake pads.
2. Clean all dirt from the brake hose-to-caliper connection.
3. Seal the brake line fitting to prevent dirt from entering the caliper.
4. Clean the outside of the caliper using fresh brake fluid and place it on a clean work surface.
5. Drain all brake fluid from the caliper.
6. Remove the retainer bolt and slide the mounting bracket off the caliper.
7. Remove the sleeve and two bushings, one from the retainer bolt and one from the groove in the caliper mounting hole. If the clips do not fall off when the bracket is removed, take them off and remove the cushions.
8. Use rags to cushion the inside of the caliper and remove the piston by applying

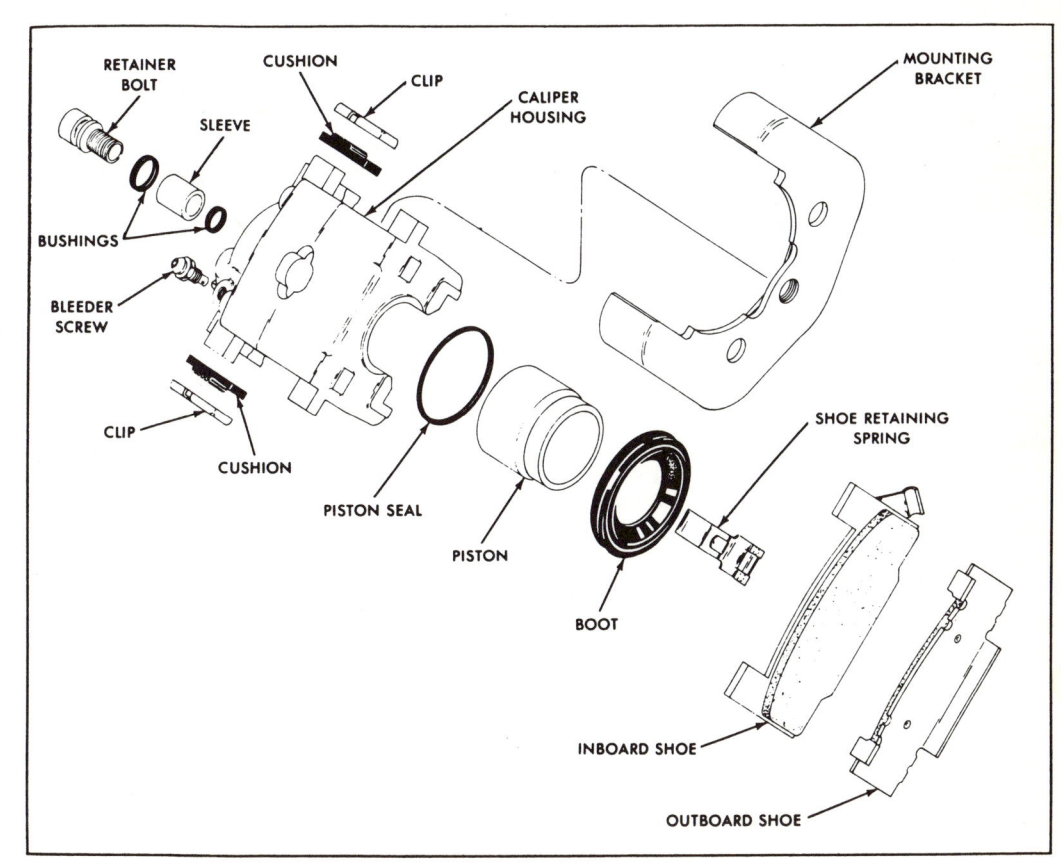

Exploded view of the caliper and brake pads (shoes)

BRAKES

compressed air into the caliper inlet hole. Use just enough pressure to ease out the piston; excessive pressure may cause damage to the piston when it flies out of the caliper. Another method of removing the piston is to depress the brake pedal slowly and gently with the hydraulic lines still connected. This will push the piston out of the caliper.

NOTE: *Never place your hands in the way of the piston as it can fly out with considerable force.*

9. Use a screwdriver to pry the piston boot out of the caliper. Extend the screwdriver across the caliper bore, under the boot, and pry it up. Be careful not to gouge the cylinder bore, or the caliper will have to be replaced.

10. Use a piece of wood or plastic (a plastic knitting needle is perfect), to remove the seal from its groove in the caliper bore. Using a metal tool will damage the bore surface.

11. Remove the bleeder valve from the caliper.

12. Buy a high quality caliper rebuilding kit, preferably original equipment type.

13. Clean all metal parts in fresh brake fluid. Never use other solvents for cleaning, as gasoline or paint thinner will ruin the rubber parts.

14. Inspect all parts for rust or other damage. The caliper bore should be free from corrosion or nicks. Replace any suspect parts. Minor stains or corrosion can be polished out of the caliper bore with *crocus cloth,* but heavily damaged pieces should be discarded.

15. Lubricate the caliper bore and the new piston seal with fresh brake fluid. Position the seal in the caliper bore groove.

16. Lubricate the piston with fresh brake fluid and assemble a new boot into the piston groove so that the fold faces the open end of the piston.

17. Insert the piston into the caliper being careful not to dislodge the seal. Force the piston down to the bottom in the bore. This requires about 50–100 lbs of force.

18. Place the outside diameter of the boot in the caliper counterbore and seat it with a bushing driver of the same diameter as the boot.

19. Install the bleeder screw.

20. Fit new cushions on the caliper lugs. Stretch the cushions over the lugs, fitting the heavy section in the lug recess, with the sawtooth edges of the cushions pointing out.

21. Liberally lubricate the sleeve and bushings, inside and out, and the unthreaded

Installing the boot in the caliper using a bushing driver

portion of the retainer bolt with silicone lubricant.

22. Fit the larger bushing in the caliper mounting hole groove and install the sleeve.

23. Position the smaller bushing in the groove in the retainer bolt.

24. Clamp the caliper in a vise, mounting lug up, across the pad openings. Fit the clips over the cushions and squeeze the mounting bracket down over the clips, lining up the retainer bolt hole.

25. Move the bracket against the retainer boss on the caliper and install the retainer bolt. Tighten the bolt to 28 ft lbs.

NOTE: *It may be very difficult to squeeze the bracket over the cushions and clips on the caliper. Start with the open end of the bracket over the ends of the clips near the boot and move the bracket towards the closed end of the piston housing.*

26. Install the caliper. Use new copper gaskets on the brake hose connection. Bleed the brakes.

Brake Disc

REMOVAL AND INSTALLATION

1. Jack up the front of the car and support it safely on jackstands.

2. Remove the wheel and tire.

3. Remove the brake caliper as previously described.

4. Remove the hub dust cap, cotter pin, spindle nut and washer, and remove the disc. Do not allow the bearing to fall out of the hub when removing the disc.

5. Remove the outer bearing with the fingers.

6. Remove the inner bearing by prying out the grease seal. Discard the seal.

7. Thoroughly clean all parts in solvent and blow dry.

8. Check the bearings for cracked separators or pitting. Check the races for scoring or pitting.

NOTE: *If it is necessary to replace either the inner or outer bearing it will also be necessary to replace the race for that bearing.*

9. Drive out the old race from the hub with a brass drift inserted behind the race in the notches in the hub.

10. Lubricate the new race with a light film of grease.

11. Use the proper tool to start the race squarely into the hub and carefully seat it.

12. Pack the inner and outer bearings with high melting point wheel bearing grease.

13. Place the inner bearing in the hub and install a new grease seal. The seal should be installed flush with the hub surface. Use a block of wood to seat the seal.

14. Install the disc over the spindle.

15. Press the outer bearing firmly into the hub by hand.

16. Install the spindle washer and nut. Adjust the wheel bearings as outlined in "Front Wheel Bearing Adjustment," following.

17. Install the brake caliper. Tighten the brake caliper mounting bolts to 70 ft lbs.

18. Install the wheel and tire.

19. Lower the car.

Front Wheel Bearings

INSPECTION

1. Raise the car and support it at the front lower control arm.

2. Spin the wheel to check for unusual noise or roughness.

3. If the bearings are noisy, tight, or excessively loose they should be cleaned, inspected, and relubricated before adjustment.

4. Grip the tire at the top and bottom and move the wheel assembly in and out on the spindle. Measure the movement of the hub, it should be 0.001–0.005 in. If not, adjust the bearings.

ADJUSTMENT

1. Raise the car and support it at the front lower control arm.

Pry the dust cover off with a large, flat-bladed screwdriver

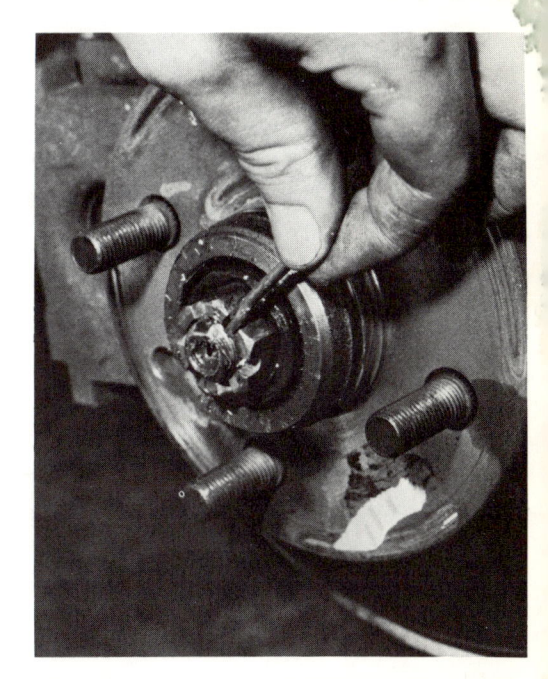

Unbend the cotter pin and remove it from the spindle nut

2. Remove the hub cap or wheel cover from the wheel. Remove the dust cap from the hub.

3. Remove the cotter pin from the spindle.

4. Spin the wheel forward by hand and

122 BRAKES

Hand-tighten (approx. 12 ft lbs), the spindle nut to seat the wheel bearings

Tap the dustcover back on with a soft-faced hammer

tighten the spindle nut to 12 ft lbs. This will fully seat the bearings.

5. Back off the nut to the "just loose" position.

6. Hand-tighten the spindle nut. Loosen the spindle nut until either hole in the spindle aligns with a slot in the nut, but not more than ½ flat.

7. Install a new cotter pin, bend the ends of the pin against the nut, and cut off any extra length to avoid interference with the dust cap.

8. Measure the end-play in the hub. Proper bearing adjustment should give 0.001–0.005 in. of end-play.

9. Install the dust cap on the hub and the hub cap or wheel cover on the wheel.

10. Lower the car.

11. Adjust the opposite front wheel bearings in the same manner.

REMOVAL AND INSTALLATION

For wheel bearing removal and installation procedure see "Brake Disc Removal and Installation".

REAR DRUM BRAKES

Drum brakes employ two brake shoes mounted on a stationary backing plate. These shoes are positioned inside a circular cast iron drum which rotates with the wheel assembly. The shoes are held in place by springs; this allows them to slide toward the drums (when they are applied) while keeping the linings and drums in alignment. The shoes are actuated by a wheel cylinder which is mounted at the top of the backing plate. When the brakes are applied, hydraulic pressure forces the wheel cylinder's two actuating links outward. Since these links bear directly against the top of the brake shoes, the tops of the shoes are then forced outward against the inner side of the drum. This action forces the bottoms of the two shoes to contact the brake drum by rotating the entire assembly slightly (known as servo action). When pressure within the wheel cylinder is relaxed, return springs pull the shoes back away from the drum.

Most modern drum brakes are designed to self-adjust themselves during application when the vehicle is moving in reverse. This motion causes both shoes to rotate very slightly with the drum, rocking an adjusting lever, thereby causing rotation of the adjusting screw by means of a star wheel.

The duo-servo brake with pin and slot adjusters is a new design used only on the Chevette.

Brake Shoes
REPLACEMENT

1. Remove the brake drum.

NOTE: *If the brake drum is stubborn in*

BRAKES 123

Remove the spring washers (arrows) before attempting to remove the drum

coming off, rotate the adjusters on the back of the brake toward the axle tube to retract the shoes from the drum.

2. Loosen the equalizer to let all tension from the parking brake cable.
3. Unhook the parking brake cable from the lever.
4. Use pliers to remove the long shoe pull back spring at the top.
5. Use pliers to remove the shoe hold down springs and retainers from the middle of each shoe.
6. Separate the shoes at the top and remove them.
7. Check that the adjusters work properly; it should take 29–36 ft lbs. torque to turn the adjusters. The adjusters and backing plate must be replaced as an assembly.
8. Lubricate the shoe contact surfaces on the backing plate and all pivot points with brake lubricant. Lubricate the parking brake cable.
9. Lubricate the pivot end of the parking brake lever and attach the lever to the shoe.
10. Connect the shoes at the bottom with the retaining spring.
11. Place the shoes in position and fasten the front shoe with the hold down spring and

Unhooking the parking brake cable

Removing the hold-down springs and retainers

Rotate adjuster bolts in direction of arrows to retract shoes

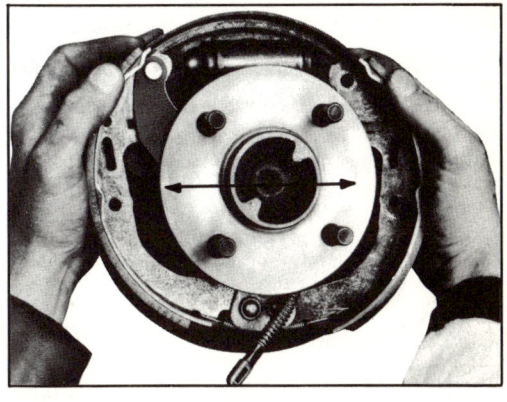

Removing the brake shoes (linings)

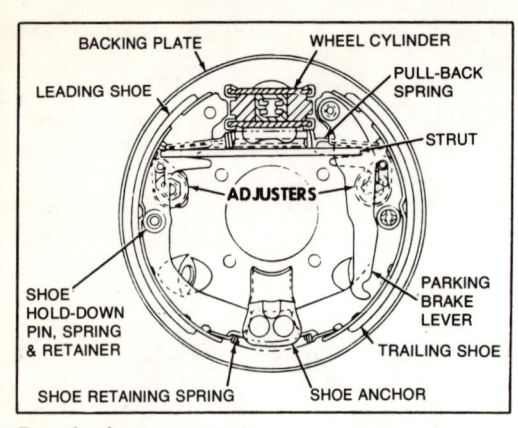

Rear brake components

retainer. Be sure that the adjuster peg is in the shoe slot.

12. Install the parking brake lever to front shoe strut. Fasten down the rear shoe with the hold down spring and retainer. Be sure that the adjuster peg is in the shoe slot.
13. Install the shoe pull back spring.
14. Attach the end of the parking brake cable to the lever.
15. Replace the drum. Adjust the brakes by applying the brake several times until the pedal is firm. Check the fluid level frequently. Adjust the parking brake.

Wheel Cylinders

It is the best practice to overhaul or replace both rear wheel cylinders if either one is found to be leaking. If this is not done, the undisturbed cylinder will probably develop a leak soon after the first repair job. New wheel cylinders are available at a price low enough to make overhaul impractical, except in emergency situations.

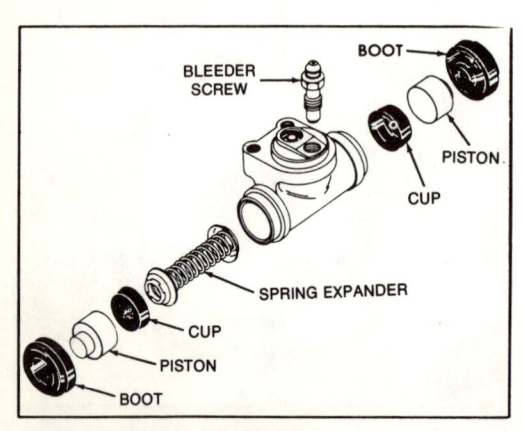

Exploded view of a wheel cylinder

OVERHAUL

1. Disassemble the brake system as described under "Brake Shoe Replacement."
2. Unbolt the wheel cylinder from the backing plate.
3. Remove and discard the rubber boots, the pistons, and the cups.
4. Clean all parts in brake fluid or denatured alcohol.
5. If there are any pits or roughness inside the cylinder, it must be replaced. Polish off any discolored area by removing the cylinder around a piece of crocus cloth held by a finger. Do not polish the cylinder in a lengthwise direction. Clean the cylinder again after polishing. Air dry.
6. Replace the piston if it is scratched or damaged in any way.
7. Lubricate the cylinder bore with clean brake fluid and insert the spring and the expanders.
8. Install the new cups with the flat side to the outside. Do not lubricate them.
9. Install the new boot onto the piston and insert the piston into the cylinder with the flat surface towards the center of the cylinder. Do not lubricate the pistons before the installation.
10. Replace the cylinder and tighten the bolts evenly.
11. Reassemble the brake system and bleed the brake hydraulic system.

PARKING BRAKE

Cable

ADJUSTMENT

1. Raise the car.
2. Apply the parking brake one notch from the fully released position.
3. Tighten the parking brake cable, equalizer adjusting nut until a light drag is felt when the rear wheels are rotated forward. The equalizer adjusting nut should be tightened to 55 in. lbs at its adjustment point.
4. Fully release the parking brake and rotate the rear wheels. There should be no drag.
5. Lower the car.

REMOVAL AND INSTALLATION

1. Raise the car.
2. Disconnect the parking brake equalizer spring and equalizer.

BRAKES 125

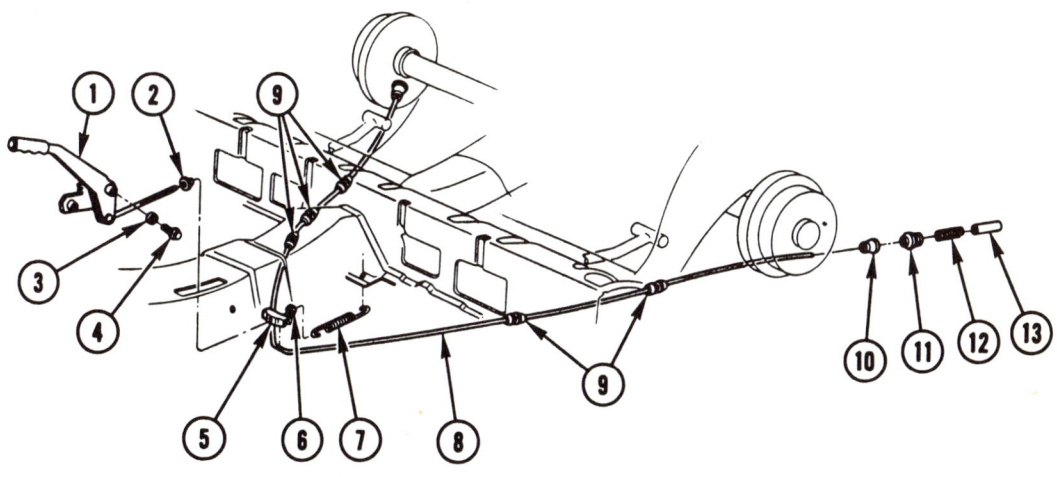

1. Parking brake lever
2. Grommet
3. Washer
4. Bolt and washer
5. Equalizer
6. Nut
7. Spring
8. Cable
9. Grommet
10. Boot
11. Grommet
12. Spring
13. Eye

Parking brake components

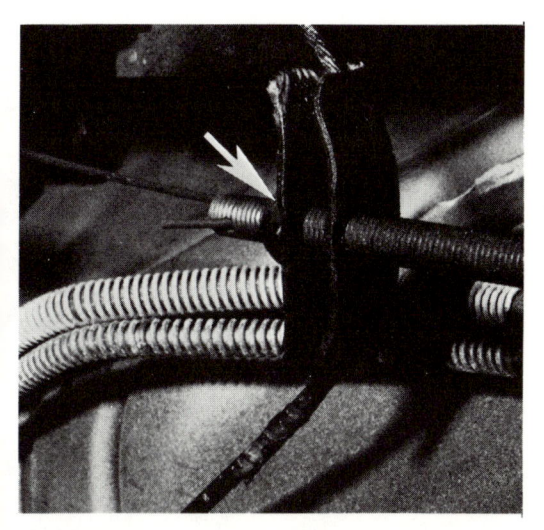

Parking brake cable is adjusted by turning the equalizer nut (arrow) in or out as necessary

3. Remove the cable from the underbody mounting brackets.
4. Remove the wheel and brake drum. With the rear brakes exposed, remove the parking brake cable from the parking brake lever.
5. Remove the spring locking clip and push out the cable grommets at the flange plate entry hole and remove the cable.
6. To install, pass the cable end through the flange plate entry hole making sure that the grommets are in place on the flange plate, and install the spring locking clips.
7. Connect the cable end to the parking brake lever.
8. Install the brake drum and the wheel.
9. Install the cable grommets at the un-

Brake Specifications

All measurements in mm, inches are given in parentheses

Year	Model	Master Cylinder Bore	WHEEL CYLINDER OR CALIPER PISTON BORE FRONT	REAR	BRAKE DISC OR DRUM DIAMETER FRONT	REAR
1976–80	All	19.05 (.750)	47.625 (1.875)	19.05 (.750)	245.87 (9.68)	200.15 (7.88)

NOTE: *Drums cannot be turned more than 0.632 mm (0.025 in.)*

BRAKES

derbody mounting brackets. On 1976–77 models, tighten the rear lower control arm bolt to 50 ft lbs; the rear control arm bracket to 50 ft lbs; the front control arm bracket to 15 ft lbs. On 1978–80 models, tighten the rear lower control arm bracket to 33 ft lbs; the rear control arm bolt to 33 ft lbs; the front control arm bracket to 16 ft lbs.

10. Install the equalizer onto the cable.
11. Install the equalizer over the parking brake lever rod and install the equalizer nut. Install the cable return spring.
12. Pre-stress the cable by applying the parking brake two or three times with heavy handle pressure.
13. Adjust the parking brake as previously described.
14. Lubricate the cable at the equalizer and at all grommets.
15. Lower the car.

Body 10

You can repair most minor auto body damage yourself. Minor damage usually falls into one of several categories: (1) small scratches and dings in the paint that can be repaired without the use of body filler, (2) deep scratches and dents that require body filler, but do not require pulling, or hammering metal back into shape and (3) rust-out repairs. The repair sequences illustrated in this chapter are typical of these types of repairs. If you want to get involved in more complicated repairs including pulling or hammering sheet metal back into shape, you will probably need more detailed instructions. Chilton's *Minor Auto Body Repair, 2nd Edition* is a comprehensive guide to repairing auto body damage yourself.

TOOLS AND SUPPLIES

The list of tools and equipment you may need to fix minor body damage ranges from very basic hand tools to a wide assortment of specialized body tools. Most minor scratches, dings and rust holes can be fixed using an electric drill, wire wheel or grinder attachment, half-round plastic file, sanding block, various grades of sandpaper (#36, which is coarse through #600, which is fine) in both wet and dry types, auto body plastic, primer, touch-up paint, spreaders, newspaper and masking tape.

Most manufacturers of auto body repair products began supplying materials to professionals. Their knowledge of the best, most-used products has been translated into body repair kits for the do-it-yourselfer. Kits are available from a number of manufacturers and contain the necessary materials in the required amounts for the repair identified on the package.

Kits are available for a wide variety of uses, including:

- Rusted out metal
- All purpose kit for dents and holes
- Dents and deep scratches
- Fiberglass repair kit
- Epoxy kit for restyling.

Kits offer the advantage of buying what you need for the job. There is little waste and little chance of materials going bad from not being used. The same manufacturers also merchandise all of the individual products used—spreaders, dent pullers, fiberglass cloth, polyester resin, cream hardener, body filler, body files, sandpaper, sanding discs and holders, primer, spray paint, etc.

CAUTION: *Most of the products you will be using contain harmful chemicals, so be extremely careful. Always read the complete label before opening the containers. When*

128 BODY

you put them away for future use, be sure they are out of children's reach!

Most auto body repair kits contain all the materials you need to do the job right in the kit. So, if you have a small rust spot or dent you want to fix, check the contents of the kit before you run out and buy any additional tools.

ALIGNING BODY PANELS

Doors

There are several methods of adjusting doors. Your vehicle will probably use one of those illustrated.

Whenever a door is removed and is to be reinstalled, you should matchmark the position of the hinges on the door pillars. The holes of the hinges and/or the hinge attaching points are usually oversize to permit alignment of doors. The striker plate is also moveable, through oversize holes, permitting up-and-down, in-and-out and fore-and-aft movement. Fore-and-aft movement is made by adding or subtracting shims from behind the striker and pillar post. The striker should be adjusted so that the door closes fully and remains closed, yet enters the lock freely.

DOOR HINGES

Don't try to cover up poor door adjustment with a striker plate adjustment. The gap on each side of the door should be equal and uniform and there should be no metal-to-metal contact as the door is opened or closed.

1. Determine which hinge bolts must be loosened to move the door in the desired direction.
2. Loosen the hinge bolt(s) just enough to allow the door to be moved with a padded pry bar.
3. Move the door a small amount and check the fit, after tightening the bolts. Be sure that there is no bind or interference with adjacent panels.
4. Repeat this until the door is properly positioned, and tighten all the bolts securely.

Hood, Trunk or Tailgate

As with doors, the outline of hinges should be scribed before removal. The hood and trunk can be aligned by loosening the hinge bolts in their slotted mounting holes and moving the hood or trunk lid as necessary.

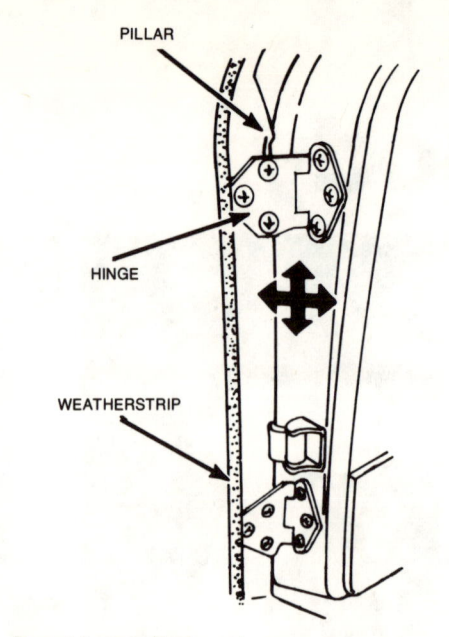

Door hinge adjustment

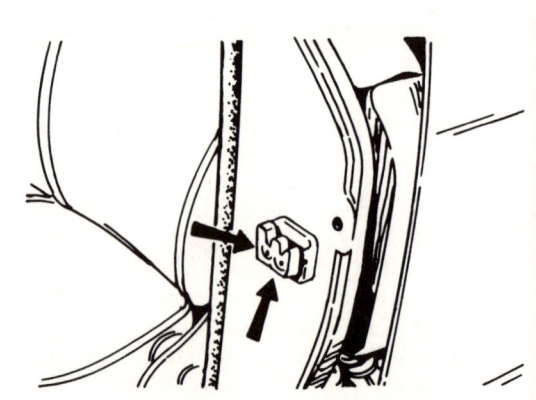

Move the door striker as indicated by arrows

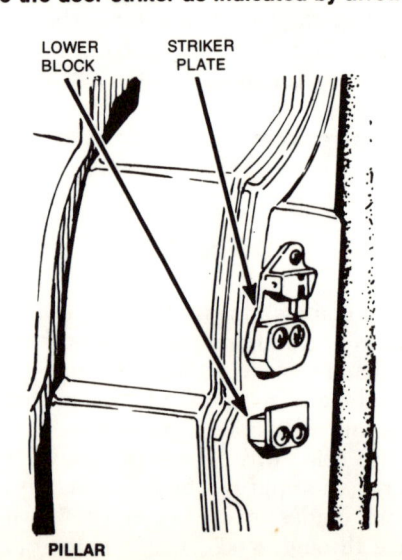

Striker plate and lower block

BODY

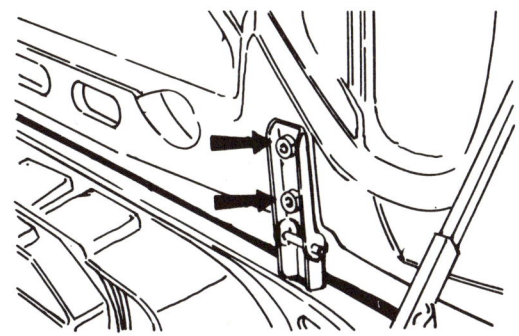

Loosen the hinge boots to permit fore-and-aft and horizontal adjustment

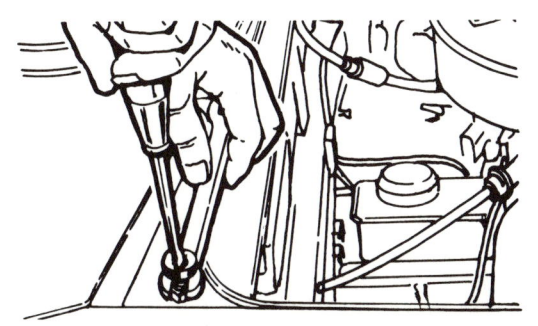

The hood is adjusted vertically by stop-screws at the front and/or rear

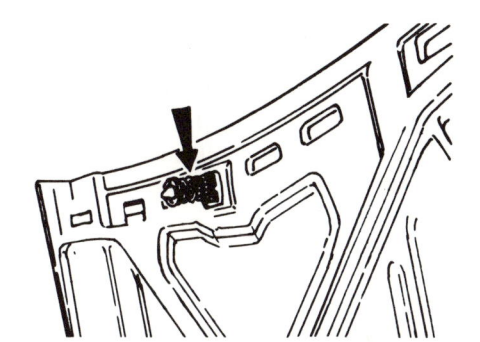

The hood pin can be adjusted for proper lock engagement

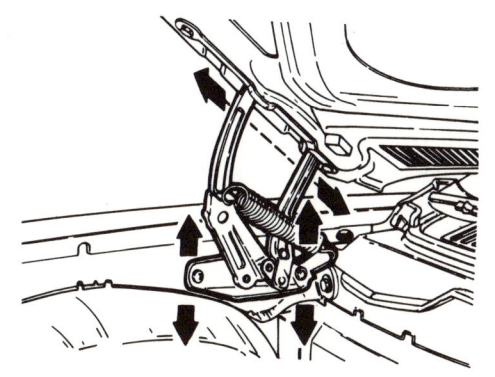

The height of the hood at the rear is adjusted by loosening the bolts that attach the hinge to the body and moving the hood up or down

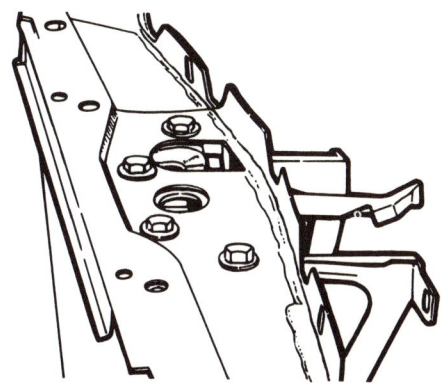

The base of the hood lock can also be repositioned slightly to give more positive lock engagement

The hood and trunk have adjustable catch locations to regulate lock engagement. Bumpers at the front and/or rear of the hood provide a vertical adjustment and the hood lockpin can be adjusted for proper engagement.

The tailgate on the station wagon can be adjusted by loosening the hinge bolts in their slotted mounting holes and moving the tailgate on its hinges. The latchplate and latch striker at the bottom of the tailgate opening can be adjusted to stop rattle. An adjustable bumper is located on each side.

RUST, UNDERCOATING, AND RUSTPROOFING

Rust

Rust is an electrochemical process. It works on ferrous metals (iron and steel) from the inside out due to exposure of unprotected surfaces to air and moisture. The possibility of rust exists practically nationwide—anywhere humidity, industrial pollution or chemical salts are present, rust can form. In coastal areas, the problem is high humidity and salt air; in snowy areas, the problem is chemical salt (de-icer) used to keep the roads clear, and in industrial areas, sulphur dioxide is present in the air from industrial pollution and is changed to sulphuric acid when it rains. The rusting process is accelerated by high temperatures, especially in snowy areas, when vehicles are driven over slushy roads and then left overnight in a heated garage.

Automotive styling also can be a contributor to rust formation. Spot welding of panels creates small pockets that trap moisture and form an environment for rust formation. Fortunately, auto manufacturers have been working hard to increase the corrosion protection of their products. Galvanized sheet metal enjoys much wider use, along with the increased use of plastic and various rust retardant coatings. Manufacturers are also designing out areas in the body where rust-forming moisture can collect.

To prevent rust, you must stop it before it gets started. On new vehicles, there are two ways to accomplish this.

First, the car or truck should be treated with a commercial rustproofing compound. There are many different brands of franchised rustproofers, but most processes involve spraying a waxy "self-healing" compound under the chassis, inside rocker panels, inside doors and fender liners and similar places where rust is likely to form. Prices for a quality rustproofing job range from $100–$250, depending on the area, the brand name and the size of the vehicle.

Ideally, the vehicle should be rustproofed as soon as possible following the purchase. The surfaces of the car or truck have begun to oxidize and deteriorate during shipping. In addition, the car may have sat on a dealer's lot or on a lot at the factory, and once the rust has progressed past the stage of light, powdery surface oxidation rustproofing is not likely to be worthwhile. Professional rustproofers feel that once rust has formed, rustproofing will simply seal in moisture already present. Most franchised rustproofing operations offer a 3–5 year warranty against rust-through, but will not support that warranty if the rustproofing is not applied within three months of the date of manufacture.

Undercoating should not be mistaken for rustproofing. Undercoating is a black, tarlike substance that is applied to the underside of a vehicle. Its basic function is to deaden noises that are transmitted from under the car. It simply cannot get into the crevices and seams where moisture tends to collect. In fact, it may clog up drainage holes and ventilation passages. Some undercoatings also tend to crack or peel with age and only create more moisture and corrosion attracting pockets.

The second thing you should do immediately after purchasing the car is apply a paint sealant. A sealant is a petroleum based product marketed under a wide variety of brand names. It has the same protective properties as a good wax, but bonds to the paint with a chemically inert layer that seals it from the air. If air can't get at the surface, oxidation cannot start.

The paint sealant kit consists of a base coat and a conditioning coat that should be applied every 6–8 months, depending on the manufacturer. The base coat must be applied before waxing, or the wax must first be removed.

Third, keep a garden hose handy for your car in winter. Use it a few times on nice days during the winter for underneath areas, and it will pay big dividends when spring arrives. Spraying under the fenders and other areas which even car washes don't reach will help remove road salt, dirt and other build-ups which help breed rust. Adjust the nozzle to a high-force spray. An old brush will help break up residue, permitting it to be washed away more easily.

It's a somewhat messy job, but worth it in the long run because rust often starts in those hidden areas.

At the same time, wash grime off the door sills and, more importantly, the under portions of the doors, plus the tailgate if you have a station wagon or truck. Applying a coat of wax to those areas at least once before and once during winter will help fend off rust.

When applying the wax to the under parts of the doors, you will note small drain holes. These holes often are plugged with undercoating or dirt. Make sure they are cleaned out to prevent water build-up inside the doors. A small punch or penknife will do the job.

Water from the high-pressure sprays in car washes sometimes can get into the housings for parking and taillights, so take a close look. If they contain water merely loosen the retaining screws and the water should run out.

BODY 131

Repairing Scratches and Small Dents

Step 1. This dent (arrow) is typical of a deep scratch or minor dent. If deep enough, the dent or scratch can be pulled out or hammered out from behind. In this case no straightening is necessary

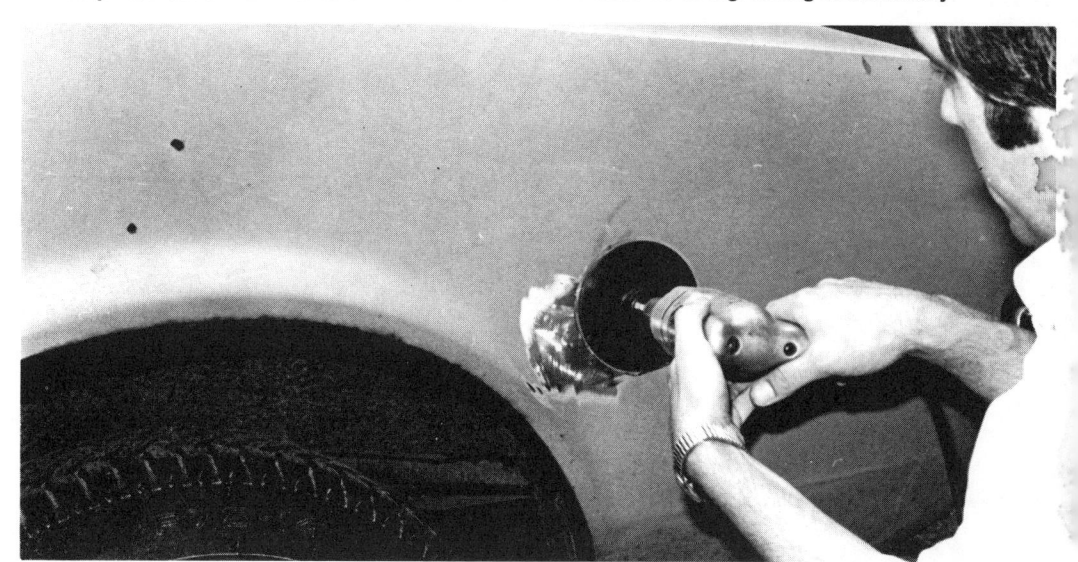

Step 2. Using an 80-grit grinding disc on an electric drill grind the paint from the surrounding area down to bare metal. This will provide a rough surface for the body filler to grab

Step 3. The area should look like this when you're finished grinding

132 BODY

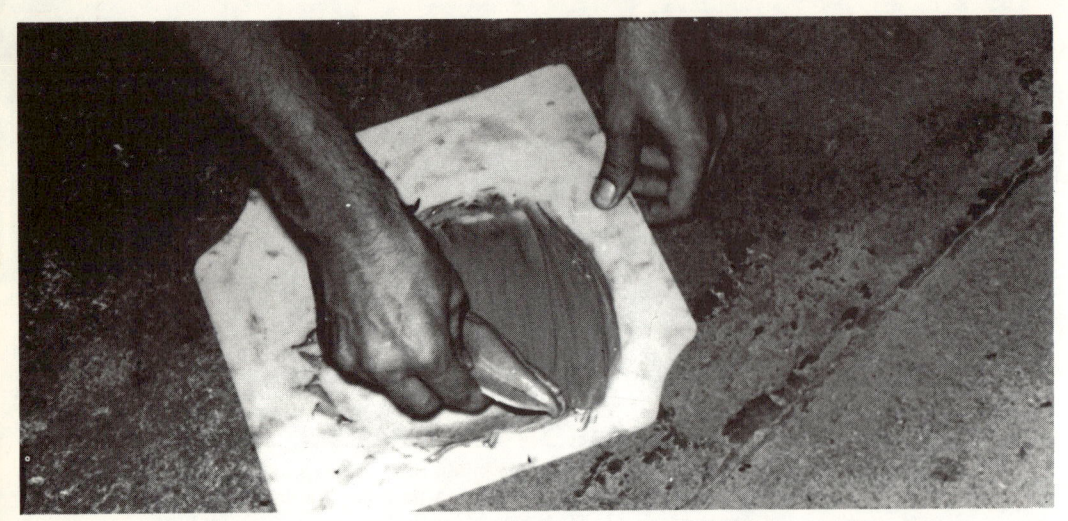

Step 4. Mix the body filler and cream hardener according to the directions

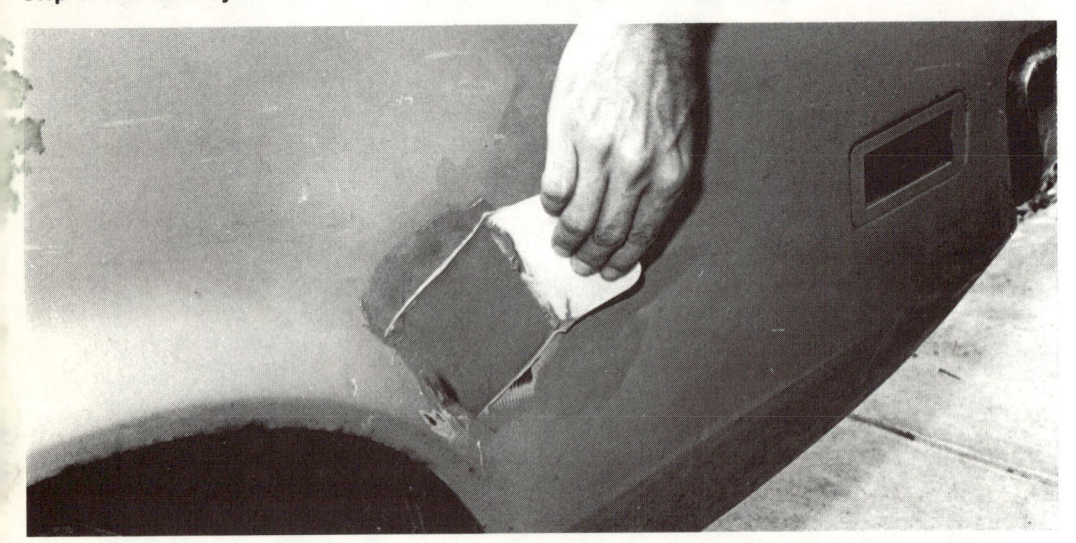

Step 5. Spread the body filler evenly over the entire area. Be sure to cover the area completely

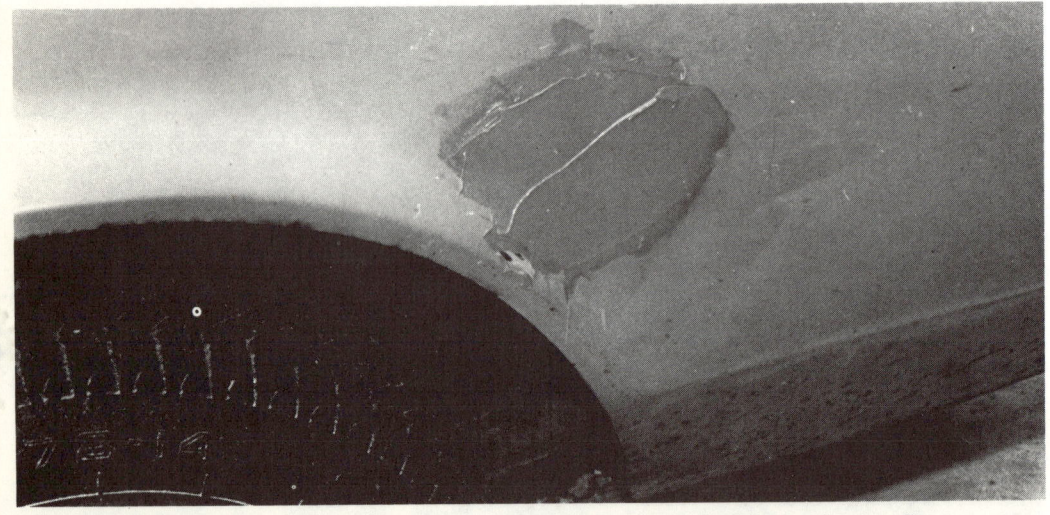

Step 6. Let the body filler dry until the surface can just be scratched with your fingernail

BODY 133

Step 7. Knock the high spots from the body filler with a body file

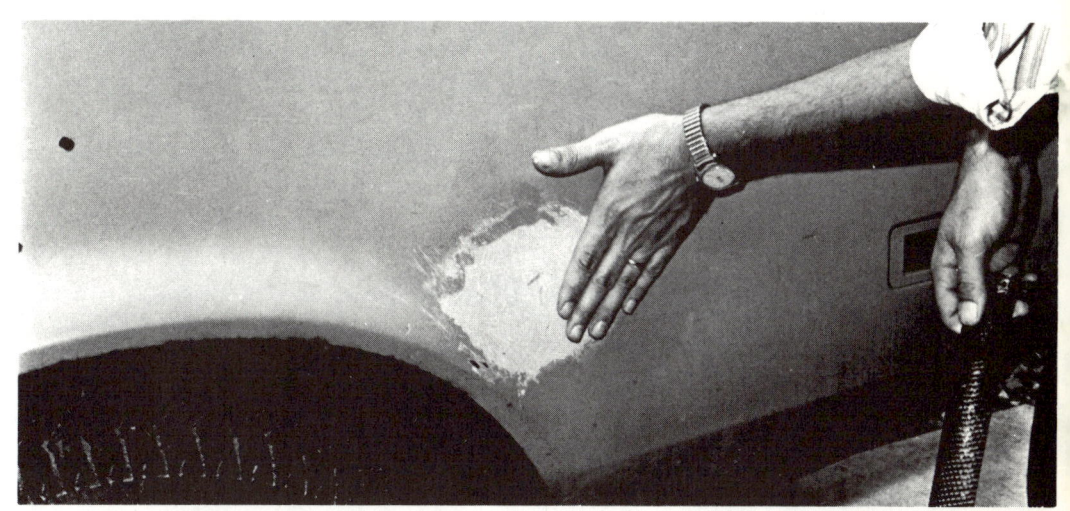

Step 8. Check frequently with the palm of your hand for high and low spots. If you wind up with low spots, you may have to apply another layer of filler

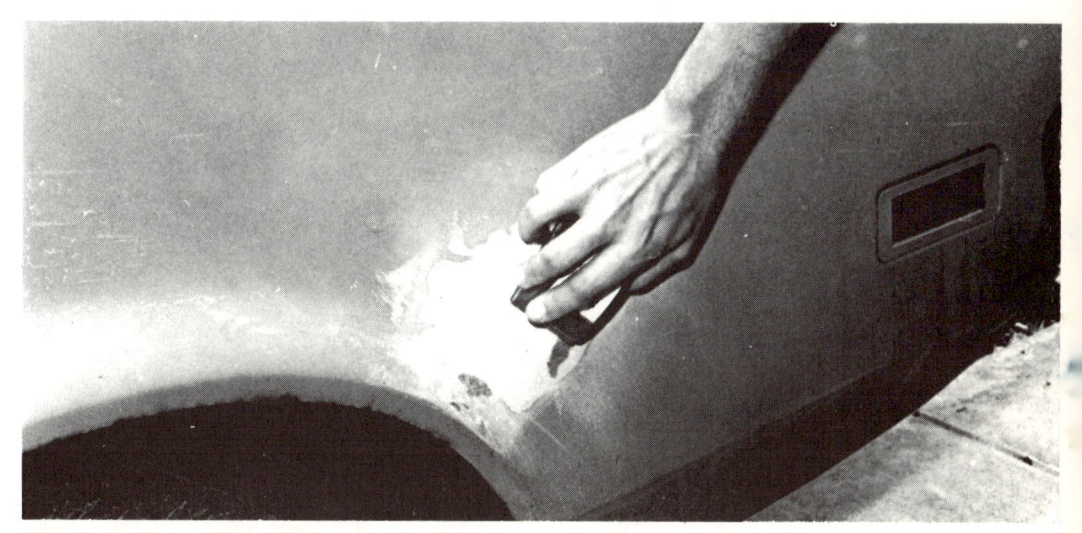

Step 9. Block sand the entire area with 320 grit paper

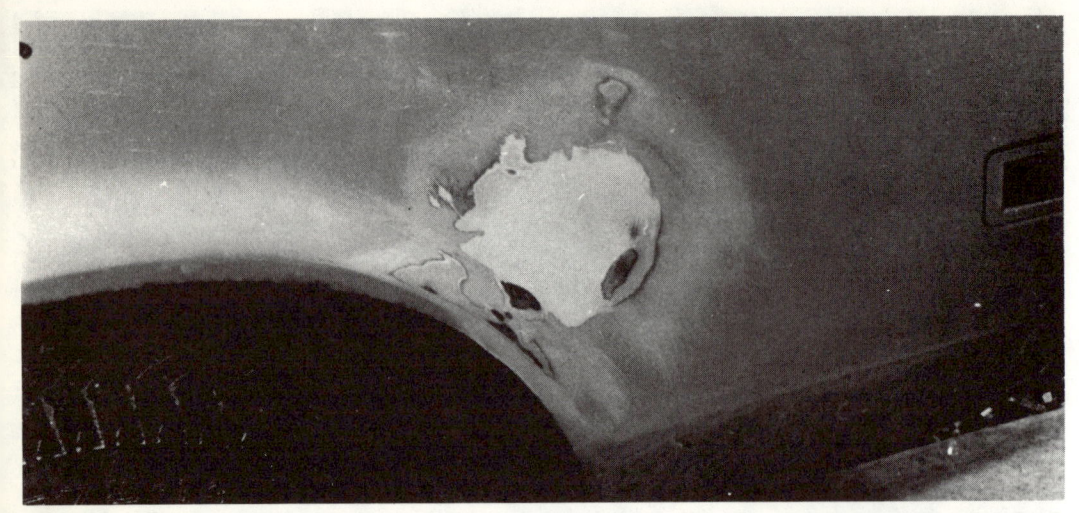

134 BODY

Step 10. When you're finished, the repair should look like this. Note the sand marks extending 2—3 inches out from the repaired area

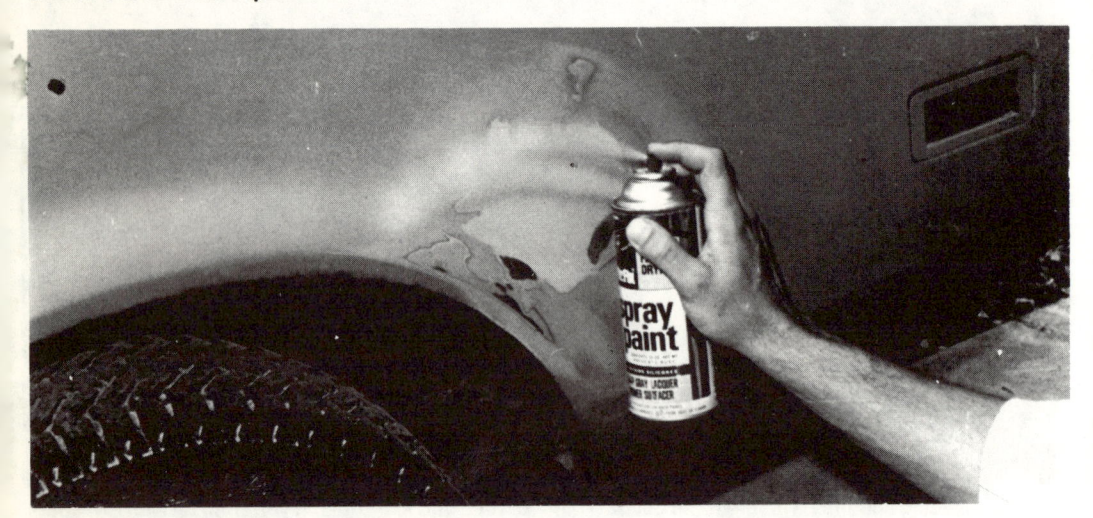

Step 11. Prime the entire area with automotive primer

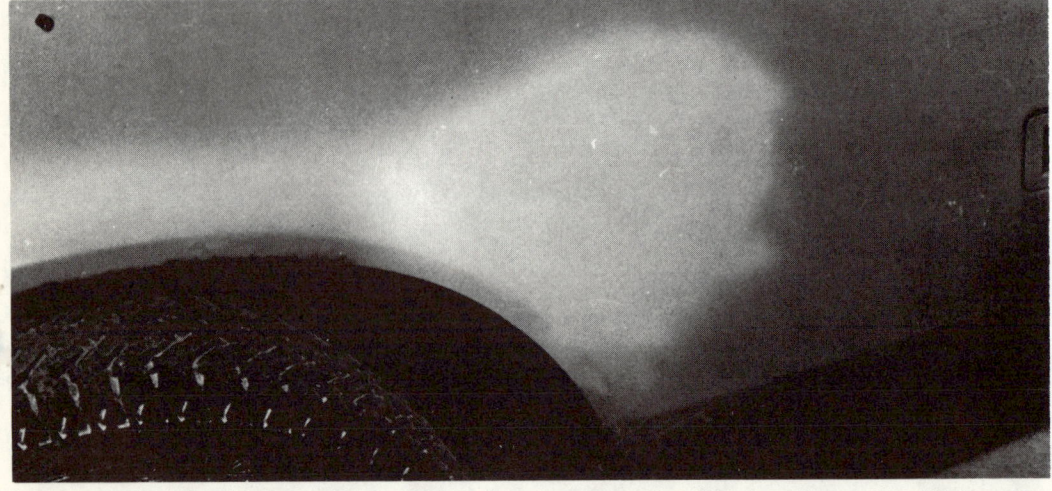

Step 12. The finished repair ready for the final paint coat. Note that the primer has covered the sanding marks (see Step 10). A repair of this size should be able to be spotpainted with good results

REPAIRING RUST HOLES

One thing you have to remember about rust: even if you grind away all the rusted metal in a panel, and repair the area with any of the kits available, *eventually* the rust will return. There are two reasons for this. One, rust is a chemical reaction that causes pressure under the repair from the inside out. That's how the blisters form. Two, the back side of the panel (and the repair) is wide open to moisture, and unpainted body filler acts like a sponge. That's why the best solution to rust problems is to remove the rusted panel and install a new one or have the rusted area cut out and a new piece of sheet metal welded in its place. The trouble with welding is the expense; sometimes it will cost more than the car or truck is worth.

One of the better solutions to do-it-yourself rust repair is the process using a fiberglass cloth repair kit (shown here). This will give a strong repair that resists cracking and moisture and is relatively easy to use. It can be used on large or small holes and also can be applied over contoured surfaces.

Step 1. Rust areas such as this are common and are easily fixed

Step 2. Grind away all traces of rust with a 24-grit grinding disc. Be sure to grind back 3—4 inches from the edge of the hole down to bare metal and be sure all traces of rust are removed

136　BODY

Step 3. Be sure all rust is removed from the edges of the metal. The edges must be ground back to un-rusted metal

Step 4. If you are going to use release film, cut a piece about 2" larger than the area you have sanded. Place the film over the repair and mark the sanded area on the film. Avoid any unnecessary wrinkling of the film

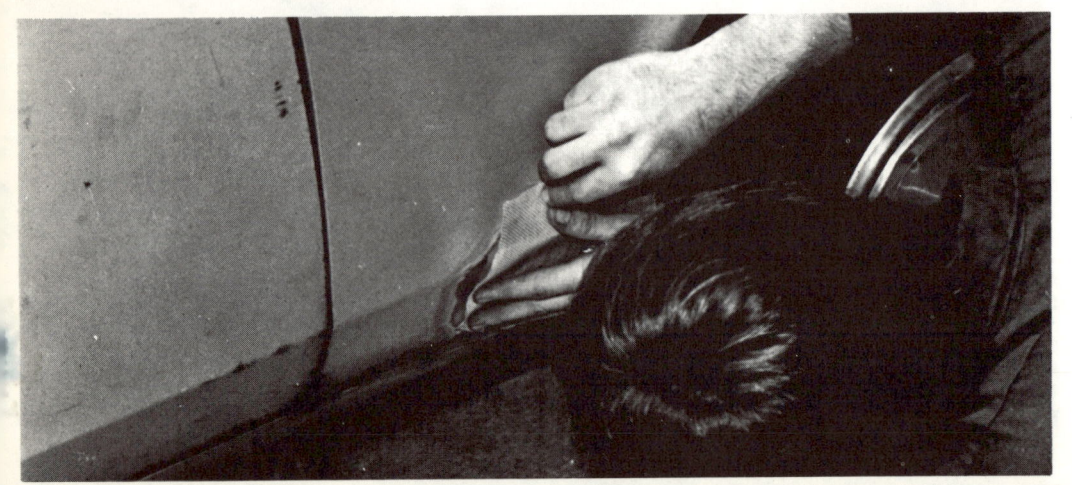

Step 5. Cut 2 pieces of fiberglass matte. One piece should be about 1" smaller than the sanded area and the second piece should be 1" smaller than the first. Use sharp scissors to avoid loose ends

BODY   137

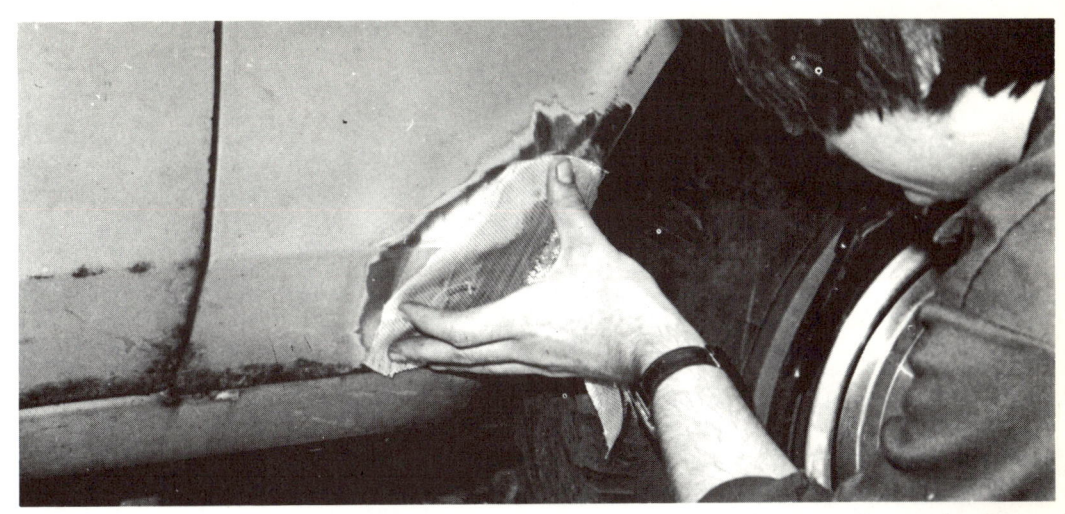

Step 6. Check the dimensions of the release film and cloth by holding them up to the repair area

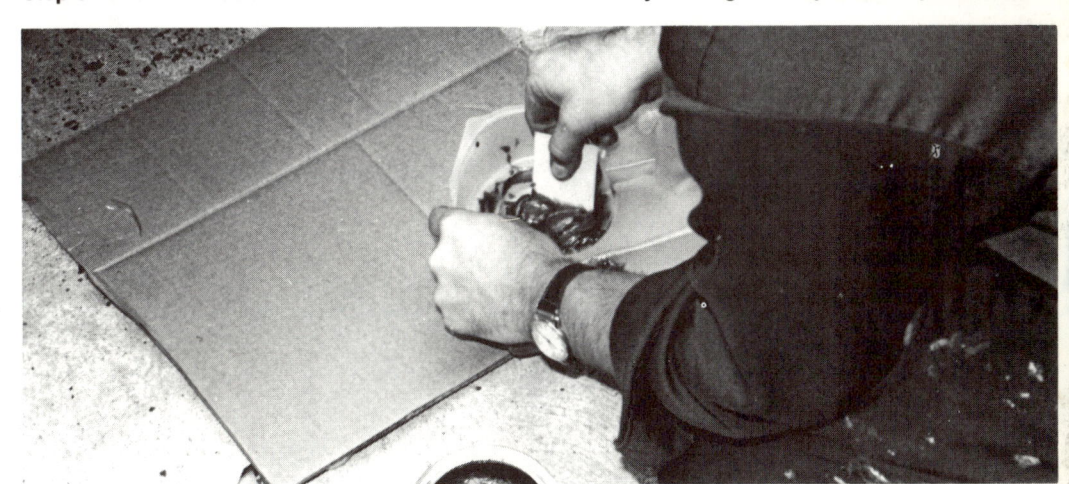

Step 7. Mix enough repair jelly and cream hardener in the mixing tray to saturate the fiberglass material or fill the repair area. Follow the directions on the container

Step 8. Lay the release sheet on a flat surface and spread an even layer of filler, large enough to cover the repair. Lay the smaller piece of fiberglass cloth in the center of the sheet and spread another layer of repair jelly over the fiberglass cloth. Repeat the operation for the larger piece of cloth. If the fiberglass cloth is not used, spread the repair jelly on the release film, concentrated in the middle of the repair

138 BODY

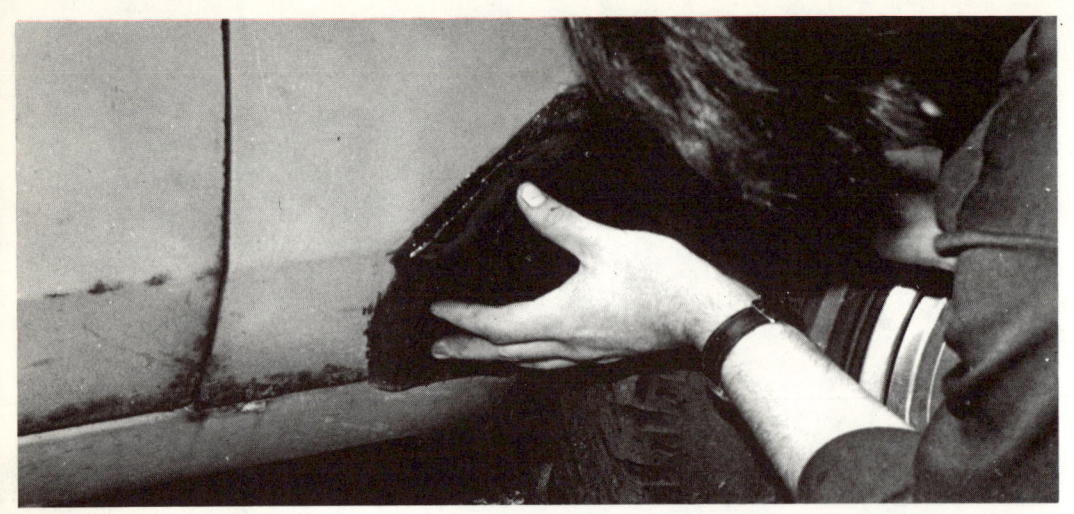

Step 9. Place the repair material over the repair area, with the release film facing outward

Step 10. Use a spreader and work from the center outward to smooth the material, following the body contours. Be sure to remove all air bubbles

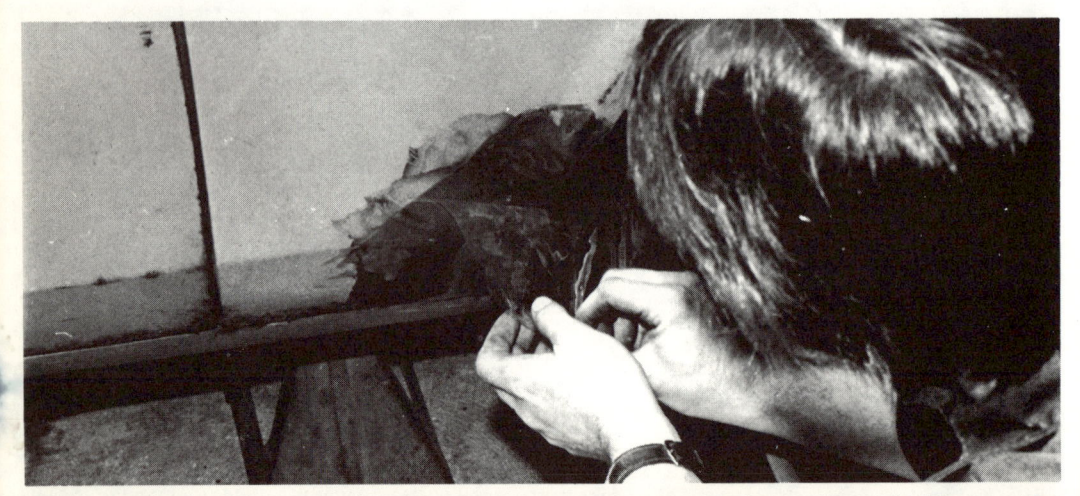

Step 11. Wait until the repair has dried tack-free and peel off the release sheet. The ideal working temperature is 65—90° F. Cooler or warmer temperatures or high humidity may require additional curing time

BODY 139

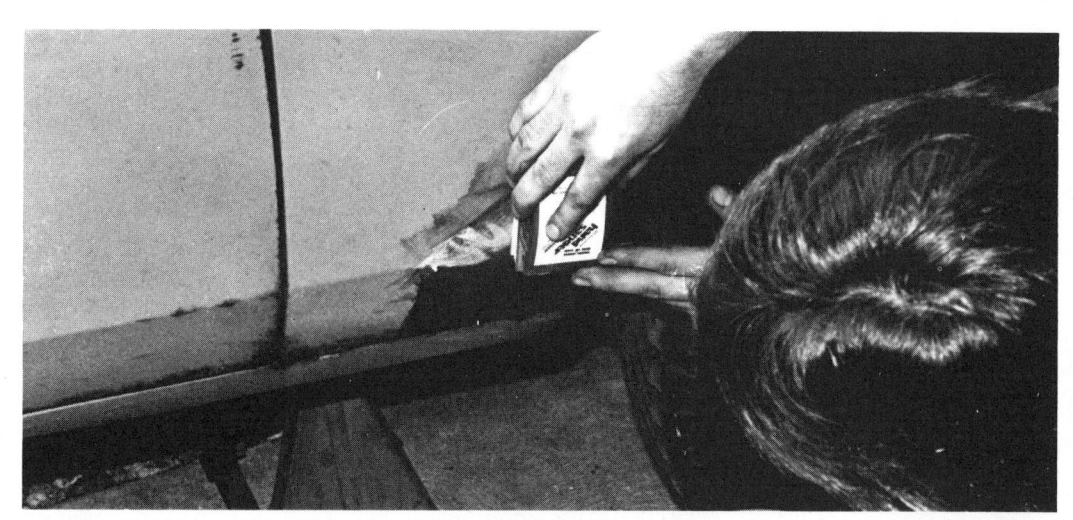

Step 12. Sand and feather-edge the entire area. The initial sanding can be done with a sanding disc on an electric drill if care is used. Finish the sanding with a block sander

Step 13. When the area is sanded smooth, mix some topcoat and hardener and apply it directly with a spreader. This will give a smooth finish and prevent the glass matte from showing through the paint

Step 14. Block sand the topcoat with finishing sandpaper

Step 15. To finish this repair, grind out the surface rust along the top edge of the rocker panel

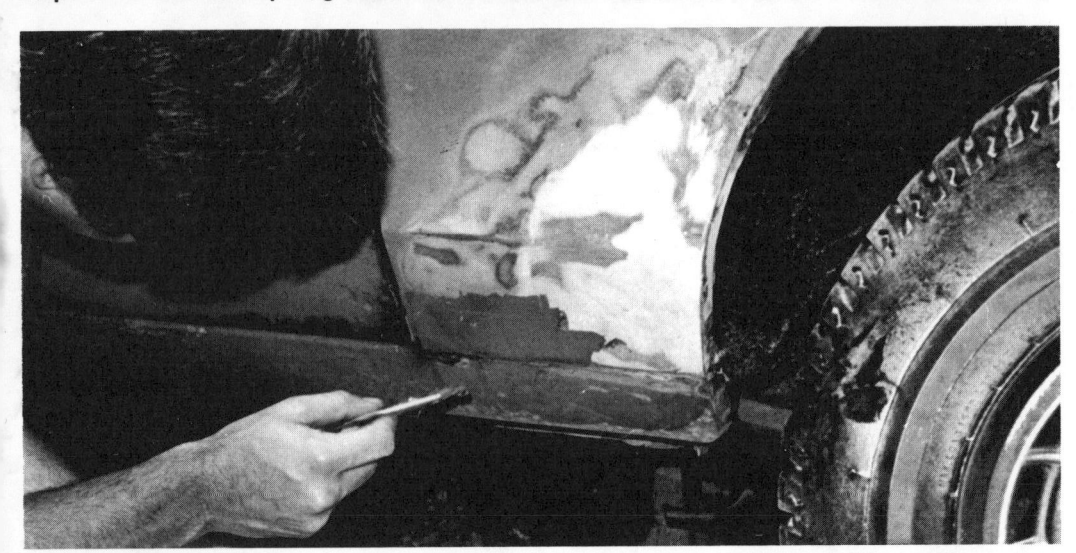

Step 16. Mix some more repair jelly and cream hardener and apply it directly over the surface

Step 17. When it dries tack-free, block sand the surface smooth

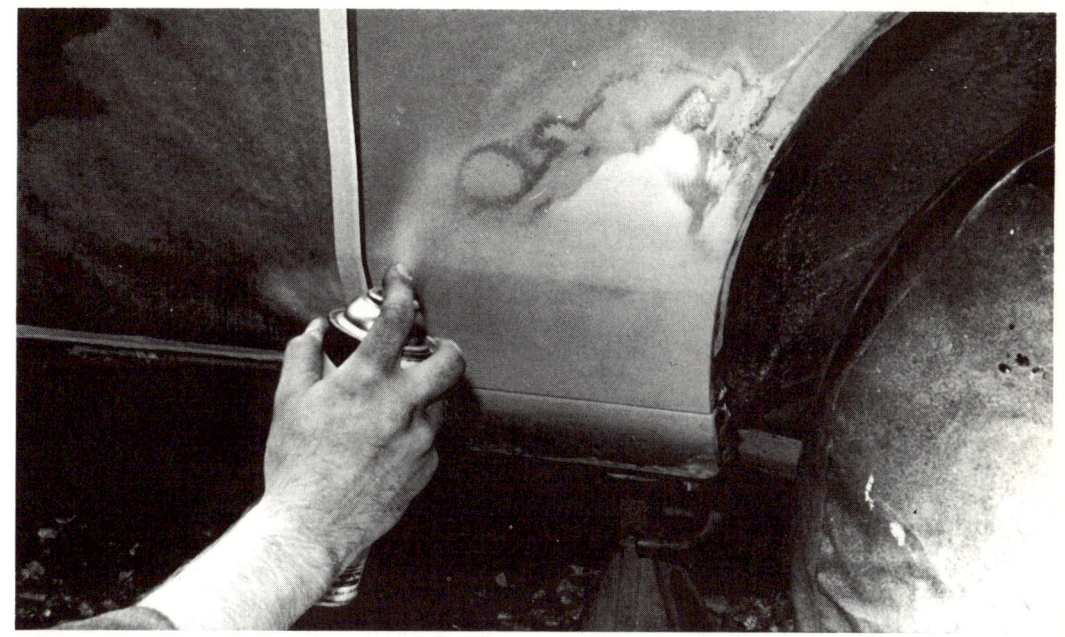

Step 18. If necessary, mask off adjacent panels and spray the entire repair with primer. You are now ready for a color coat

AUTO BODY CARE

There are hundreds—maybe thousands—of products on the market, all designed to protect or aid your car's finish in some manner. There are as many different products as there are ways to use them, but they all have one thing in common—the surface must be clean.

Washing

The primary ingredient for washing your car is water, preferably "soft" water. In many areas of the country, the local water supply is "hard" containing many minerals. The little rings or film that is left on your car's surface after it has dried is the result of "hard" water.

Since you usually can't change the local water supply, the next best thing is to dry the surface before it has a chance to dry itself.

Into the water you usually add soap. Don't use detergents or common, coarse soaps. Your car's paint never truly dries out, but is always evaporating residual oils into the air. Harsh detergents will remove these oils, causing the paint to dry faster than normal. Instead use warm water and a non-detergent soap made especially for waxed surfaces or a liquid soap made for waxed surfaces or a liquid soap made for washing dishes by hand.

Other products that can be used on painted surfaces include baking soda or plain soda water for stubborn dirt.

Wash the car completely, starting at the top, and rinse it completely clean. Abrasive grit should be loaded off under water pressure; scrubbing grit off will scratch the finish. The best washing tool is a sponge, cleaning mitt or soft towel. Whichever you choose, replace it often as each tends to absorb grease and dirt.

Other ways to get a better wash include:

• Don't wash your car in the sun or when the finish is hot.

• Use water pressure to remove caked-on dirt.

• Remove tree-sap and bird effluence immediately. Such substances will eat through wax, polish and paint.

One of the best implements to dry your car is a turkish towel or an old, soft bath towel. Anything with a deep nap will hold any dirt in suspension and not grind it into the paint.

Harder cloths will only grind the grit into the paint making more scratches. Always start drying at the top, followed by the hood and trunk and sides. You'll find there's always more dirt near the rocker panels and wheelwells which will wind up on the rest of the car if you dry these areas first.

Cleaners, Waxes and Polishes

Before going any farther you should know the function of various products.

Cleaners—remove the top layer of dead pigment or paint.

Rubbing or polishing compounds—used to remove stubborn dirt, get rid of minor scratches, smooth away imperfections and partially restore badly weathered paint.

Polishes—contain no abrasives or waxes; they shine the paint by adding oils to the paint.

Waxes—are a protective coating for the polish.

CLEANERS AND COMPOUNDS

Before you apply any wax, you'll have to remove oxidation, road film and other types of pollutants that washing alone will not remove.

The paint on your car never dries completely. There are always residual oils evaporating from the paint into the air. When enough oils are present in the paint, it has a healthy shine (gloss). When too many oils evaporate the paint takes on a whitish cast known as oxidation. The idea of polishing and waxing is to keep enough oil present in the painted surface to prevent oxidation; but when it occurs, the only recourse is to remove the top layer of "dead" paint, exposing the healthy paint underneath.

Products to remove oxidation and road film are sold under a variety of generic names—polishes, cleaner, rubbing compound, cleaner/polish, polish/cleaner, self-polishing wax, pre-wax cleaner, finish restorer and many more. Regardless of name there are two types of cleaners—abrasive cleaners (sometimes called polishing or rubbing compounds) that remove oxidation by grinding away the top layer of "dead" paint, or chemical cleaners that dissolve the "dead" pigment, allowing it to be wiped away.

Abrasive cleaners, by their nature, leave thousands of minute scratches in the finish, which must be polished out later. These should only be used in extreme cases, but are usually the only thing to use on badly oxidized paint finishes. Chemical cleaners are much milder but are not strong enough for severe cases of oxidation or weathered paint.

The most popular cleaners are liquid or paste abrasive polishing and rubbing compounds. Polishing compounds have a finer abrasive grit for medium duty work. Rubbing compounds are a coarser abrasive and for heavy duty work. Unless you are familiar with how to use compounds, be very careful. Excessive rubbing with any type of compound or cleaner can grind right through the paint to primer or bare metal. Follow the directions on the container—depending on type, the cleaner may or may not be OK for your paint. For example, some cleaners are not formulated for acrylic lacquer finishes.

When a small area needs compounding or heavy polishing, it's best to do the job by hand. Some people prefer a powered buffer for large areas. Avoid cutting through the paint along styling edges on the body. Small, hand operations where the compound is applied and rubbed using cloth folded into a thick ball allow you to work in straight lines along such edges.

To avoid cutting through on the edges when using a power buffer, try masking tape. Just cover the edge with tape while using power. Then finish the job by hand with the tape removed. Even then work carefully. The paint tends to be a lot thinner along the sharp ridges stamped into the panels.

Whether compounding by machine or by hand, only work on a small area and apply the compound sparingly. If the materials are spread too thin, or allowed to sit too long, they dry out. Once dry they lose the ability to deliver a smooth, clean finish. Also, dried out polish tends to cause the buffer to stick in one spot. This in turn can burn or cut through the finish.

WAXES AND POLISHES

Your car's finish can be protected in a number of ways. A cleaner/wax or polish/cleaner followed by wax or variations of each all provide good results. The two-step approach (polish followed by wax) is probably slightly better but consumes more time and effort. Properly fed with oils, your paint should never need cleaning, but despite the best polishing job, it won't last unless it's protected with wax. Without wax, polish must be renewed at least once a month to prevent oxidation. Years ago (some still swear by it today), the best wax was made from the Brazilian palm, the Carnuba, favored for its vegetable base and high melting point. However, modern synthetic waxes are harder, which means they protect against moisture better, and chemically inert silicone is used for a long lasting protection. The only problem with silicone wax is that it penetrates all layers of paint. To repaint or touch up a panel or car protected by silicone wax, you have to completely strip the finish to avoid "fisheyes."

Under normal conditions, silicone waxes will last 4–6 months, but you have to be careful of wax build-up from too much waxing. Too thick a coat of wax is just as bad as no wax at all; it stops the paint from breathing.

Combination cleaners/waxes have become popular lately because they remove the old layer of wax plus light oxidation, while putting on a fresh coat of wax at the same time. Some cleaners/waxes contain abrasive cleaners which require caution, although many cleaner/waxes use a chemical cleaner.

Applying Wax or Polish

You may view polishing and waxing your car as a pleasant way to spend an afternoon, or as a boring chore, but it has to be done to keep the paint on your car. Caring for the paint doesn't require special tools, but you should follow a few rules.

1. Use a good quality wax.
2. Before applying any wax or polish, be sure the surface is completely clean. Just because the car looks clean, doesn't mean it's ready for polish or wax.
3. If the finish on your car is weathered, dull, or oxidized, it will probably have to be compounded to remove the old or oxidized paint. If the paint is simply dulled from lack of care, one of the non-abrasive cleaners known as polishing compounds will do the trick. If the paint is severely scratched or really dull, you'll probably have to use a rubbing compound to prepare the finish for waxing. If you're not sure which one to use, use the polishing compound, since you can easily ruin the finish by using too strong a compound.
4. Don't apply wax, polish or compound in direct sunlight, even if the directions on the can say you can. Most waxes will not cure properly in bright sunlight and you'll probably end up with a blotchy looking finish.
5. Don't rub the wax off too soon. The result will be a wet, dull looking finish. Let the wax dry thoroughly before buffing it off.
6. A constant debate among car enthusiasts is how wax should be applied. Some maintain pastes or liquids should be applied in a circular motion, but body shop experts have long thought that this approach results in barely detectable circular abrasions, especially on cars that are waxed frequently. They advise rubbing in straight lines, especially if any kind of cleaner is involved.
7. If an applicator is not supplied with the wax, use a piece of soft cheesecloth or very soft lint-free material. The same applies to buffing the surface.

SPECIAL SURFACES

One-step combination cleaner and wax formulas shouldn't be used on many of the special surfaces which abound on cars. The one-step materials contain abrasives to achieve a clean surface under the wax top coat. The abrasives are so mild that you could clean a car every week for a couple of years without fear of rubbing through the paint. But this same level of abrasiveness might, through repeated use, damage decals used for special trim effects. This includes wide stripes, wood-grain trim and other appliques.

Painted plastics must be cleaned with care. If a cleaner is too aggressive it will cut through the paint and expose the primer. If bright trim such as polished aluminum or chrome is painted, cleaning must be performed with even greater care. If rubbing compound is being used, it will cut faster than polish.

Abrasive cleaners will dull an acrylic finish. The best way to clean these newer finishes is with a non-abrasive liquid polish. Only dirt and oxidation, not paint, will be removed.

Taking a few minutes to read the instructions on the can of polish or wax will help prevent making serious mistakes. Not all preparations will work on all surfaces. And some are intended for power application while others will only work when applied by hand.

Don't get the idea that just pouring on some polish and then hitting it with a buffer will suffice. Power equipment speeds the operation. But it also adds a measure of risk. It's very easy to damage the finish if you use the wrong methods or materials.

Caring for Chrome

Read the label on the container. Many products are formulated specifically for chrome, but others contain abrasives that will scratch the chrome finish. If it isn't recommended for chrome, don't use it.

Never use steel wool or kitchen soap pads to clean chrome. Be careful not to get chrome cleaner on paint or interior vinyl surfaces. If you do, get it off immediately.

Troubleshooting 11

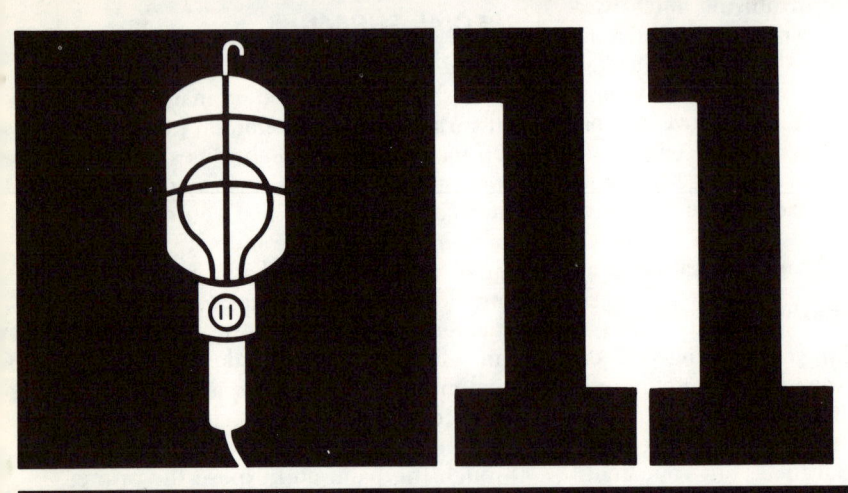

This section is designed to aid in the quick, accurate diagnosis of automotive problems. While automotive repairs can be made by many people, accurate troubleshooting is a rare skill for the amateur and professional alike.

In its simplest state, troubleshooting is an exercise in logic. It is essential to realize that an automobile is really composed of a series of systems. Some of these systems are interrelated; others are not. Automobiles operate within a framework of logical rules and physical laws, and the key to troubleshooting is a good understanding of all the automotive systems.

This section breaks the car or truck down into its component systems, allowing the problem to be isolated. The charts and diagnostic road maps list the most common problems and the most probable causes of trouble. Obviously it would be impossible to list every possible problem that could happen along with every possible cause, but it will locate MOST problems and eliminate a lot of unnecessary guesswork. The systematic format will locate problems within a given system, but, because many automotive systems are interrelated, the solution to your particular problem may be found in a number of systems on the car or truck.

USING THE TROUBLESHOOTING CHARTS

This book contains all of the specific information that the average do-it-yourself mechanic needs to repair and maintain his or her car or truck. The troubleshooting charts are designed to be used in conjunction with the specific procedures and information in the text. For instance, troubleshooting a point-type ignition system is fairly standard for all models, but you may be directed to the text to find procedures for troubleshooting an individual type of electronic ignition. You will also have to refer to the specification charts throughout the book for specifications applicable to your car or truck.

TOOLS AND EQUIPMENT

The tools illustrated in Chapter 1 (plus two more diagnostic pieces) will be adequate to troubleshoot most problems. The two other tools needed are a voltmeter and an ohmmeter. These can be purchased separately or in combination, known as a VOM meter.

In the event that other tools are required, they will be noted in the procedures.

TROUBLESHOOTING

Troubleshooting Engine Problems
See Chapters 2, 3, 4 for more information and service procedures.

Index to Systems

System	To Test	Group
Battery	Engine need not be running	1
Starting system	Engine need not be running	2
Primary electrical system	Engine need not be running	3
Secondary electrical system	Engine need not be running	4
Fuel system	Engine need not be running	5
Engine compression	Engine need not be running	6
Engine vacuum	Engine must be running	7
Secondary electrical system	Engine must be running	8
Valve train	Engine must be running	9
Exhaust system	Engine must be running	10
Cooling system	Engine must be running	11
Engine lubrication	Engine must be running	12

Index to Problems

Problem: Symptom	Begin at Specific Diagnosis, Number
Engine Won't Start:	
Starter doesn't turn	1.1, 2.1
Starter turns, engine doesn't	2.1
Starter turns engine very slowly	1.1, 2.4
Starter turns engine normally	3.1, 4.1
Starter turns engine very quickly	6.1
Engine fires intermittently	4.1
Engine fires consistently	5.1, 6.1
Engine Runs Poorly:	
Hard starting	3.1, 4.1, 5.1, 8.1
Rough idle	4.1, 5.1, 8.1
Stalling	3.1, 4.1, 5.1, 8.1
Engine dies at high speeds	4.1, 5.1
Hesitation (on acceleration from standing stop)	5.1, 8.1
Poor pickup	4.1, 5.1, 8.1
Lack of power	3.1, 4.1, 5.1, 8.1
Backfire through the carburetor	4.1, 8.1, 9.1
Backfire through the exhaust	4.1, 8.1, 9.1
Blue exhaust gases	6.1, 7.1
Black exhaust gases	5.1
Running on (after the ignition is shut off)	3.1, 8.1
Susceptible to moisture	4.1
Engine misfires under load	4.1, 7.1, 8.4, 9.1
Engine misfires at speed	4.1, 8.4
Engine misfires at idle	3.1, 4.1, 5.1, 7.1, 8.4

Sample Section

Test and Procedure	Results and Indications	Proceed to
4.1—Check for spark: Hold each spark plug wire approximately ¼" from ground with gloves or a heavy, dry rag. Crank the engine and observe the spark.	→ If no spark is evident:	→4.2
	→ If spark is good in some cases:	→4.3
	→ If spark is good in all cases:	→4.6

TROUBLESHOOTING

Specific Diagnosis

This section is arranged so that following each test, instructions are given to proceed to another, until a problem is diagnosed.

Section 1—Battery

Test and Procedure	Results and Indications	Proceed to
1.1—Inspect the battery visually for case condition (corrosion, cracks) and water level.	If case is cracked, replace battery:	1.4
	If the case is intact, remove corrosion with a solution of baking soda and water (**CAUTION:** *do not get the solution into the battery*), and fill with water:	1.2
Inspect the battery case		
1.2—Check the battery cable connections: Insert a screwdriver between the battery post and the cable clamp. Turn the headlights on high beam, and observe them as the screwdriver is gently twisted to ensure good metal to metal contact.	If the lights brighten, remove and clean the clamp and post; coat the post with petroleum jelly, install and tighten the clamp:	1.4
	If no improvement is noted:	1.3
TESTING BATTERY CABLE CONNECTIONS USING A SCREWDRIVER		
1.3—Test the state of charge of the battery using an individual cell tester or hydrometer.	If indicated, charge the battery. **NOTE:** *If no obvious reason exists for the low state of charge (i.e., battery age, prolonged storage), proceed to:*	1.4

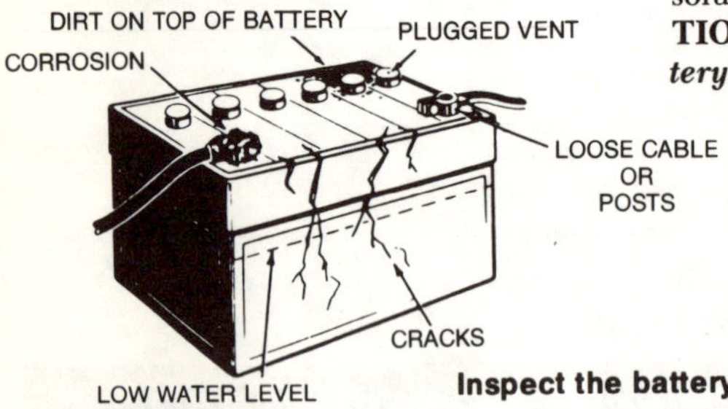

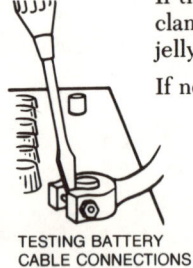

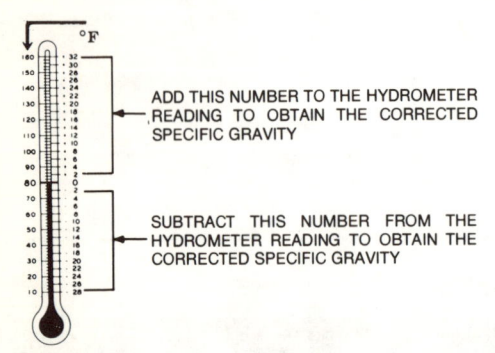

Specific Gravity (@ 80° F.)

ADD THIS NUMBER TO THE HYDROMETER READING TO OBTAIN THE CORRECTED SPECIFIC GRAVITY

SUBTRACT THIS NUMBER FROM THE HYDROMETER READING TO OBTAIN THE CORRECTED SPECIFIC GRAVITY

Minimum	Battery Charge
1.260	100% Charged
1.230	75% Charged
1.200	50% Charged
1.170	25% Charged
1.140	Very Little Power Left
1.110	Completely Discharged

The effects of temperature on battery specific gravity (left) and amount of battery charge in relation to specific gravity (right)

Test and Procedure	Results and Indications	Proceed to
1.4—Visually inspect battery cables for cracking, bad connection to ground, or bad connection to starter.	If necessary, tighten connections or replace the cables:	2.1

TROUBLESHOOTING

Section 2—Starting System
See Chapter 3 for service procedures

Test and Procedure	Results and Indications	Proceed to
Note: Tests in Group 2 are performed with coil high tension lead disconnected to prevent accidental starting.		
2.1—Test the starter motor and solenoid: Connect a jumper from the battery post of the solenoid (or relay) to the starter post of the solenoid (or relay).	If starter turns the engine normally:	2.2
	If the starter buzzes, or turns the engine very slowly:	2.4
	If no response, replace the solenoid (or relay).	3.1
	If the starter turns, but the engine doesn't, ensure that the flywheel ring gear is intact. If the gear is undamaged, replace the starter drive.	3.1
2.2—Determine whether ignition override switches are functioning properly (clutch start switch, neutral safety switch), by connecting a jumper across the switch(es), and turning the ignition switch to "start".	If starter operates, adjust or replace switch:	3.1
	If the starter doesn't operate:	2.3
2.3—Check the ignition switch "start" position: Connect a 12V test lamp or voltmeter between the starter post of the solenoid (or relay) and ground. Turn the ignition switch to the "start" position, and jiggle the key.	If the lamp doesn't light or the meter needle doesn't move when the switch is turned, check the ignition switch for loose connections, cracked insulation, or broken wires. Repair or replace as necessary:	3.1
	If the lamp flickers or needle moves when the key is jiggled, replace the ignition switch.	3.3

Checking the ignition switch "start" position

STARTER RELAY (IF EQUIPPED)

2.4—Remove and bench test the starter, according to specifications in the engine electrical section.	If the starter does not meet specifications, repair or replace as needed:	3.1
	If the starter is operating properly:	2.5
2.5—Determine whether the engine can turn freely: Remove the spark plugs, and check for water in the cylinders. Check for water on the dipstick, or oil in the radiator. Attempt to turn the engine using an 18" flex drive and socket on the crankshaft pulley nut or bolt.	If the engine will turn freely only with the spark plugs out, and hydrostatic lock (water in the cylinders) is ruled out, check valve timing:	9.2
	If engine will not turn freely, and it is known that the clutch and transmission are free, the engine must be disassembled for further evaluation:	Chapter 3

TROUBLESHOOTING

Section 3—Primary Electrical System

Test and Procedure	Results and Indications	Proceed to
3.1—Check the ignition switch "on" position: Connect a jumper wire between the distributor side of the coil and ground, and a 12V test lamp between the switch side of the coil and ground. Remove the high tension lead from the coil. Turn the ignition switch on and jiggle the key.	If the lamp lights: If the lamp flickers when the key is jiggled, replace the ignition switch: If the lamp doesn't light, check for loose or open connections. If none are found, remove the ignition switch and check for continuity. If the switch is faulty, replace it:	3.2 3.3 3.3

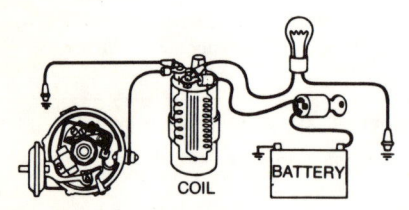

Checking the ignition switch "on" position

| 3.2—Check the ballast resistor or resistance wire for an open circuit, using an ohmmeter. See Chapter 3 for specific tests. | Replace the resistor or resistance wire if the resistance is zero. **NOTE:** *Some ignition systems have no ballast resistor.* | 3.3 |

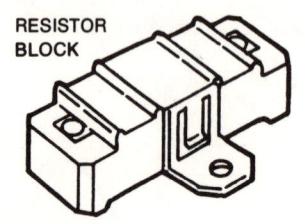

Two types of resistors

| 3.3—On point-type ignition systems, visually inspect the breaker points for burning, pitting or excessive wear. Gray coloring of the point contact surfaces is normal. Rotate the crankshaft until the contact heel rests on a high point of the distributor cam and adjust the point gap to specifications. On electronic ignition models, remove the distributor cap and visually inspect the armature. Ensure that the armature pin is in place, and that the armature is on tight and rotates when the engine is cranked. Make sure there are no cracks, chips or rounded edges on the armature. | If the breaker points are intact, clean the contact surfaces with fine emery cloth, and adjust the point gap to specifications. If the points are worn, replace them. On electronic systems, replace any parts which appear defective. If condition persists: | 3.4 |

TROUBLESHOOTING 149

Test and Procedure	Results and Indications	Proceed to
3.4—On point-type ignition systems, connect a dwell-meter between the distributor primary lead and ground. Crank the engine and observe the point dwell angle. On electronic ignition systems, conduct a stator (magnetic pickup assembly) test. See Chapter 3.	On point-type systems, adjust the dwell angle if necessary. **NOTE:** *Increasing the point gap decreases the dwell angle and vice-versa.*	3.6
	If the dwell meter shows little or no reading;	3.5
	On electronic ignition systems, if the stator is bad, replace the stator. If the stator is good, proceed to the other tests in Chapter 3.	

Dwell is a function of point gap

3.5—On the point-type ignition systems, check the condenser for short: connect an ohmeter across the condenser body and the pigtail lead.	If any reading other than infinite is noted, replace the condenser	3.6

Checking the condenser for short

3.6—Test the coil primary resistance: On point-type ignition systems, connect an ohmmeter across the coil primary terminals, and read the resistance on the low scale. Note whether an external ballast resistor or resistance wire is used. On electronic ignition systems, test the coil primary resistance as in Chapter 3.	Point-type ignition coils utilizing ballast resistors or resistance wires should have approximately 1.0 ohms resistance. Coils with internal resistors should have approximately 4.0 ohms resistance. If values far from the above are noted, replace the coil.	4.1

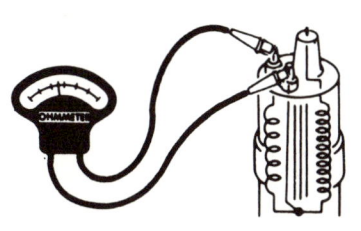

Check the coil primary resistance

150 TROUBLESHOOTING

Section 4—Secondary Electrical System
See Chapters 2–3 for service procedures

Test and Procedure	Results and Indications	Proceed to
4.1—Check for spark: Hold each spark plug wire approximately ¼" from ground with gloves or a heavy, dry rag. Crank the engine, and observe the spark.	If no spark is evident:	4.2
	If spark is good in some cylinders:	4.3
	If spark is good in all cylinders:	4.6

Check for spark at the plugs

4.2—Check for spark at the coil high tension lead: Remove the coil high tension lead from the distributor and position it approximately ¼" from ground. Crank the engine and observe spark. **CAUTION: This test should not be performed on engines equipped with electronic ignition.**	If the spark is good and consistent:	4.3
	If the spark is good but intermittent, test the primary electrical system starting at 3.3:	3.3
	If the spark is weak or non-existent, replace the coil high tension lead, clean and tighten all connections and retest. If no improvement is noted:	4.4
4.3—Visually inspect the distributor cap and rotor for burned or corroded contacts, cracks, carbon tracks, or moisture. Also check the fit of the rotor on the distributor shaft (where applicable).	If moisture is present, dry thoroughly, and retest per 4.1:	4.1
	If burned or excessively corroded contacts, cracks, or carbon tracks are noted, replace the defective part(s) and retest per 4.1:	4.1
	If the rotor and cap appear intact, or are only slightly corroded, clean the contacts thoroughly (including the cap towers and spark plug wire ends) and retest per 4.1:	
	If the spark is good in all cases:	4.6
	If the spark is poor in all cases:	4.5

Inspect the distributor cap and rotor

TROUBLESHOOTING 151

Test and Procedure	Results and Indications	Proceed to
4.4—Check the coil secondary resistance: On point-type systems connect an ohmmeter across the distributor side of the coil and the coil tower. Read the resistance on the high scale of the ohmmeter. On electronic ignition systems, see Chapter 3 for specific tests.	The resistance of a satisfactory coil should be between 4,000 and 10,000 ohms. If resistance is considerably higher (i.e., 40,000 ohms) replace the coil and retest per 4.1. **NOTE:** *This does not apply to high performance coils.*	

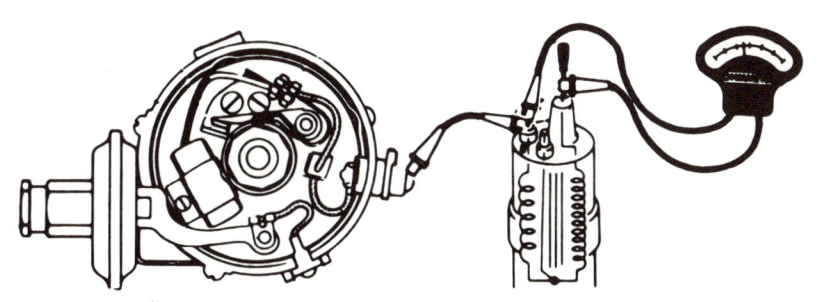

Testing the coil secondary resistance

4.5—Visually inspect the spark plug wires for cracking or brittleness. Ensure that no two wires are positioned so as to cause induction firing (adjacent and parallel). Remove each wire, one by one, and check resistance with an ohmmeter.	Replace any cracked or brittle wires. If any of the wires are defective, replace the entire set. Replace any wires with excessive resistance (over $8000\,\Omega$ per foot for suppression wire), and separate any wires that might cause induction firing.	4.6

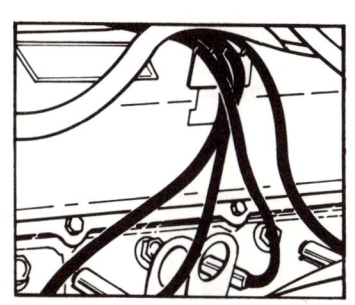

Misfiring can be the result of spark plug leads to adjacent, consecutively firing cylinders running parallel and too close together

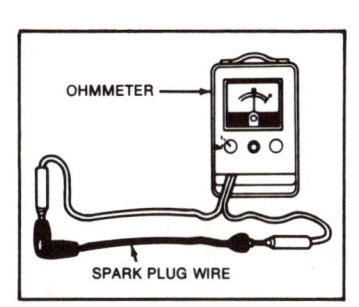

On point-type ignition systems, check the spark plug wires as shown. On electronic ignitions, do not remove the wire from the distributor cap terminal; instead, test through the cap

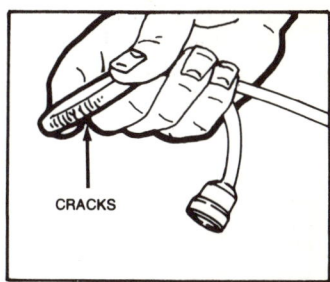

Spark plug wires can be checked visually by bending them in a loop over your finger. This will reveal any cracks, burned or broken insulation. Any wire with cracked insulation should be replaced

4.6—Remove the spark plugs, noting the cylinders from which they were removed, and evaluate according to the color photos in the middle of this book.	See following.	**See following.**

152 TROUBLESHOOTING

Test and Procedure	Results and Indications	Proceed to
4.7—Examine the location of all the plugs.	The following diagrams illustrate some of the conditions that the location of plugs will reveal.	**4.8**

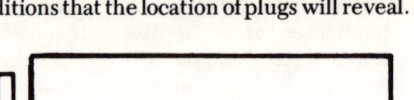

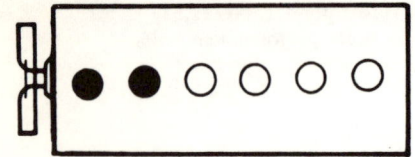

Two adjacent plugs are fouled in a 6-cylinder engine, 4-cylinder engine or either bank of a V-8. This is probably due to a blown head gasket between the two cylinders

The two center plugs in a 6-cylinder engine are fouled. Raw fuel may be "boiled" out of the carburetor into the intake manifold after the engine is shut-off. Stop-start driving can also foul the center plugs, due to overly rich mixture. Proper float level, a new float needle and seat or use of an insulating spacer may help this problem

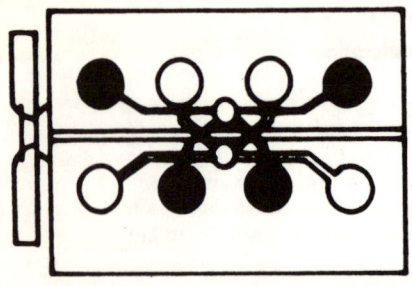

An unbalanced carburetor is indicated. Following the fuel flow on this particular design shows that the cylinders fed by the right-hand barrel are fouled from overly rich mixture, while the cylinders fed by the left-hand barrel are normal

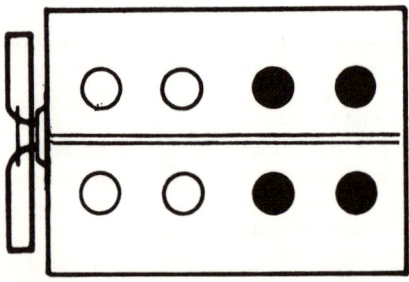

If the four rear plugs are overheated, a cooling system problem is suggested. A thorough cleaning of the cooling system may restore coolant circulation and cure the problem

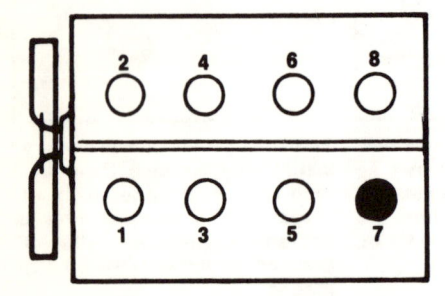

Finding one plug overheated may indicate an intake manifold leak near the affected cylinder. If the overheated plug is the second of two adjacent, consecutively firing plugs, it could be the result of ignition cross-firing. Separating the leads to these two plugs will eliminate cross-fire

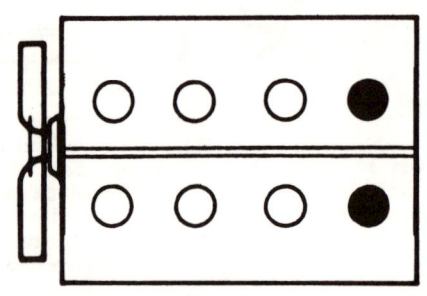

Occasionally, the two rear plugs in large, lightly used V-8's will become oil fouled. High oil consumption and smoky exhaust may also be noticed. It is probably due to plugged oil drain holes in the rear of the cylinder head, causing oil to be sucked in around the valve stems. This usually occurs in the rear cylinders first, because the engine slants that way

TROUBLESHOOTING 153

Test and Procedure	Results and Indications	Proceed to
4.8—Determine the static ignition timing. Using the crankshaft pulley timing marks as a guide, locate top dead center on the compression stroke of the number one cylinder.	The rotor should be pointing toward the No. 1 tower in the distributor cap, and, on electronic ignitions, the armature spoke for that cylinder should be lined up with the stator.	4.8
4.9—Check coil polarity: Connect a voltmeter negative lead to the coil high tension lead, and the positive lead to ground (**NOTE:** *Reverse the hook-up for positive ground systems*). Crank the engine momentarily. **Checking coil polarity**	If the voltmeter reads up-scale, the polarity is correct: If the voltmeter reads down-scale, reverse the coil polarity (switch the primary leads):	5.1 5.1

Section 5—Fuel System
See Chapter 4 for service procedures

Test and Procedure	Results and Indications	Proceed to
5.1—Determine that the air filter is functioning efficiently: Hold paper elements up to a strong light, and attempt to see light through the filter.	Clean permanent air filters in solvent (or manufacturer's recommendation), and allow to dry. Replace paper elements through which light cannot be seen:	5.2
5.2—Determine whether a flooding condition exists: Flooding is identified by a strong gasoline odor, and excessive gasoline present in the throttle bore(s) of the carburetor. **If the engine floods repeatedly, check the choke butterfly flap**	If flooding is not evident: If flooding is evident, permit the gasoline to dry for a few moments and restart. If flooding doesn't recur: If flooding is persistent:	5.3 5.7 5.5
5.3—Check that fuel is reaching the carburetor: Detach the fuel line at the carburetor inlet. Hold the end of the line in a cup (not styrofoam), and crank the engine. **Check the fuel pump by disconnecting the output line (fuel pump-to-carburetor) at the carburetor and operating the starter briefly**	If fuel flows smoothly: If fuel doesn't flow (**NOTE:** *Make sure that there is fuel in the tank*), or flows erratically:	5.7 5.4

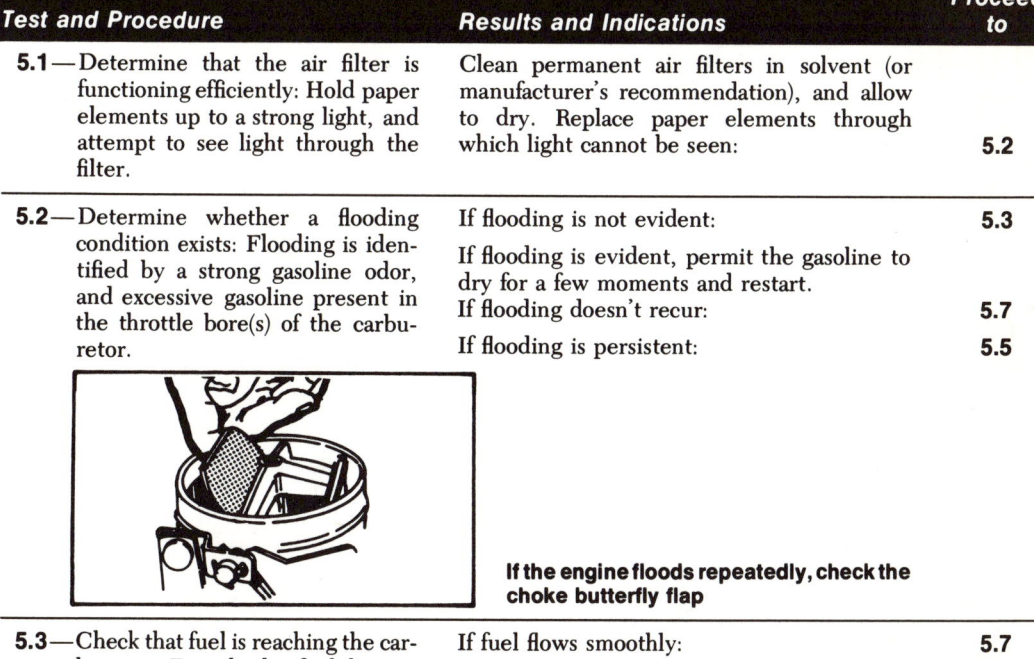

TROUBLESHOOTING

Test and Procedure	Results and Indications	Proceed to
5.4—Test the fuel pump: Disconnect all fuel lines from the fuel pump. Hold a finger over the input fitting, crank the engine (with electric pump, turn the ignition or pump on); and feel for suction.	If suction is evident, blow out the fuel line to the tank with low pressure compressed air until bubbling is heard from the fuel filler neck. Also blow out the carburetor fuel line (both ends disconnected):	5.7
	If no suction is evident, replace or repair the fuel pump: NOTE: *Repeated oil fouling of the spark plugs, or a no-start condition, could be the result of a ruptured vacuum booster pump diaphragm, through which oil or gasoline is being drawn into the intake manifold (where applicable).*	5.7
5.5—Occasionally, small specks of dirt will clog the small jets and orifices in the carburetor. With the engine cold, hold a flat piece of wood or similar material over the carburetor, where possible, and crank the engine.	If the engine starts, but runs roughly the engine is probably not run enough. If the engine won't start:	5.9
5.6—Check the needle and seat: Tap the carburetor in the area of the needle and seat.	If flooding stops, a gasoline additive (e.g., Gumout) will often cure the problem:	5.7
	If flooding continues, check the fuel pump for excessive pressure at the carburetor (according to specifications). If the pressure is normal, the needle and seat must be removed and checked, and/or the float level adjusted:	5.7
5.7—Test the accelerator pump by looking into the throttle bores while operating the throttle.	If the accelerator pump appears to be operating normally:	5.8
	If the accelerator pump is not operating, the pump must be reconditioned. Where possible, service the pump with the carburetor(s) installed on the engine. If necessary, remove the carburetor. Prior to removal:	5.8

Check for gas at the carburetor by looking down the carburetor throat while someone moves the accelerator

5.8—Determine whether the carburetor main fuel system is functioning: Spray a commercial starting fluid into the carburetor while attempting to start the engine.	If the engine starts, runs for a few seconds, and dies:	5.9
	If the engine doesn't start:	6.1

TROUBLESHOOTING 155

Test and Procedure	Results and Indications	Proceed to
5.9—Uncommon fuel system malfunctions: See below:	If the problem is solved:	6.1
	If the problem remains, remove and recondition the carburetor.	

Condition	Indication	Test	Prevailing Weather Conditions	Remedy
Vapor lock	Engine will not restart shortly after running.	Cool the components of the fuel system until the engine starts. Vapor lock can be cured faster by draping a wet cloth over a mechanical fuel pump.	Hot to very hot	Ensure that the exhaust manifold heat control valve is operating. Check with the vehicle manufacturer for the recommended solution to vapor lock on the model in question.
Carburetor icing	Engine will not idle, stalls at low speeds.	Visually inspect the throttle plate area of the throttle bores for frost.	High humidity, 32–40° F.	Ensure that the exhaust manifold heat control valve is operating, and that the intake manifold heat riser is not blocked.
Water in the fuel	Engine sputters and stalls; may not start.	Pump a small amount of fuel into a glass jar. Allow to stand, and inspect for droplets or a layer of water.	High humidity, extreme temperature changes.	For droplets, use one or two cans of commercial gas line anti-freeze. For a layer of water, the tank must be drained, and the fuel lines blown out with compressed air.

Section 6—Engine Compression
See Chapter 3 for service procedures

6.1—Test engine compression: Remove all spark plugs. Block the throttle wide open. Insert a compression gauge into a spark plug port, crank the engine to obtain the maximum reading, and record.	If compression is within limits on all cylinders:	7.1
	If gauge reading is extremely low on all cylinders:	6.2
	If gauge reading is low on one or two cylinders: (If gauge readings are identical and low on two or more adjacent cylinders, the head gasket must be replaced.)	6.2

Checking compression

6.2—Test engine compression (wet): Squirt approximately 30 cc. of engine oil into each cylinder, and retest per 6.1.	If the readings improve, worn or cracked rings or broken pistons are indicated:	See Chapter 3
	If the readings do not improve, burned or excessively carboned valves or a jumped timing chain are indicated: NOTE: *A jumped timing chain is often indicated by difficult cranking.*	7.1

TROUBLESHOOTING

Section 7—Engine Vacuum
See Chapter 3 for service procedures

Test and Procedure	Results and Indications	Proceed to
7.1—Attach a vacuum gauge to the intake manifold beyond the throttle plate. Start the engine, and observe the action of the needle over the range of engine speeds.	See below.	See below

Normal engine
INDICATION: normal engine in good condition
Proceed to: 8.1
Gauge reading: steady, from 17–22 in./Hg.

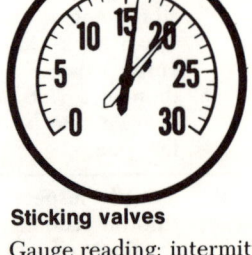

Sticking valves
INDICATION: sticking valves or ignition miss
Proceed to: 9.1, 8.3
Gauge reading: intermittent fluctuation at idle

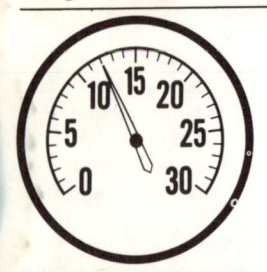

Incorrect valve timing
INDICATION: late ignition or valve timing, low compression, stuck throttle valve, leaking carburetor or manifold gasket
Proceed to: 6.1
Gauge reading: low (10–15 in./Hg) but steady

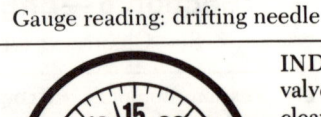

Carburetor requires adjustment
INDICATION: improper carburetor adjustment or minor intake leak.
Proceed to: 7.2
Gauge reading: drifting needle

Blown head gasket
INDICATION: ignition miss, blown cylinder head gasket, leaking valve or weak valve spring
Proceed to: 8.3, 6.1
Gauge reading: needle fluctuates as engine speed increases

Burnt or leaking valves
INDICATION: burnt valve or faulty valve clearance. Needle will fall when defective valve operates
Proceed to: 9.1
Gauge reading: steady needle, but drops regularly

Clogged exhaust system
INDICATION: choked muffler, excessive back pressure in system
Proceed to: 10.1
Gauge reading: gradual drop in reading at idle

Worn valve guides
INDICATION: worn valve guides
Proceed to: 9.1
Gauge reading: needle vibrates excessively at idle, but steadies as engine speed increases

White pointer = steady gauge hand   Black pointer = fluctuating gauge hand

TROUBLESHOOTING

Test and Procedure	Results and Indications	Proceed to
7.2—Attach a vacuum gauge per 7.1, and test for an intake manifold leak. Squirt a small amount of oil around the intake manifold gaskets, carburetor gaskets, plugs and fittings. Observe the action of the vacuum gauge.	If the reading improves, replace the indicated gasket, or seal the indicated fitting or plug: If the reading remains low:	8.1 7.3
7.3—Test all vacuum hoses and accessories for leaks as described in 7.2. Also check the carburetor body (dashpots, automatic choke mechanism, throttle shafts) for leaks in the same manner.	If the reading improves, service or replace the offending part(s): If the reading remains low:	8.1 6.1

Section 8—Secondary Electrical System
See Chapter 2 for service procedures

Test and Procedure	Results and Indications	Proceed to
8.1—Remove the distributor cap and check to make sure that the rotor turns when the engine is cranked. Visually inspect the distributor components.	Clean, tighten or replace any components which appear defective.	8.2
8.2—Connect a timing light (per manufacturer's recommendation) and check the dynamic ignition timing. Disconnect and plug the vacuum hose(s) to the distributor if specified, start the engine, and observe the timing marks at the specified engine speed.	If the timing is not correct, adjust to specifications by rotating the distributor in the engine: (Advance timing by rotating distributor opposite normal direction of rotor rotation, retard timing by rotating distributor in same direction as rotor rotation.)	8.3
8.3—Check the operation of the distributor advance mechanism(s): To test the mechanical advance, disconnect the vacuum lines from the distributor advance unit and observe the timing marks with a timing light as the engine speed is increased from idle. If the mark moves smoothly, without hesitation, it may be assumed that the mechanical advance is functioning properly. To test vacuum advance and/or retard systems, alternately crimp and release the vacuum line, and observe the timing mark for movement. If movement is noted, the system is operating.	If the systems are functioning: If the systems are not functioning, remove the distributor, and test on a distributor tester:	8.4 8.4
8.4—Locate an ignition miss: With the engine running, remove each spark plug wire, one at a time, until one is found that doesn't cause the engine to roughen and slow down.	When the missing cylinder is identified:	4.1

TROUBLESHOOTING

Section 9—Valve Train
See Chapter 3 for service procedures

Test and Procedure	Results and Indications	Proceed to
9.1—Evaluate the valve train: Remove the valve cover, and ensure that the valves are adjusted to specifications. A mechanic's stethoscope may be used to aid in the diagnosis of the valve train. By pushing the probe on or near push rods or rockers, valve noise often can be isolated. A timing light also may be used to diagnose valve problems. Connect the light according to manufacturer's recommendations, and start the engine. Vary the firing moment of the light by increasing the engine speed (and therefore the ignition advance), and moving the trigger from cylinder to cylinder. Observe the movement of each valve.	Sticking valves or erratic valve train motion can be observed with the timing light. The cylinder head must be disassembled for repairs.	**See Chapter 3**
9.2—Check the valve timing: Locate top dead center of the No. 1 piston, and install a degree wheel or tape on the crankshaft pulley or damper with zero corresponding to an index mark on the engine. Rotate the crankshaft in its direction of rotation, and observe the opening of the No. 1 cylinder intake valve. The opening should correspond with the correct mark on the degree wheel according to specifications.	If the timing is not correct, the timing cover must be removed for further investigation.	**See Chapter 3**

Section 10—Exhaust System

Test and Procedure	Results and Indications	Proceed to
10.1—Determine whether the exhaust manifold heat control valve is operating: Operate the valve by hand to determine whether it is free to move. If the valve is free, run the engine to operating temperature and observe the action of the valve, to ensure that it is opening.	If the valve sticks, spray it with a suitable solvent, open and close the valve to free it, and retest. If the valve functions properly: If the valve does not free, or does not operate, replace the valve:	10.2 10.2
10.2—Ensure that there are no exhaust restrictions: Visually inspect the exhaust system for kinks, dents, or crushing. Also note that gases are flowing freely from the tailpipe at all engine speeds, indicating no restriction in the muffler or resonator.	Replace any damaged portion of the system:	11.1

TROUBLESHOOTING

Section 11—Cooling System
See Chapter 3 for service procedures

Test and Procedure	Results and Indications	Proceed to
11.1—Visually inspect the fan belt for glazing, cracks, and fraying, and replace if necessary. Tighten the belt so that the longest span has approximately ½" play at its midpoint under thumb pressure (see Chapter 1).	Replace or tighten the fan belt as necessary: *Checking belt tension*	11.2
11.2—Check the fluid level of the cooling system.	If full or slightly low, fill as necessary: If extremely low:	11.5 11.3
11.3—Visually inspect the external portions of the cooling system (radiator, radiator hoses, thermostat elbow, water pump seals, heater hoses, etc.) for leaks. If none are found, pressurize the cooling system to 14–15 psi.	If cooling system holds the pressure: If cooling system loses pressure rapidly, reinspect external parts of the system for leaks under pressure. If none are found, check dipstick for coolant in crankcase. If no coolant is present, but pressure loss continues: If coolant is evident in crankcase, remove cylinder head(s), and check gasket(s). If gaskets are intact, block and cylinder head(s) should be checked for cracks or holes. If the gasket(s) is blown, replace, and purge the crankcase of coolant: **NOTE:** *Occasionally, due to atmospheric and driving conditions, condensation of water can occur in the crankcase. This causes the oil to appear milky white. To remedy, run the engine until hot, and change the oil and oil filter.*	11.5 11.4 12.6
11.4—Check for combustion leaks into the cooling system: Pressurize the cooling system as above. Start the engine, and observe the pressure gauge. If the needle fluctuates, remove each spark plug wire, one at a time, noting which cylinder(s) reduce or eliminate the fluctuation.	Cylinders which reduce or eliminate the fluctuation, when the spark plug wire is removed, are leaking into the cooling system. Replace the head gasket on the affected cylinder bank(s). *Pressurizing the cooling system*	

160 TROUBLESHOOTING

Test and Procedure	Results and Indications	Proceed to
11.5—Check the radiator pressure cap: Attach a radiator pressure tester to the radiator cap (wet the seal prior to installation). Quickly pump up the pressure, noting the point at which the cap releases.	If the cap releases within ± 1 psi of the specified rating, it is operating properly:	11.6
	If the cap releases at more than ± 1 psi of the specified rating, it should be replaced:	11.6

Checking radiator pressure cap

11.6—Test the thermostat: Start the engine cold, remove the radiator cap, and insert a thermometer into the radiator. Allow the engine to idle. After a short while, there will be a sudden, rapid increase in coolant temperature. The temperature at which this sharp rise stops is the thermostat opening temperature.	If the thermostat opens at or about the specified temperature:	11.7
	If the temperature doesn't increase: (If the temperature increases slowly and gradually, replace the thermostat.)	11.7
11.7—Check the water pump: Remove the thermostat elbow and the thermostat, disconnect the coil high tension lead (to prevent starting), and crank the engine momentarily.	If coolant flows, replace the thermostat and retest per 11.6:	11.6
	If coolant doesn't flow, reverse flush the cooling system to alleviate any blockage that might exist. If system is not blocked, and coolant will not flow, replace the water pump.	

Section 12—Lubrication
See Chapter 3 for service procedures

Test and Procedure	Results and Indications	Proceed to
12.1—Check the oil pressure gauge or warning light: If the gauge shows low pressure, or the light is on for no obvious reason, remove the oil pressure sender. Install an accurate oil pressure gauge and run the engine momentarily.	If oil pressure builds normally, run engine for a few moments to determine that it is functioning normally, and replace the sender.	—
	If the pressure remains low:	12.2
	If the pressure surges:	12.3
	If the oil pressure is zero:	12.3
12.2—Visually inspect the oil: If the oil is watery or very thin, milky, or foamy, replace the oil and oil filter.	If the oil is normal:	12.3
	If after replacing oil the pressure remains low:	12.3
	If after replacing oil the pressure becomes normal:	—

Test and Procedure	Results and Indications	Proceed to
12.3—Inspect the oil pressure relief valve and spring, to ensure that it is not sticking or stuck. Remove and thoroughly clean the valve, spring, and the valve body.	If the oil pressure improves: If no improvement is noted:	— 12.4
12.4—Check to ensure that the oil pump is not cavitating (sucking air instead of oil): See that the crankcase is neither over nor underfull, and that the pickup in the sump is in the proper position and free from sludge.	Fill or drain the crankcase to the proper capacity, and clean the pickup screen in solvent if necessary. If no improvement is noted:	12.5
12.5—Inspect the oil pump drive and the oil pump:	If the pump drive or the oil pump appear to be defective, service as necessary and retest per 12.1:	12.1
	If the pump drive and pump appear to be operating normally, the engine should be disassembled to determine where blockage exists:	See Chapter 3
12.6—Purge the engine of ethylene glycol coolant: Completely drain the crankcase and the oil filter. Obtain a commercial butyl cellosolve base solvent, designated for this purpose, and follow the instructions precisely. Following this, install a new oil filter and refill the crankcase with the proper weight oil. The next oil and filter change should follow shortly thereafter (1000 miles).		

TROUBLESHOOTING EMISSION CONTROL SYSTEMS

See Chapter 4 for procedures applicable to individual emission control systems used on specific combinations of engine/transmission/model.

TROUBLESHOOTING THE CARBURETOR

See Chapter 4 for service procedures

Carburetor problems cannot be effectively isolated unless all other engine systems (particularly ignition and emission) are functioning properly and the engine is properly tuned.

TROUBLESHOOTING

Condition	Possible Cause
Engine cranks, but does not start	1. Improper starting procedure 2. No fuel in tank 3. Clogged fuel line or filter 4. Defective fuel pump 5. Choke valve not closing properly 6. Engine flooded 7. Choke valve not unloading 8. Throttle linkage not making full travel 9. Stuck needle or float 10. Leaking float needle or seat 11. Improper float adjustment
Engine stalls	1. Improperly adjusted idle speed or mixture **Engine hot** 2. Improperly adjusted dashpot 3. Defective or improperly adjusted solenoid 4. Incorrect fuel level in fuel bowl 5. Fuel pump pressure too high 6. Leaking float needle seat 7. Secondary throttle valve stuck open 8. Air or fuel leaks 9. Idle air bleeds plugged or missing 10. Idle passages plugged **Engine Cold** 11. Incorrectly adjusted choke 12. Improperly adjusted fast idle speed 13. Air leaks 14. Plugged idle or idle air passages 15. Stuck choke valve or binding linkage 16. Stuck secondary throttle valves 17. Engine flooding—high fuel level 18. Leaking or misaligned float
Engine hesitates on acceleration	1. Clogged fuel filter 2. Leaking fuel pump diaphragm 3. Low fuel pump pressure 4. Secondary throttle valves stuck, bent or misadjusted 5. Sticking or binding air valve 6. Defective accelerator pump 7. Vacuum leaks 8. Clogged air filter 9. Incorrect choke adjustment (engine cold)
Engine feels sluggish or flat on acceleration	1. Improperly adjusted idle speed or mixture 2. Clogged fuel filter 3. Defective accelerator pump 4. Dirty, plugged or incorrect main metering jets 5. Bent or sticking main metering rods 6. Sticking throttle valves 7. Stuck heat riser 8. Binding or stuck air valve 9. Dirty, plugged or incorrect secondary jets 10. Bent or sticking secondary metering rods. 11. Throttle body or manifold heat passages plugged 12. Improperly adjusted choke or choke vacuum break.
Carburetor floods	1. Defective fuel pump. Pressure too high. 2. Stuck choke valve 3. Dirty, worn or damaged float or needle valve/seat 4. Incorrect float/fuel level 5. Leaking float bowl

TROUBLESHOOTING

Condition	Possible Cause
Engine idles roughly and stalls	1. Incorrect idle speed 2. Clogged fuel filter 3. Dirt in fuel system or carburetor 4. Loose carburetor screws or attaching bolts 5. Broken carburetor gaskets 6. Air leaks 7. Dirty carburetor 8. Worn idle mixture needles 9. Throttle valves stuck open 10. Incorrectly adjusted float or fuel level 11. Clogged air filter
Engine runs unevenly or surges	1. Defective fuel pump 2. Dirty or clogged fuel filter 3. Plugged, loose or incorrect main metering jets or rods 4. Air leaks 5. Bent or sticking main metering rods 6. Stuck power piston 7. Incorrect float adjustment 8. Incorrect idle speed or mixture 9. Dirty or plugged idle system passages 10. Hard, brittle or broken gaskets 11. Loose attaching or mounting screws 12. Stuck or misaligned secondary throttle valves
Poor fuel economy	1. Poor driving habits 2. Stuck choke valve 3. Binding choke linkage 4. Stuck heat riser 5. Incorrect idle mixture 6. Defective accelerator pump 7. Air leaks 8. Plugged, loose or incorrect main metering jets 9. Improperly adjusted float or fuel level 10. Bent, misaligned or fuel-clogged float 11. Leaking float needle seat 12. Fuel leak 13. Accelerator pump discharge ball not seating properly 14. Incorrect main jets
Engine lacks high speed performance or power	1. Incorrect throttle linkage adjustment 2. Stuck or binding power piston 3. Defective accelerator pump 4. Air leaks 5. Incorrect float setting or fuel level 6. Dirty, plugged, worn or incorrect main metering jets or rods 7. Binding or sticking air valve 8. Brittle or cracked gaskets 9. Bent, incorrect or improperly adjusted secondary metering rods 10. Clogged fuel filter 11. Clogged air filter 12. Defective fuel pump

TROUBLESHOOTING FUEL INJECTION PROBLEMS

Each fuel injection system has its own unique components and test procedures, for which it is impossible to generalize. Refer to Chapter 4 of this Repair & Tune-Up Guide for specific test and repair procedures, if the vehicle is equipped with fuel injection.

TROUBLESHOOTING ELECTRICAL PROBLEMS

See Chapter 5 for service procedures

For any electrical system to operate, it must make a complete circuit. This simply means that the power flow from the battery must make a complete circle. When an electrical component is operating, power flows from the battery to the component, passes through the component causing it to perform its function (lighting a light bulb), and then returns to the battery through the ground of the circuit. This ground is usually (but not always) the metal part of the car or truck on which the electrical component is mounted.

Perhaps the easiest way to visualize this is to think of connecting a light bulb with two wires attached to it to the battery. If one of the two wires attached to the light bulb were attached to the negative post of the battery and the other were attached to the positive post of the battery, you would have a complete circuit. Current from the battery would flow to the light bulb, causing it to light, and return to the negative post of the battery.

The normal automotive circuit differs from this simple example in two ways. First, instead of having a return wire from the bulb to the battery, the light bulb returns the current to the battery through the chassis of the vehicle. Since the negative battery cable is attached to the chassis and the chassis is made of electrically conductive metal, the chassis of the vehicle can serve as a ground wire to complete the circuit. Secondly, most automotive circuits contain switches to turn components on and off as required.

Every complete circuit from a power source must include a component which is using the power from the power source. If you were to disconnect the light bulb from the wires and touch the two wires together (don't do this) the power supply wire to the component would be grounded before the normal ground connection for the circuit.

Because grounding a wire from a power source makes a complete circuit—less the required component to use the power—this phenomenon is called a short circuit. Common causes are: broken insulation (exposing the metal wire to a metal part of the car or truck), or a shorted switch.

Some electrical components which require a large amount of current to operate also have a relay in their circuit. Since these circuits carry a large amount of current, the thickness of the wire in the circuit (gauge size) is also greater. If this large wire were connected from the component to the control switch on the instrument panel, and then back to the component, a voltage drop would occur in the circuit. To prevent this potential drop in voltage, an electromagnetic switch (relay) is used. The large wires in the circuit are connected from the battery to one side of the relay, and from the opposite side of the relay to the component. The relay is normally open, preventing current from passing through the circuit. An additional, smaller, wire is connected from the relay to the control switch for the circuit. When the control switch is turned on, it grounds the smaller wire from the relay and completes the circuit. This closes the relay and allows current to flow from the battery to the component. The horn, headlight, and starter circuits are three which use relays.

It is possible for larger surges of current to pass through the electrical system of your car or truck. If this surge of current were to reach an electrical component, it could burn it out. To prevent this, fuses, circuit breakers or fusible links are connected into the current supply wires of most of the major electrical systems. When an electrical current of excessive power passes through the component's fuse, the fuse blows out and breaks the circuit, saving the component from destruction.

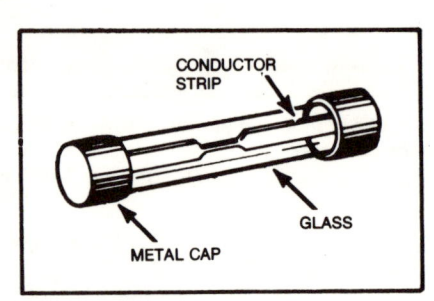

Typical automotive fuse

A circuit breaker is basically a self-repairing fuse. The circuit breaker opens the circuit the same way a fuse does. However, when either the short is removed from the circuit or the surge subsides, the circuit breaker resets itself and does not have to be replaced as a fuse does.

A fuse link is a wire that acts as a fuse. It is normally connected between the starter relay and the main wiring harness. This connection is usually under the hood. The fuse link (if installed) protects all the

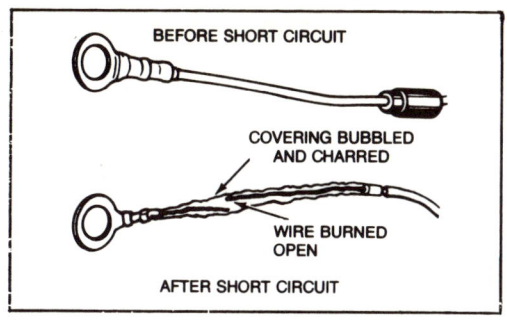

Most fusible links show a charred, melted insulation when they burn out

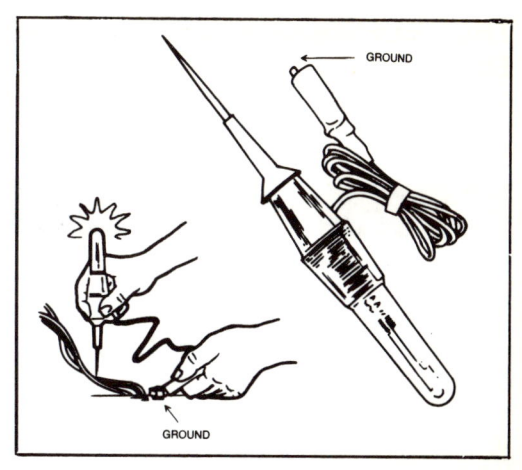

The test light will show the presence of current when touched to a hot wire and grounded at the other end

chassis electrical components, and is the probable cause of trouble when none of the electrical components function, unless the battery is disconnected or dead.

Electrical problems generally fall into one of three areas:

1. The component that is not functioning is not receiving current.
2. The component itself is not functioning.
3. The component is not properly grounded.

The electrical system can be checked with a test light and a jumper wire. A test light is a device that looks like a pointed screwdriver with a wire attached to it and has a light bulb in its handle. A jumper wire is a piece of insulated wire with an alligator clip attached to each end.

If a component is not working, you must follow a systematic plan to determine which of the three causes is the villain.

1. Turn on the switch that controls the inoperable component.
2. Disconnect the power supply wire from the component.
3. Attach the ground wire on the test light to a good metal ground.
4. Touch the probe end of the test light to the end of the power supply wire that was disconnected from the component. If the component is receiving current, the test light will go on.

NOTE: *Some components work only when the ignition switch is turned on.*

If the test light does not go on, then the problem is in the circuit between the battery and the component. This includes all the switches, fuses, and relays in the system. Follow the wire that runs back to the battery. The problem is an open circuit between the battery and the component. If the fuse is blown and, when replaced, immediately blows again, there is a short circuit in the system which must be located and repaired. If there is a switch in the system, bypass it with a jumper wire. This is done by connecting one end of the jumper wire to the power supply wire into the switch and the other end of the jumper wire to the wire coming out of the switch. If the test light lights with the jumper wire installed, the switch or whatever was bypassed is defective.

NOTE: *Never substitute the jumper wire for the component, since it is required to use the power from the power source.*

5. If the bulb in the test light goes on, then the current is getting to the component that is not working. This eliminates the first of the three possible causes. Connect the power supply wire and connect a jumper wire from the component to a good metal ground. Do this with the switch which controls the component turned on, and also the ignition switch turned on if it is required for the component to work. If the component works with the jumper wire installed, then it has a bad ground. This is usually caused by the metal area on which the component mounts to the chassis being coated with some type of foreign matter.

6. If neither test located the source of the trouble, then the component itself is defective. Remember that for any electrical system to work, all connections must be clean and tight.

TROUBLESHOOTING

Troubleshooting Basic Turn Signal and Flasher Problems
See Chapter 5 for service procedures

Most problems in the turn signals or flasher system can be reduced to defective flashers or bulbs, which are easily replaced. Occasionally, the turn signal switch will prove defective.

F = Front   R = Rear   ● = Lights off   ○ = Lights on

Condition		Possible Cause
Turn signals light, but do not flash	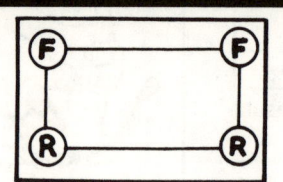	Defective flasher
No turn signals light on either side	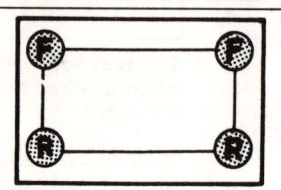	Blown fuse. Replace if defective. Defective flasher. Check by substitution. Open circuit, short circuit or poor ground.
Both turn signals on one side don't work	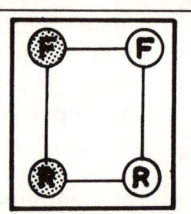	Bad bulbs. Bad ground in both (or either) housings.
One turn signal light on one side doesn't work	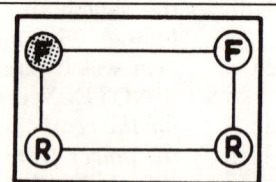	Defective bulb. Corrosion in socket. Clean contacts. Poor ground at socket.
Turn signal flashes too fast or too slowly	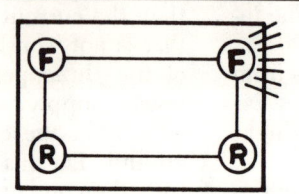	Check any bulb on the side flashing too fast. A heavy-duty bulb is probably installed in place of a regular bulb. Check the bulb flashing too slowly. A standard bulb was probably installed in place of a heavy-duty bulb. Loose connections or corrosion at the bulb socket.
Indicator lights don't work in either direction		Check if the turn signals are working. Check the dash indicator lights. Check the flasher by substitution.
One indicator light doesn't light		On systems with one dash indicator: See if the lights work on the same side. Often the filaments have been reversed in systems combining stoplights with taillights and turn signals. Check the flasher by substitution. On systems with two indicators: Check the bulbs on the same side. Check the indicator light bulb. Check the flasher by substitution.

TROUBLESHOOTING

Troubleshooting Lighting Problems
See Chapter 5 for service procedures

Condition	Possible Cause
One or more lights don't work, but others do	1. Defective bulb(s) 2. Blown fuse(s) 3. Dirty fuse clips or light sockets 4. Poor ground circuit
Lights burn out quickly	1. Incorrect voltage regulator setting or defective regulator 2. Poor battery/alternator connections
Lights go dim	1. Low/discharged battery 2. Alternator not charging 3. Corroded sockets or connections 4. Low voltage output
Lights flicker	1. Loose connection 2. Poor ground. (Run ground wire from light housing to frame) 3. Circuit breaker operating (short circuit)
Lights "flare"—Some flare is normal on acceleration—If excessive, see "Lights Burn Out Quickly"	High voltage setting
Lights glare—approaching drivers are blinded	1. Lights adjusted too high 2. Rear springs or shocks sagging 3. Rear tires soft

Troubleshooting Dash Gauge Problems

Most problems can be traced to a defective sending unit or faulty wiring. Occasionally, the gauge itself is at fault. See Chapter 5 for service procedures.

Condition	Possible Cause
COOLANT TEMPERATURE GAUGE	
Gauge reads erratically or not at all	1. Loose or dirty connections 2. Defective sending unit. 3. Defective gauge. To test a bi-metal gauge, remove the wire from the sending unit. Ground the wire for an instant. If the gauge registers, replace the sending unit. To test a magnetic gauge, disconnect the wire at the sending unit. With ignition ON gauge should register COLD. Ground the wire; gauge should register HOT.
AMMETER GAUGE—TURN HEADLIGHTS ON (DO NOT START ENGINE). NOTE REACTION	
Ammeter shows charge Ammeter shows discharge Ammeter does not move	1. Connections reversed on gauge 2. Ammeter is OK 3. Loose connections or faulty wiring 4. Defective gauge

TROUBLESHOOTING

Condition	Possible Cause

OIL PRESSURE GAUGE

Gauge does not register or is inaccurate	1. On mechanical gauge, Bourdon tube may be bent or kinked. 2. Low oil pressure. Remove sending unit. Idle the engine briefly. If no oil flows from sending unit hole, problem is in engine. 3. Defective gauge. Remove the wire from the sending unit and ground it for an instant with the ignition ON. A good gauge will go to the top of the scale. 4. Defective wiring. Check the wiring to the gauge. If it's OK and the gauge doesn't register when grounded, replace the gauge. 5. Defective sending unit.

ALL GAUGES

All gauges do not operate All gauges read low or erratically All gauges pegged	1. Blown fuse 2. Defective instrument regulator 3. Defective or dirty instrument voltage regulator 4. Loss of ground between instrument voltage regulator and frame 5. Defective instrument regulator

WARNING LIGHTS

Light(s) do not come on when ignition is ON, but engine is not started Light comes on with engine running	1. Defective bulb 2. Defective wire 3. Defective sending unit. Disconnect the wire from the sending unit and ground it. Replace the sending unit if the light comes on with the ignition ON. 4. Problem in individual system 5. Defective sending unit

Troubleshooting Clutch Problems

It is false economy to replace individual clutch components. The pressure plate, clutch plate and throwout bearing should be replaced as a set, and the flywheel face inspected, whenever the clutch is overhauled. See Chapter 6 for service procedures.

Condition	Possible Cause
Clutch chatter	1. Grease on driven plate (disc) facing 2. Binding clutch linkage or cable 3. Loose, damaged facings on driven plate (disc) 4. Engine mounts loose 5. Incorrect height adjustment of pressure plate release levers 6. Clutch housing or housing to transmission adapter misalignment 7. Loose driven plate hub
Clutch grabbing	1. Oil, grease on driven plate (disc) facing 2. Broken pressure plate 3. Warped or binding driven plate. Driven plate binding on clutch shaft
Clutch slips	1. Lack of lubrication in clutch linkage or cable (linkage or cable binds, causes incomplete engagement) 2. Incorrect pedal, or linkage adjustment 3. Broken pressure plate springs 4. Weak pressure plate springs 5. Grease on driven plate facings (disc)

TROUBLESHOOTING

Troubleshooting Clutch Problems (cont.)

Condition	Possible Cause
Incomplete clutch release	1. Incorrect pedal or linkage adjustment or linkage or cable binding 2. Incorrect height adjustment on pressure plate release levers 3. Loose, broken facings on driven plate (disc) 4. Bent, dished, warped driven plate caused by overheating
Grinding, whirring grating noise when pedal is depressed	1. Worn or defective throwout bearing 2. Starter drive teeth contacting flywheel ring gear teeth. Look for milled or polished teeth on ring gear.
Squeal, howl, trumpeting noise when pedal is being released (occurs during first inch to inch and one-half of pedal travel)	Pilot bushing worn or lack of lubricant. If bushing appears OK, polish bushing with emery cloth, soak lube wick in oil, lube bushing with oil, apply film of chassis grease to clutch shaft pilot hub, reassemble. NOTE: Bushing wear may be due to misalignment of clutch housing or housing to transmission adapter
Vibration or clutch pedal pulsation with clutch disengaged (pedal fully depressed)	1. Worn or defective engine transmission mounts 2. Flywheel run out. (Flywheel run out at face not to exceed 0.005") 3. Damaged or defective clutch components

Troubleshooting Manual Transmission Problems
See Chapter 6 for service procedures

Condition	Possible Cause
Transmission jumps out of gear	1. Misalignment of transmission case or clutch housing. 2. Worn pilot bearing in crankshaft. 3. Bent transmission shaft. 4. Worn high speed sliding gear. 5. Worn teeth or end-play in clutch shaft. 6. Insufficient spring tension on shifter rail plunger. 7. Bent or loose shifter fork. 8. Gears not engaging completely. 9. Loose or worn bearings on clutch shaft or mainshaft. 10. Worn gear teeth. 11. Worn or damaged detent balls.
Transmission sticks in gear	1. Clutch not releasing fully. 2. Burred or battered teeth on clutch shaft, or sliding sleeve. 3. Burred or battered transmission mainshaft. 4. Frozen synchronizing clutch. 5. Stuck shifter rail plunger. 6. Gearshift lever twisting and binding shifter rail. 7. Battered teeth on high speed sliding gear or on sleeve. 8. Improper lubrication, or lack of lubrication. 9. Corroded transmission parts. 10. Defective mainshaft pilot bearing. 11. Locked gear bearings will give same effect as stuck in gear.
Transmission gears will not synchronize	1. Binding pilot bearing on mainshaft, will synchronize in high gear only. 2. Clutch not releasing fully. 3. Detent spring weak or broken. 4. Weak or broken springs under balls in sliding gear sleeve. 5. Binding bearing on clutch shaft, or binding countershaft. 6. Binding pilot bearing in crankshaft. 7. Badly worn gear teeth. 8. Improper lubrication. 9. Constant mesh gear not turning freely on transmission mainshaft. Will synchronize in that gear only.

170 TROUBLESHOOTING

Condition	Possible Cause
Gears spinning when shifting into gear from neutral	1. Clutch not releasing fully. 2. In some cases an extremely light lubricant in transmission will cause gears to continue to spin for a short time after clutch is released. 3. Binding pilot bearing in crankshaft.
Transmission noisy in all gears	1. Insufficient lubricant, or improper lubricant. 2. Worn countergear bearings. 3. Worn or damaged main drive gear or countergear. 4. Damaged main drive gear or mainshaft bearings. 5. Worn or damaged countergear anti-lash plate.
Transmission noisy in neutral only	1. Damaged main drive gear bearing. 2. Damaged or loose mainshaft pilot bearing. 3. Worn or damaged countergear anti-lash plate. 4. Worn countergear bearings.
Transmission noisy in one gear only	1. Damaged or worn constant mesh gears. 2. Worn or damaged countergear bearings. 3. Damaged or worn synchronizer.
Transmission noisy in reverse only	1. Worn or damaged reverse idler gear or idler bushing. 2. Worn or damaged mainshaft reverse gear. 3. Worn or damaged reverse countergear. 4. Damaged shift mechanism.

TROUBLESHOOTING AUTOMATIC TRANSMISSION PROBLEMS

Keeping alert to changes in the operating characteristics of the transmission (changing shift points, noises, etc.) can prevent small problems from becoming large ones. If the problem cannot be traced to loose bolts, fluid level, misadjusted linkage, clogged filters or similar problems, you should probably seek professional service.

Transmission Fluid Indications

The appearance and odor of the transmission fluid can give valuable clues to the overall condition of the transmission. Always note the appearance of the fluid when you check the fluid level or change the fluid. Rub a small amount of fluid between your fingers to feel for grit and smell the fluid on the dipstick.

If the fluid appears:	It indicates:
Clear and red colored	Normal operation
Discolored (extremely dark red or brownish) or smells burned	Band or clutch pack failure, usually caused by an overheated transmission. Hauling very heavy loads with insufficient power or failure to change the fluid often result in overheating. Do not confuse this appearance with newer fluids that have a darker red color and a strong odor (though not a burned odor).
Foamy or aerated (light in color and full of bubbles)	1. The level is too high (gear train is churning oil) 2. An internal air leak (air is mixing with the fluid). Have the transmission checked professionally.
Solid residue in the fluid	Defective bands, clutch pack or bearings. Bits of band material or metal abrasives are clinging to the dipstick. Have the transmission checked professionally.
Varnish coating on the dipstick	The transmission fluid is overheating

TROUBLESHOOTING DRIVE AXLE PROBLEMS

First, determine when the noise is most noticeable.

Drive Noise: Produced under vehicle acceleration.

Coast Noise: Produced while coasting with a closed throttle.

Float Noise: Occurs while maintaining constant speed (just enough to keep speed constant) on a level road.

External Noise Elimination

It is advisable to make a thorough road test to determine whether the noise originates in the rear axle or whether it originates from the tires, engine, transmission, wheel bearings or road surface. Noise originating from other places cannot be corrected by servicing the rear axle.

ROAD NOISE

Brick or rough surfaced concrete roads produce noises that seem to come from the rear axle. Road noise is usually identical in Drive or Coast and driving on a different type of road will tell whether the road is the problem.

TIRE NOISE

Tire noise can be mistaken as rear axle noise, even though the tires on the front are at fault. Snow tread and mud tread tires or tires worn unevenly will frequently cause vibrations which seem to originate elsewhere; *temporarily, and for test purposes only,* inflate the tires to 40–50 lbs. This will significantly alter the noise produced by the tires, but will not alter noise from the rear axle. Noises from the rear axle will normally cease at speeds below 30 mph on coast, while tire noise will continue at lower tone as speed is decreased. The rear axle noise will usually change from drive conditions to coast conditions, while tire noise will not. Do not forget to lower the tire pressure to normal after the test is complete.

ENGINE/TRANSMISSION NOISE

Determine at what speed the noise is most pronounced, then stop in a quiet place. With the transmission in Neutral, run the engine through speeds corresponding to road speeds where the noise was noticed. Noises produced with the vehicle standing still are coming from the engine or transmission.

FRONT WHEEL BEARINGS

Front wheel bearing noises, sometimes confused with rear axle noises, will not change when comparing drive and coast conditions. While holding the speed steady, lightly apply the footbrake. This will often cause wheel bearing noise to lessen, as some of the weight is taken off the bearing. Front wheel bearings are easily checked by jacking up the wheels and spinning the wheels. Shaking the wheels will also determine if the wheel bearings are excessively loose.

REAR AXLE NOISES

Eliminating other possible sources can narrow the cause to the rear axle, which normally produces noise from worn gears or bearings. Gear noises tend to peak in a narrow speed range, while bearing noises will usually vary in pitch with engine speeds.

Noise Diagnosis

The Noise Is:	Most Probably Produced By:
1. Identical under Drive or Coast	Road surface, tires or front wheel bearings
2. Different depending on road surface	Road surface or tires
3. Lower as speed is lowered	Tires
4. Similar when standing or moving	Engine or transmission
5. A vibration	Unbalanced tires, rear wheel bearing, unbalanced driveshaft or worn U-joint
6. A knock or click about every two tire revolutions	Rear wheel bearing
7. Most pronounced on turns	Damaged differential gears
8. A steady low-pitched whirring or scraping, starting at low speeds	Damaged or worn pinion bearing
9. A chattering vibration on turns	Wrong differential lubricant or worn clutch plates (limited slip rear axle)
10. Noticed only in Drive, Coast or Float conditions	Worn ring gear and/or pinion gear

TROUBLESHOOTING

Troubleshooting Steering & Suspension Problems

Condition	Possible Cause
Hard steering (wheel is hard to turn)	1. Improper tire pressure 2. Loose or glazed pump drive belt 3. Low or incorrect fluid 4. Loose, bent or poorly lubricated front end parts 5. Improper front end alignment (excessive caster) 6. Bind in steering column or linkage 7. Kinked hydraulic hose 8. Air in hydraulic system 9. Low pump output or leaks in system 10. Obstruction in lines 11. Pump valves sticking or out of adjustment 12. Incorrect wheel alignment
Loose steering (too much play in steering wheel)	1. Loose wheel bearings 2. Faulty shocks 3. Worn linkage or suspension components 4. Loose steering gear mounting or linkage points 5. Steering mechanism worn or improperly adjusted 6. Valve spool improperly adjusted 7. Worn ball joints, tie-rod ends, etc.
Veers or wanders (pulls to one side with hands off steering wheel)	1. Improper tire pressure 2. Improper front end alignment 3. Dragging or improperly adjusted brakes 4. Bent frame 5. Improper rear end alignment 6. Faulty shocks or springs 7. Loose or bent front end components 8. Play in Pitman arm 9. Steering gear mountings loose 10. Loose wheel bearings 11. Binding Pitman arm 12. Spool valve sticking or improperly adjusted 13. Worn ball joints
Wheel oscillation or vibration transmitted through steering wheel	1. Low or uneven tire pressure 2. Loose wheel bearings 3. Improper front end alignment 4. Bent spindle 5. Worn, bent or broken front end components 6. Tires out of round or out of balance 7. Excessive lateral runout in disc brake rotor 8. Loose or bent shock absorber or strut
Noises (see also "Troubleshooting Drive Axle Problems")	1. Loose belts 2. Low fluid, air in system 3. Foreign matter in system 4. Improper lubrication 5. Interference or chafing in linkage 6. Steering gear mountings loose 7. Incorrect adjustment or wear in gear box 8. Faulty valves or wear in pump 9. Kinked hydraulic lines 10. Worn wheel bearings
Poor return of steering	1. Over-inflated tires 2. Improperly aligned front end (excessive caster) 3. Binding in steering column 4. No lubrication in front end 5. Steering gear adjusted too tight
Uneven tire wear (see "How To Read Tire Wear")	1. Incorrect tire pressure 2. Improperly aligned front end 3. Tires out-of-balance 4. Bent or worn suspension parts

TROUBLESHOOTING

HOW TO READ TIRE WEAR

The way your tires wear is a good indicator of other parts of the suspension. Abnormal wear patterns are often caused by the need for simple tire maintenance, or for front end alignment.

Excessive wear at the center of the tread indicates that the air pressure in the tire is consistently too high. The tire is riding on the center of the tread and wearing it prematurely. Occasionally, this wear pattern can result from outrageously wide tires on narrow rims. The cure for this is to replace either the tires or the wheels.

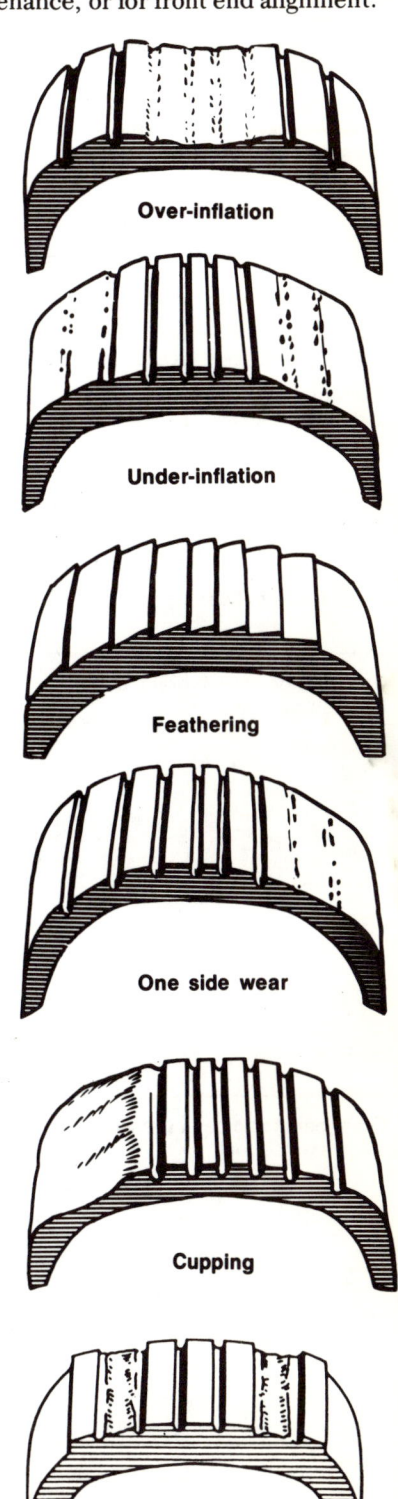

Over-inflation

This type of wear usually results from consistent under-inflation. When a tire is under-inflated, there is too much contact with the road by the outer treads, which wear prematurely. When this type of wear occurs, and the tire pressure is known to be consistently correct, a bent or worn steering component or the need for wheel alignment could be indicated.

Under-inflation

Feathering is a condition when the edge of each tread rib develops a slightly rounded edge on one side and a sharp edge on the other. By running your hand over the tire, you can usually feel the sharper edges before you'll be able to see them. The most common causes of feathering are incorrect toe-in setting or deteriorated bushings in the front suspension.

Feathering

When an inner or outer rib wears faster than the rest of the tire, the need for wheel alignment is indicated. There is excessive camber in the front suspension, causing the wheel to lean too much putting excessive load on one side of the tire. Misalignment could also be due to sagging springs, worn ball joints, or worn control arm bushings. Be sure the vehicle is loaded the way it's normally driven when you have the wheels aligned.

One side wear

Cups or scalloped dips appearing around the edge of the tread almost always indicate worn (sometimes bent) suspension parts. Adjustment of wheel alignment alone will seldom cure the problem. Any worn component that connects the wheel to the suspension can cause this type of wear. Occasionally, wheels that are out of balance will wear like this, but wheel imbalance usually shows up as bald spots between the outside edges and center of the tread.

Cupping

Second-rib wear is usually found only in radial tires, and appears where the steel belts end in relation to the tread. It can be kept to a minimum by paying careful attention to tire pressure and frequently rotating the tires. This is often considered normal wear but excessive amounts indicate that the tires are too wide for the wheels.

Second-rib wear

TROUBLESHOOTING

Troubleshooting Disc Brake Problems

Condition	Possible Cause
Noise—groan—brake noise emanating when slowly releasing brakes (creep-groan)	Not detrimental to function of disc brakes—no corrective action required. (This noise may be eliminated by slightly increasing or decreasing brake pedal efforts.)
Rattle—brake noise or rattle emanating at low speeds on rough roads, (front wheels only).	1. Shoe anti-rattle spring missing or not properly positioned. 2. Excessive clearance between shoe and caliper. 3. Soft or broken caliper seals. 4. Deformed or misaligned disc. 5. Loose caliper.
Scraping	1. Mounting bolts too long. 2. Loose wheel bearings. 3. Bent, loose, or misaligned splash shield.
Front brakes heat up during driving and fail to release	1. Operator riding brake pedal. 2. Stop light switch improperly adjusted. 3. Sticking pedal linkage. 4. Frozen or seized piston. 5. Residual pressure valve in master cylinder. 6. Power brake malfunction. 7. Proportioning valve malfunction.
Leaky brake caliper	1. Damaged or worn caliper piston seal. 2. Scores or corrosion on surface of cylinder bore.
Grabbing or uneven brake action—Brakes pull to one side	1. Causes listed under "Brakes Pull". 2. Power brake malfunction. 3. Low fluid level in master cylinder. 4. Air in hydraulic system. 5. Brake fluid, oil or grease on linings. 6. Unmatched linings. 7. Distorted brake pads. 8. Frozen or seized pistons. 9. Incorrect tire pressure. 10. Front end out of alignment. 11. Broken rear spring. 12. Brake caliper pistons sticking. 13. Restricted hose or line. 14. Caliper not in proper alignment to braking disc. 15. Stuck or malfunctioning metering valve. 16. Soft or broken caliper seals. 17. Loose caliper.
Brake pedal can be depressed without braking effect	1. Air in hydraulic system or improper bleeding procedure. 2. Leak past primary cup in master cylinder. 3. Leak in system. 4. Rear brakes out of adjustment. 5. Bleeder screw open.
Excessive pedal travel	1. Air, leak, or insufficient fluid in system or caliper. 2. Warped or excessively tapered shoe and lining assembly. 3. Excessive disc runout. 4. Rear brake adjustment required. 5. Loose wheel bearing adjustment. 6. Damaged caliper piston seal. 7. Improper brake fluid (boil). 8. Power brake malfunction. 9. Weak or soft hoses.

Troubleshooting Disc Brake Problems (cont.)

Condition	Possible Cause
Brake roughness or chatter (pedal pumping)	1. Excessive thickness variation of braking disc. 2. Excessive lateral runout of braking disc. 3. Rear brake drums out-of-round. 4. Excessive front bearing clearance.
Excessive pedal effort	1. Brake fluid, oil or grease on linings. 2. Incorrect lining. 3. Frozen or seized pistons. 4. Power brake malfunction. 5. Kinked or collapsed hose or line. 6. Stuck metering valve. 7. Scored caliper or master cylinder bore. 8. Seized caliper pistons.
Brake pedal fades (pedal travel increases with foot on brake)	1. Rough master cylinder or caliper bore. 2. Loose or broken hydraulic lines/connections. 3. Air in hydraulic system. 4. Fluid level low. 5. Weak or soft hoses. 6. Inferior quality brake shoes or fluid. 7. Worn master cylinder piston cups or seals.

Troubleshooting Drum Brakes

Condition	Possible Cause
Pedal goes to floor	1. Fluid low in reservoir. 2. Air in hydraulic system. 3. Improperly adjusted brake. 4. Leaking wheel cylinders. 5. Loose or broken brake lines. 6. Leaking or worn master cylinder. 7. Excessively worn brake lining.
Spongy brake pedal	1. Air in hydraulic system. 2. Improper brake fluid (low boiling point). 3. Excessively worn or cracked brake drums. 4. Broken pedal pivot bushing.
Brakes pulling	1. Contaminated lining. 2. Front end out of alignment. 3. Incorrect brake adjustment. 4. Unmatched brake lining. 5. Brake drums out of round. 6. Brake shoes distorted. 7. Restricted brake hose or line. 8. Broken rear spring. 9. Worn brake linings. 10. Uneven lining wear. 11. Glazed brake lining. 12. Excessive brake lining dust. 13. Heat spotted brake drums. 14. Weak brake return springs. 15. Faulty automatic adjusters. 16. Low or incorrect tire pressure.

TROUBLESHOOTING

Condition	Possible Cause
Squealing brakes	1. Glazed brake lining. 2. Saturated brake lining. 3. Weak or broken brake shoe retaining spring. 4. Broken or weak brake shoe return spring. 5. Incorrect brake lining. 6. Distorted brake shoes. 7. Bent support plate. 8. Dust in brakes or scored brake drums. 9. Linings worn below limit. 10. Uneven brake lining wear. 11. Heat spotted brake drums.
Chirping brakes	1. Out of round drum or eccentric axle flange pilot.
Dragging brakes	1. Incorrect wheel or parking brake adjustment. 2. Parking brakes engaged or improperly adjusted. 3. Weak or broken brake shoe return spring. 4. Brake pedal binding. 5. Master cylinder cup sticking. 6. Obstructed master cylinder relief port. 7. Saturated brake lining. 8. Bent or out of round brake drum. 9. Contaminated or improper brake fluid. 10. Sticking wheel cylinder pistons. 11. Driver riding brake pedal. 12. Defective proportioning valve. 13. Insufficient brake shoe lubricant.
Hard pedal	1. Brake booster inoperative. 2. Incorrect brake lining. 3. Restricted brake line or hose. 4. Frozen brake pedal linkage. 5. Stuck wheel cylinder. 6. Binding pedal linkage. 7. Faulty proportioning valve.
Wheel locks	1. Contaminated brake lining. 2. Loose or torn brake lining. 3. Wheel cylinder cups sticking. 4. Incorrect wheel bearing adjustment. 5. Faulty proportioning valve.
Brakes fade (high speed)	1. Incorrect lining. 2. Overheated brake drums. 3. Incorrect brake fluid (low boiling temperature). 4. Saturated brake lining. 5. Leak in hydraulic system. 6. Faulty automatic adjusters.
Pedal pulsates	1. Bent or out of round brake drum.
Brake chatter and shoe knock	1. Out of round brake drum. 2. Loose support plate. 3. Bent support plate. 4. Distorted brake shoes. 5. Machine grooves in contact face of brake drum (Shoe Knock). 6. Contaminated brake lining. 7. Missing or loose components. 8. Incorrect lining material. 9. Out-of-round brake drums. 10. Heat spotted or scored brake drums. 11. Out-of-balance wheels.

TROUBLESHOOTING

Troubleshooting Drum Brakes (cont.)

Condition	Possible Cause
Brakes do not self adjust	1. Adjuster screw frozen in thread. 2. Adjuster screw corroded at thrust washer. 3. Adjuster lever does not engage star wheel. 4. Adjuster installed on wrong wheel.
Brake light glows	1. Leak in the hydraulic system. 2. Air in the system. 3. Improperly adjusted master cylinder pushrod. 4. Uneven lining wear. 5. Failure to center combination valve or proportioning valve.

Appendix

General Conversion Table

Multiply by	To convert	To	
2.54	Inches	Centimeters	.3937
30.48	Feet	Centimeters	.0328
.914	Yards	Meters	1.094
1.609	Miles	Kilometers	.621
.645	Square inches	Square cm.	.155
.836	Square yards	Square meters	1.196
16.39	Cubic inches	Cubic cm.	.061
28.3	Cubic feet	Liters	.0353
.4536	Pounds	Kilograms	2.2045
4.226	Gallons	Liters	.264
.068	Lbs./sq. in. (psi)	Atmospheres	14.7
.138	Foot pounds	Kg. m.	7.23
1.014	H.P. (DIN)	H.P. (SAE)	.9861
—	To obtain	From	Multiply by

Note: 1 cm. equals 10 mm.; 1 mm. equals .0394".

Conversion—Common Fractions to Decimals and Millimeters

Common Fractions	Decimal Fractions	Millimeters (approx.)	Common Fractions	Decimal Fractions	Millimeters (approx.)	Common Fractions	Decimal Fractions	Millimeters (approx.)
1/128	.008	0.20	11/32	.344	8.73	43/64	.672	17.07
1/64	.016	0.40	23/64	.359	9.13	11/16	.688	17.46
1/32	.031	0.79	3/8	.375	9.53	45/64	.703	17.86
3/64	.047	1.19	25/64	.391	9.92	23/32	.719	18.26
1/16	.063	1.59	13/32	.406	10.32	47/64	.734	18.65
5/64	.078	1.98	27/64	.422	10.72	3/4	.750	19.05
3/32	.094	2.38	7/16	.438	11.11	49/64	.766	19.45
7/64	.109	2.78	29/64	.453	11.51	25/32	.781	19.84
1/8	.125	3.18	15/32	.469	11.91	51/64	.797	20.24
9/64	.141	3.57	31/64	.484	12.30	13/16	.813	20.64
5/32	.156	3.97	1/2	.500	12.70	53/64	.828	21.03
11/64	.172	4.37	33/64	.516	13.10	27/32	.844	21.43
3/16	.188	4.76	17/32	.531	13.49	55/64	.859	21.83
13/64	.203	5.16	35/64	.547	13.89	7/8	.875	22.23
7/32	.219	5.56	9/16	.563	14.29	57/64	.891	22.62
15/64	.234	5.95	37/64	.578	14.68	29/32	.906	23.02
1/4	.250	6.35	19/32	.594	15.08	59/64	.922	23.42
17/64	.266	6.75	39/64	.609	15.48	15/16	.938	23.81
9/32	.281	7.14	5/8	.625	15.88	61/64	.953	24.21
19/64	.297	7.54	41/64	.641	16.27	31/32	.969	24.61
5/16	.313	7.94	21/32	.656	16.67	63/64	.984	25.00
21/64	.328	8.33						

APPENDIX 179

Conversion—Millimeters to Decimal Inches

mm	inches	mm	inches	mm	inches	mm	inches	mm	inches
1	.039 370	31	1.220 470	61	2.401 570	91	3.582 670	210	8.267 700
2	.078 740	32	1.259 840	62	2.440 940	92	3.622 040	220	8.661 400
3	.118 110	33	1.299 210	63	2.480 310	93	3.661 410	230	9.055 100
4	.157 480	34	1.338 580	64	2.519 680	94	3.700 780	240	9.448 800
5	.196 850	35	1.377 949	65	2.559 050	95	3.740 150	250	9.842 500
6	.236 220	36	1.417 319	66	2.598 420	96	3.779 520	260	10.236 200
7	.275 590	37	1.456 689	67	2.637 790	97	3.818 890	270	10.629 900
8	.314 960	38	1.496 050	68	2.677 160	98	3.858 260	280	11.032 600
9	.354 330	39	1.535 430	69	2.716 530	99	3.897 630	290	11.417 300
10	.393 700	40	1.574 800	70	2.755 900	100	3.937 000	300	11.811 000
11	.433 070	41	1.614 170	71	2.795 270	105	4.133 848	310	12.204 700
12	.472 440	42	1.653 540	72	2.834 640	110	4.330 700	320	12.598 400
13	.511 810	43	1.692 910	73	2.874 010	115	4.527 550	330	12.992 100
14	.551 180	44	1.732 280	74	2.913 380	120	4.724 400	340	13.385 800
15	.590 550	45	1.771 650	75	2.952 750	125	4.921 250	350	13.779 500
16	.629 920	46	1.811 020	76	2.992 120	130	5.118 100	360	14.173 200
17	.669 290	47	1.850 390	77	3.031 490	135	5.314 950	370	14.566 900
18	.708 660	48	1.889 760	78	3.070 860	140	5.511 800	380	14.960 600
19	.748 030	49	1.929 130	79	3.110 230	145	5.708 650	390	15.354 300
20	.787 400	50	1.968 500	80	3.149 600	150	5.905 500	400	15.748 000
21	.826 770	51	2.007 870	81	3.188 970	155	6.102 350	500	19.685 000
22	.866 140	52	2.047 240	82	3.228 340	160	6.299 200	600	23.622 000
23	.905 510	53	2.086 610	83	3.267 710	165	6.496 050	700	27.559 000
24	.944 880	54	2.125 980	84	3.307 080	170	6.692 900	800	31.496 000
25	.984 250	55	2.165 350	85	3.346 450	175	6.889 750	900	35.433 000
26	1.023 620	56	2.204 720	86	3.385 820	180	7.086 600	1000	39.370 000
27	1.062 990	57	2.244 090	87	3.425 190	185	7.283 450	2000	78.740 000
28	1.102 360	58	2.283 460	88	3.464 560	190	7.480 300	3000	118.110 000
29	1.141 730	59	2.322 830	89	3.503 903	195	7.677 150	4000	157.480 000
30	1.181 100	60	2.362 200	90	3.543 300	200	7.874 000	5000	196.850 000

To change decimal millimeters to decimal inches, position the decimal point where desired on either side of the millimeter measurement shown and reset the inches decimal by the same number of digits in the same direction. For example, to convert 0.001 mm to decimal inches, reset the decimal behind the 1 mm (shown on the chart) to 0.001; change the decimal inch equivalent (0.039″ shown) to 0.000039″.

Tap Drill Sizes

National Fine or S.A.E.

Screw & Tap Size	Threads Per Inch	Use Drill Number
No. 5	44	.37
No. 6	40	.33
No. 8	36	.29
No. 10	32	.21
No. 12	28	.15
1/4	28	3
5/16	24	1
3/8	24	Q
7/16	20	W
1/2	20	29/64
9/16	18	33/64
5/8	18	37/64
3/4	16	11/16
7/8	14	13/16
1 1/8	12	1 3/64
1 1/4	12	1 11/64
1 1/2	12	1 27/64

Tap Drill Sizes

National Coarse or U.S.S.

Screw & Tap Size	Threads Per Inch	Use Drill Number
No. 5	40	.39
No. 6	32	.36
No. 8	32	.29
No. 10	24	.25
No. 12	24	.17
1/4	20	8
5/16	18	F
3/8	16	5/16
7/16	14	U
1/2	13	27/64
9/16	12	31/64
5/8	11	17/32
3/4	10	21/32
7/8	9	49/64
1	8	7/8
1 1/8	7	63/64
1 1/4	7	1 17/64
1 1/2	6	1 11/32

Decimal Equivalent Size of the Number Drills

Drill No.	Decimal Equivalent	Drill No.	Decimal Equivalent	Drill No.	Decimal Equivalent
80	.0135	53	.0595	26	.1470
79	.0145	52	.0635	25	.1495
78	.0160	51	.0670	24	.1520
77	.0180	50	.0700	23	.1540
76	.0200	49	.0730	22	.1570
75	.0210	48	.0760	21	.1590
74	.0225	47	.0785	20	.1610
73	.0240	46	.0810	19	.1660
72	.0250	45	.0820	18	.1695
71	.0260	44	.0860	17	.1730
70	.0280	43	.0890	16	.1770
69	.0292	42	.0935	15	.1800
68	.0310	41	.0960	14	.1820
67	.0320	40	.0980	13	.1850
66	.0330	39	.0995	12	.1890
65	.0350	38	.1015	11	.1910
64	.0360	37	.1040	10	.1935
63	.0370	36	.1065	9	.1960
62	.0380	35	.1100	8	.1990
61	.0390	34	.1110	7	.2010
60	.0400	33	.1130	6	.2040
59	.0410	32	.1160	5	.2055
58	.0420	31	.1200	4	.2090
57	.0430	30	.1285	3	.2130
56	.0465	29	.1360	2	.2210
55	.0520	28	.1405	1	.2280
54	.0550	27	.1440		

Decimal Equivalent Size of the Letter Drills

Letter Drill	Decimal Equivalent	Letter Drill	Decimal Equivalent	Letter Drill	Decimal Equivalent
A	.234	J	.277	S	.348
B	.238	K	.281	T	.358
C	.242	L	.290	U	.368
D	.246	M	.295	V	.377
E	.250	N	.302	W	.386
F	.257	O	.316	X	.397
G	.261	P	.323	Y	.404
H	.266	Q	.332	Z	.413
I	.272	R	.339		

APPENDIX 181

Anti-Freeze Chart

Temperatures Shown in Degrees Fahrenheit +32 is Freezing

Cooling System Capacity Quarts	1	2	3	4	5	6	7	8	9	10	11	12	13	14
10	+24°	+16°	+4°	−12°	−34°	−62°								
11	+25	+18	+8	−6	−23	−47		\multicolumn{7}{l}{For capacities over 30 quarts divide true capacity by 3. Find quarts Anti-Freeze for the ⅓ and multiply by 3 for quarts to add.}
12	+26	+19	+10	0	−15	−34	−57°							
13	+27	+21	+13	+3	−9	−25	−45							
14			+15	+6	−5	−18	−34							
15			+16	+8	0	−12	−26							
16			+17	+10	+2	−8	−19	−34	−52°					
17			+18	+12	+5	−4	−14	−27	−42					
18			+19	+14	+7	0	−10	−21	−34	−50°				
19			+20	+15	+9	+2	−7	−16	−28	−42				
20				+16	+10	+4	−3	−12	−22	−34	−48°			
21				+17	+12	+6	0	−9	−17	−28	−41			
22				+18	+13	+8	+2	−6	−14	−23	−34	−47°		
23				+19	+14	+9	+4	−3	−10	−19	−29	−40		
24				+19	+15	+10	+5	0	−8	−15	−23	−34	−46°	
25				+20	+16	+12	+7	+1	−5	−12	−20	−29	−40	−50°
26					+17	+13	+8	+3	−3	−9	−16	−25	−34	−44
27					+18	+14	+9	+5	−1	−7	−13	−21	−29	−39
28					+18	+15	+10	+6	+1	−5	−11	−18	−25	−34
29					+19	+16	+12	+7	+2	−3	−8	−15	−22	−29
30					+20	+17	+13	+8	+4	−1	−6	−12	−18	−25

For capacities under 10 quarts multiply true capacity by 3. Find quarts Anti-Freeze for the tripled volume and divide by 3 for quarts to add.

To Increase the Freezing Protection of Anti-Freeze Solutions Already Installed

Number of Quarts of ETHYLENE GLYCOL Anti-Freeze Required to Increase Protection

Cooling System Capacity Quarts	\multicolumn{5}{c}{From +20° F. to}	\multicolumn{5}{c}{From +10° F. to}	\multicolumn{4}{c}{From 0° F. to}
	0°	−10°	−20°	−30°	−40°	0°	−10°	−20°	−30°	−40°	−10°	−20°	−30°	−40°
10	1¾	2¼	3	3½	3¾	¾	1½	2¼	2¾	3¼	¾	1½	2	2½
12	2	2¾	3½	4	4½	1	1¾	2½	3¼	3¾	1	1¾	2½	3¼
14	2¼	3¼	4	4¾	5½	1¼	2	3	3¾	4½	1	2	3	3½
16	2½	3½	4½	5¼	6	1¼	2½	3½	4¼	5¼	1¼	2¼	3¼	4
18	3	4	5	6	7	1½	2¾	4	5	5¾	1½	2½	3¾	4¾
20	3¼	4½	5¾	6¾	7½	1¾	3	4¼	5½	6½	1½	2¾	4¼	5¼
22	3½	5	6¼	7¼	8¼	1¾	3¼	4¾	6	7¼	1¾	3¼	4½	5½
24	4	5½	7	8	9	2	3½	5	6½	7½	1¾	3½	5	6
26	4¼	6	7½	8¾	10	2	4	5½	7	8¼	2	3¾	5½	6¾
28	4½	6¼	8	9½	10½	2¼	4¼	6	7½	9	2	4	5¾	7¼
30	5	6¾	8½	10	11½	2½	4½	6½	8	9½	2¼	4¼	6¼	7¾

Test radiator solution with proper hydrometer. Determine from the table the number of quarts of solution to be drawn off from a full cooling system and replace with undiluted anti-freeze, to give the desired increased protection. For example, to increase protection of a 22-quart cooling system containing Ethylene Glycol (permanent type) anti-freeze, from +20° F. to −20° F. will require the replacement of 6¼ quarts of solution with undiluted anti-freeze.

Index

A

Air cleaner, 3
Air conditioning, 6
Alternator, 27
Automatic transmission
    Adjustment, 94
    Filter change, 14, 96
    Pan removal, 14, 96
Axle
    Fluid recommendations, 15
    Lubricant level, 15
Axle shaft
    Bearings and seals, 98

B

Ball joints
    Lower, 101
    Upper, 104
Battery
    Jump starting, 16
    Maintenance, 9, 31
Belt tension adjustment, 5
Body, 127
Brakes
    Adjustment, 114
    Bleeding, 116
    Caliper, 118
    Distribution switch, 117
    Fluid level, 7
    Fluid recommendations, 7
    Front brakes, 118
    Master cylinder, 114
    Parking brake, 124
    Rear brakes, 122
Bulbs, 84

C

Camber, 105
Camshaft and bearings, 44
Capacities, 9
Carburetor
    Adjustment, 23, 75
    Overhaul, 78
    Replacement, 75
    Specifications, 78
Caster, 105
Catalytic converter, 74
Charging system, 27
Chassis lubrication, 15
Choke, 77
Clutch
    Adjustment, 88
    Replacement, 87
Clutch cable, 90
Connecting rod and bearings, 61
Control arm
    Upper, 104
    Lower, 102

Cooling system, 48
Crankcase ventilation (PCV), 4, 70
Crankshaft, 60
Cylinder head
    Reconditioning, 54
    Removal and installation, 37
    Torque sequence, 41

D

Dents and scratches, 131
Differential
    Fluid change, 15
Distributor
    Removal and installation, 26
Door panels, 128
Drive axle, 98
Drivshaft, 97

E

Electrical
    Chassis, 81
    Engine, 26
Electronic ignition, 21
Emission controls, 70
Engine
    Camshaft, 44
    Cylinder head torque sequence, 41
    Exhaust manifold, 42
    Front cover, 44
    Identification, 2
    Intake manifold, 41
    Oil recommendations, 6
    Pistons and rings, 45
    Rebuilding, 51
    Removal and installation, 33
    Specifications, 32
    Timing belt and cover, 42
    Tune-up, 18
Evaporative canister, 4, 74
Exhaust manifold, 42

F

Fan belt adjustment, 5
Firing order, 27
Fluid level checks
    Battery, 9
    Coolant, 8
    Engine oil, 6
    Master cylinder, 7
    Rear axle, 8, 15
    Steering gear, 8
    Transmission, 7, 14
Fluid recommendations, 11
Front suspension
    Ball joints, 101, 104
    lower control arm, 102
    Shock absorber, 101
    Spring, 102

INDEX

Upper control arm, 104
Wheel alignment, 105
Front wheel bearing, 121
Fuel filter, 10
Fuel pump, 75
Fuel system, 75
Fuel tank, 80
Fuses and flashers, 85

G
Gearshift linkage adjustment, 94

H
Hand brake, 124
Headlights, 84
Headlight switch, 83
Heater, 81

I
Identification
   Vehicle, 2
   Engine, 2
   Transmission, 2
Idle speed and mixture, 23
Ignition switch, 112
Instrument cluster, 83
Intake manifold, 41

J
Jacking points, 17
Jump starting, 16

L
Lights, 84-85
Light bulb specifications, 85
Lock cylinder, 112
Lower control arm, 102
Lubrication
   Chassis, 15
   Differential, 15
   Engine, 14
   Transmission, 14

M
Maintenance intervals, 11
Manifolds
   Intake, 41
   Exhaust, 42
Manual transmission, 91
Master cylinder, 114
Model identification, 2

N
Neutral safety switch, 93

O
Oil and fuel recommendations, 11
Oil change, 12
Oil filter (engine), 13
Oil pan, 46
Oil pump, 47
Oil level (engine), 6

P
Parking brake
Parking lights, turn signal bulbs, 84
Pistons and rings
   Installation, 45, 64
   Positioning, 45, 64
PCV valve, 4, 70
Pushing, 16

R
Radiator, 49
Radio, 82
Rear axle, 98
Rear suspension
   Control arm, 108
   Shock absorber, 106
   Springs, 106
   Stabilizer, 108
   Track rod, 108
Regulator, 29
Rear main oil seal, 48
Rings, 45, 64
Routine maintenance, 3
Rust spots, 135

S
Safety notice, ii
Scratches and dents, 131
Serial number location, 2
Shock absorbers
   Front, 101
   Rear, 106
Spark plugs, 18
Specifications
   Alternator and regulator, 28
   Brakes, 125
   Capacities, 9
   Carburetor, 78
   Crankshaft and connecting rod, 34
   Fuses, 86
   General engine, 32
   Light bulb, 85
   Piston and ring, 35
   Torque, 35
   Tune-up, 19
   Valve, 34
   Wheel alignment, 106
Springs
   Front, 102
   Rear, 106
Stabilizer, 105

INDEX

Starter, 29
Steering
   Rack and pinion assembly, 109
   Wheel, 110
Stripped threads, 52

T

Thermostat, 50
Timing belt, 42
Timing (ignition), 22
Tires, 9
Tools, 2
Towing, 16
Transmission
   Automatic, 93
   Manual, 91
   Fluid change, 14, 96
Troubleshooting, 144
Tune-up
   Procedures, 18
   Specifications, 19
Turn signal switch, 110

U

U-joints, 97

V

Valves
   Adjustment, 23
   Service, 37, 41, 55
   Specifications, 34
Vehicle identification, 2

W

Water pump, 49
Wheel alignment, 105
Wheel bearings, 121
Wheel cylinders, 124
Windshield wipers
   Blade, 83
   Motor, 82
   Switch, 111